Games, Simulations and Playful Learning in Business Education

Games, Simulations and Playful Learning in Business Education

Edited by

Caroline Elliott

Professor of Economics, Department of Economics, University of Warwick and Visiting Professor, Aston Business School, Aston University, UK

Jon Guest

Senior Teaching Fellow, Department of Economics, Finance and Entrepreneurship, Aston Business School, Aston University, UK

Elinor Vettraino

Programme Director in Business Enterprise Development, Centre for Innovation in Enterprise Education, Aston Business School, Aston University, UK

Cheltenham, UK • Northampton, MA, USA

Published by
Edward Elgar Publishing Limited
The Lypiatts
15 Lansdown Road
Cheltenham
Glos GL50 2JA
UK

Edward Elgar Publishing, Inc.
William Pratt House
9 Dewey Court
Northampton
Massachusetts 01060
USA

Paperback edition 2022

A catalogue record for this book
is available from the British Library

Library of Congress Control Number: 2021939240

This book is available electronically in the **Elgar**online
Business subject collection
http://dx.doi.org/10.4337/9781800372702

ISBN 978 1 80037 269 6 (cased)
ISBN 978 1 80037 270 2 (eBook)
ISBN 978 1 0353 0181 2 (paperback)

Printed and bound by CPI Group (UK) Ltd, Croydon, CR0 4YY

Contents

Figures

Tables

Contributors

Ozlem Arikan Department of Accounting, Aston Business School, Aston University

Matt Davies Department of Accounting, Aston Business School, Aston University

Caroline Elliott Department of Economics, University of Warwick and Aston Business School, Aston University

Jason Evans Department of Economics, Finance and Entrepreneurship, Aston Business School, Aston University

Jon Guest Department of Economics, Finance and Entrepreneurship, Aston Business School, Aston University

Bahar Ali Kazmi Department of Work and Organisations, Aston Business School, Aston University

Clive Kerridge Department of Marketing and Strategy, Aston Business School, Aston University

Pieter Koornhof Aston Law School, Aston University

Maria Kozlovskaya Department of Economics, Finance and Entrepreneurship, Aston Business School, Aston University

Kris Lines Aston Law School, Aston University

Ivo De Loo Department of Accounting, Aston Business School, Aston University

Matthew Olczak Department of Economics, Finance and Entrepreneurship, Aston Business School, Aston University

Panagiotis Petridis Department of Operations and Information Management, Aston Business School, Aston University

Martin Potts Department of Accounting, Aston Business School, Aston University

Jude Preston Department of Work and Organisations, Aston Business School, Aston University

Frances Rosairo Department of Accounting, Aston Business School, Aston University

Lauren Traczykowski Aston Law School, Aston University

Chris Umfreville Aston Law School, Aston University

Elinor Vettraino Centre for Innovation in Enterprise Education, Aston Business School, Aston University

David Yates Department of Accounting, Aston Business School, Aston University

Preface

Caroline Elliott

When I started work at Aston Business School, speaking to colleagues across the Business School I was struck by the number of colleagues using games, experiments and simulations to enhance the learning and teaching in their modules. Some colleagues very effectively use very simple games and experiments like the ones I have used for many years in my own teaching, but I was also impressed by the number of colleagues using, and in some cases developing, sophisticated games and simulations to be played online, including through mobile phone game apps. This led to the development of A-Game, 'Aston Games in Education'. It is commonplace for universities, faculties and departments to have specialist research centres, but while I am sure there are similar teaching and learning specialised centres bringing together colleagues with a shared interest in a specific pedagogy I didn't know of any. A-Game brings together colleagues from across Aston Business School and Aston Law School, providing opportunities for us to share our best practice. While increasingly we also host external speakers, this book offers an opportunity for us to share what we hope are innovative and effective uses of games, experiments and simulations across Aston Business School.

Increasingly, A-Game has also embraced developments in playful learning, helping us all appreciate the differences, and sometimes the blurriness, between the uses of games and simulations and playful learning in our teaching. Hence, it was natural for this book also to discuss potential uses and benefits of playful learning in higher education.

In the text that follows there are separate sections that, in turn, provide advice on how best to incorporate games, simulations and playful learning into business education. We use the term business education broadly. It encompasses the use of games, simulations and playful learning in Economics and Law, as well as in business disciplines such as Accounting, Marketing, Strategy, etc. As with the previously Edward Elgar published, edited book, *Learning and Teaching in Higher Education: Perspectives from a Business School*, this book is written solely by Aston Business and Law School colleagues. Further, as with the previously published book, chapters are interspersed with short practical thoughts and tips on how best to incorporate games, simulations and playful learning. This book provides an opportunity to celebrate and recognise the great quality academics, learning and teaching at Aston University.

Finally, some thanks. First, thank you to Kathy Daniels who had the original idea for Aston Business and Law School colleagues solely to write a book on how to teach in a business school. Second, and very importantly, a big thank you to Angie Daniels, who looked after the details of putting the book together, always with a smile, a joke and much patience. Finally, to Elinor, Jon and all the authors who were so generous and happy to offer to contribute to this book.

1. Introduction on games, serious games, simulation and gamification

Panagiotis Petridis and Lauren Traczykowski

INTRODUCTION

Over the last 20 years, games have arguably become the largest form of entertainment, surpassing the movie industry (Maslow 1954; Isfe 2010). The starkest increase in annual revenue for the games industry has occurred in the last year (2020) in which the global pandemic forced us to stay home and entertain ourselves (Perez 2020). AAA titles such as *Call of Duty*, *Assassin's Creed* and *Grand Theft Auto* have budgets of billions and are played by millions of people. For example, *Grand Theft Auto Five* generated more than US$815 million in worldwide revenue in the first 24 hours of release, surpassing blockbuster movie releases in the same time period (Ejinsight 2020). So we have to wonder, why do people play games and what attracts the players to those games? And what does this tell us about the necessity to bring games and play into our classrooms?

WHY DO PEOPLE PLAY GAMES?

The answer to this question is very complicated and is linked with human evolution. Humans have developed basic needs over the centuries which are closely linked to our survival, existence and continued evolution. Abraham Maslow developed a five-tier model of human needs, often depicted as a pyramid, to make sense of these needs (Maslow 1954).

The bottom four levels of this five-stage model are referred to as deficiency needs; the top level is referred to as a growth need. The pyramid should be read bottom to top; each lower level needs to be met before we progress upward. When the deficiency needs are fulfilled the individual can move to the growth need. Evolution has wired our brains in such a way that it rewards us when we reinforce healthy behaviours (for example, eating when we are hungry, or drinking water when we are thirsty) by releasing dopamine, a neurotransmitter associated with a pleasant feeling and linked with motivation (Gottfried 2011).

Source: Maslow (1954).

Figure 1.1   Maslow's hierarchy of needs

It is as if our bodies are helping us to distinguish positive behaviour by rewarding it with an induction of pleasurable brain chemicals.

However, growth needs do not stem from a lack of something, but rather from a desire to grow as a person. The growth needs are linked with our psychological needs. For example, one individual may have a strong desire to become a famous musician, or a famous athlete, etc. The 'need' or 'desire' is particular to the individual. Thus, if we feel that we are achieving our objective and we are getting good results, our brains will reward us with the release of dopamine. In order to measure our successes, we tend to compare them against a set of metrics (i.e. we tend to measure our success against other people, or against a set of objectives that we set ourselves).

Games in general (either video games or otherwise) are designed to deal with those issues, because they have a set of rules to follow and are played against other people or computers, and the outcome can be easily measured. I still remember the excitement I felt when I was winning at a game of hide and seek. I feel the same excitement as an adult when I complete a mission on *Borderlands 3* or *World of Warcraft*.

Mihaly Csikszentmihalyi, a pioneer in positive psychology, has developed the 'flow state', which according to him is: "being completely involved in an activity for its own sake. The ego falls away. Time flies. Every action, movement, and thought follows inevitably from the previous one, like playing jazz. Your whole being is involved, and you're using your skills to the utmost"

(*Wired Magazine* 1996). So, when we play a game or are performing an immersive activity, when we are fully involved and enjoying the activity, and we are completely absorbed by this activity, and 'in the zone', we are in the flow state.

The flow state is shown in the figure below, and it provides the ideal condition where we can meet the flow state. Time flies without us noticing when we are in the flow state. People who play games, including me, can strongly relate to that feeling. So it is apparent that this can be beneficial to learners and not only gamers. In this case the 'gamers' of the educational platform will be our students. The aim of a game-based 'education' is to provide students with knowledge in different subjects and disciplines, and additionally provide them with the skills and digital competences necessary to navigate the digital world (Anette Braun et al. 2020). Carefully aligning the challenge level of the proposed educational tasks with the skill level required for the completion of the task could allow the student to reach the flow state. That will allow the student to be more immersed in the task, and therefore will allow the student to learn by completing the activity.

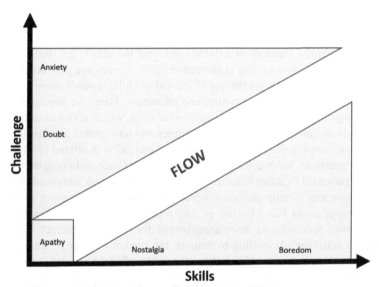

Source: Csikszentmihalyi 1975; Csikszentmihalyi and Kubey 1981.

Figure 1.2   *The flow state*

PLEASURE-CREATION AS A PEDAGOGICAL APPROACH

Education is the ultimate mechanism for individual growth. This is even more relevant when we realise that education increases the rate at which a country's GDP increases (Coen Teulings 2008). In a recent study from a high-level expert group involved in the 'Kronberg Declaration', it was identified that traditional education will be revolutionised by radically changing models of knowledge acquisition, the role of teachers and trainers, as well as the institutional framework and methods of assessment (Anette Braun et al. 2020). It has also been reported that "learners would play an increasingly active role in acquiring and sharing knowledge, creating and disseminating content, and that teachers would increasingly act as managers of learning processes and as trainers" (Anette Braun et al. 2020). So it is apparent that playful learning experiences, including games, gamification and simulation in correlation with new technologies such as virtual reality, augmented reality, mixed reality, haptic devices and artificial intelligence will revolutionise the way that we deliver content to our students (Anette Braun et al. 2020).

If we know that games and play lead to pleasurable releases of dopamine, then it makes sense to integrate play and games into our teaching. The 'flow state' is freedom – freedom to achieve some goal but also to get there in your own time and in your own way (Unterhalter 2003). Games and play are thereby potential tools to encourage the use of individual skills towards some ultimate goal and can be applied to training and education. Here, we investigate the recent surge in playful and games-based education, which is linked to technological advancement, the popularity of games and how games are developed.

First, the surge in playful and games-based education is related to advancements in computer hardware and the affordability of such technologies. Today we have powerful PCs that can run high fidelity worlds with increased realism. We can use our mobile phones – which are 30 or 40 times more powerful than a ten-year-old PC – on the go and without any hassle. In the last ten years, novel technologies have transformed the way we interact with our everyday activities. According to Statista, the current number of smartphone users in the world today is 3.5 billion; this means that 44.81% of the world's population owns a smartphone. Games account for 43% of all smartphone use (Bankmycell 2020).

Second, games, video games in particular, are incredibly popular. A recent study from the International Software Federation of Europe (Isfe 2010) revealed that more than 51% of Europeans aged between six and 64 play video games and the average age of video game players in the EU is 31 years old. The survey revealed that 45% of EU video game players are female, and that the average game play time was 8.6 hours per day, with increases predicted. The popularity of video games, especially among younger demographics, makes them an ideal medium for educational programmes aimed at hard-to-reach demographics (Petridis et al. 2015; Lameras et al. 2017). Non-video games have also seen increased popularity in recent years (Petridis et al. 2015).

The third reason is closely related with the game mechanics. Games are designed in such a way that their main focus is to maximise the amount of pleasure and fun that we get from them. The power of games to immerse, engage and motivate (Garris et al. 2002) and the capabilities of games to foster and facilitate critical thinking, problem-solving skills, innovation, emotional intelligence, awareness and behavioural change have led more games of this nature to be deployed in real-life scenarios. A game's ability (Panzoli et al. 2010; Petridis et al. 2015; Lameras et al. 2017) to change perceptions and views (de Freitas and Neumann 2011) has created a more positive approach to the application of games or the application of 'game elements' in non-entertainment contexts.

Increases in game usage in non-entertainment contexts, such as training (e.g. Mautone et al. 2008), are transforming everyday lives through improving efficiency, increasing knowledge, obtaining new skills (Lameras et al. 2017). The increasing use of multimedia tools in education and training offers the opportunity to present content in multiple formats such as text, images, video, audio, gaming. This provides the educator with more flexibility in how s/he integrates teaching and training strategies, learning outcomes, assessment methodologies and feedback mechanisms. Key aspects are the use of a range of tools, resources and services in a pedagogical manner to enhance the students' experience (Stéphanie Philippe et al. 2020).

WAYS TO PLAY: PLAYFUL LEARNING, SERIOUS GAMES, SIMULATION AND GAMIFICATION

Before I discuss *ways* to play, let's discuss play more generally. Bateson analysed language and play in nonhuman animals. Humans signal to each other and we recognise that a signal is a signal: a handshake, a hug, a cry. These are the precursors of language which, concomitantly, provide us with the opportunity to experience things like empathy. Bateson's research on signals and languages with nonhuman animals brought him to a zoo in San Francisco. Here, monkeys were play fighting. He knew that it was play and not real by the signals provided. (Consider that there is the threat of violence, but no intention for real harm; deception and strategy may be further contributing factors to our understanding of certain interactions as being related to, but not the same as, real interactions and hence stand as play.)

Play actions look like the real actions, but we know that they are not. Bateson further extrapolated from this that a monkey's playful nip at the other's ear "denotes the bite, but does not denote that which would be denoted by the bite" whilst at the same time providing the recipient with an understanding of what was meant (Bateson 1976). As long as the participants continue to play, the play continues. There are no rules about when the goal or learning outcome has been achieved. The monkeys learn whatever it is they want to learn, or don't; play is not hindered by the learning or non-learning.

Play

Play is the heart of games, simulations and any other 'playful' endeavour. Huinzingua offers this definition of play: "a free activity standing quite consciously outside 'ordinary' life as being 'not serious', but at the same time absorbing the player intensely and utterly" (Alvarez et al. 2011; Huizinga 2016). Play can exist without games; games cannot exist without play. It is a mechanism of engagement and understanding about the world around us; it consists of people, 'complex interrelations', art, fantasy, etc. (Frasca 2003; Sicart 2014). Sicart argues that play is autotelic: it has the notion of goals and a space within which it takes place (2014). With games, there are rules, winners and losers; with play, there may be rules, but they aren't rigid and they do not need to aim at winning versus losing (Frasca 2003; Sicart 2014). Play is free-form and unbounded: we learn from it what we need to learn without a clear goal in sight (Whitton and Moseley 2019).

The value and importance of 'practising' skills and learning while/as doing is the noted benefit of play. This is hugely important when we consider the best way to learn, practise and test student skills. In general, the mechanism for achieving the learning outcome (games, simulation or play) is as irrelevant as the type of gun used to kill someone in war. What is most important is the learning achieved. We need not only reinforce standard, 'serious' mechanisms for learning if other mechanisms exist. Hence, the analysis herein is intended as a contribution to and a strengthening of our discipline-specific expertise, with a focus specifically on play. Play is not better or more important than games but rather it is an alternative mechanism for improving the quality of learning which can add to the variety and skills adopted of those participating.

Serious Games

Games are closely linked with play. 'Serious games' represent a dramatic convergence of games, e-learning technologies and pedagogical models to provide a rich, immersive virtual environment. By combining sophisticated theories of education with cutting-edge technology, serious games have tackled a wide range of challenges ranging from corporate training and education through to emergency medical response (Petridis et al. 2015). The broadest definition of a serious game, therefore, is perhaps best defined as a game played for a purpose other than entertainment. Zyda (2005) provides a broad-stroke definition of a serious game as "a mental contest, played with a computer in accordance with specific rules that uses entertainment to further government or corporate training, education, health, public policy, and strategic communication objectives" (Petridis et al. 2015). Serious games are games designed not just to entertain, but also to solve a problem. Referencing Abt (1970), Bogost (1970) includes a definition in his book *Persuasive Games* as games that "have an explicit and carefully through-out educational purpose and are not intended to be played primarily for amusement".

Well-designed serious games can make learning fun, challenging and rewarding. Serious games designers are faced with the challenge of designing a game which is fun, tied up with pedagogical elements (Petridis et al. 2015). The methodology, then, must safeguard against both these failure conditions: on the one hand, it must ensure the game retains the engaging characteristics that make game-based learning an optimal selection for the learning context; on the other, it must ensure that effective pedagogy is implemented in a synergistic fashion with gameplay elements. Thus the importance of formal design methodologies for serious games is well documented (Petridis et al. 2015). A central challenge in creating a prescriptive approach is being able to sufficiently evidence context independent of development models, since a proven approach for one serious game may not be applicable to another, given the broad range of topic areas and learner demographics (Petridis et al. 2015). Existing e-learning development methodologies have met with limited success when transposed to serious gaming, as they emphasise instructional content with little affordance for the unique way in which games attract and retain learners (Petridis et al. 2015).

In order to create a successful serious game we need to ensure involvement from stakeholders throughout the development process. Therefore, care should be taken to support stakeholder involvement regardless of development context, supporting, where possible, co-location and open channels of communication between all parties (Petridis et al. 2015; Lameras et al. 2017). Ultimately, the design and implementation of effective serious games must be grounded in pedagogy, as well as technology, and therefore future work should address the many issues surrounding the equation of learning requirements to these identified technical features. Towards this end, future studies will focus on the analysis of the impact of the various engines and their functionalities on targeted learner groups (Petridis et al. 2015).

Simulation

Simulation sits at the intersection between serious games and play because of its situation between reality and fantasy (Pelletier and Kneebone 2016). Simulation aims at realness, and hence is devoted to the 'seriousness' of that which is being modelled, allowing for the reality of emotion and human behaviour (Frasca 2003). By opening the space, and relaxing a sense of rules, real play is possible. *Hutspiel, T.E.M.P.E.R, ARPA-AGILE COIN GAME* were early video games – and, more recently, we would include *Call of Duty* – which helped players understand aspects of war, conflict, strategy and response (Alvarez et al. 2011). These high fidelity/immersive simulations contribute to an understanding of the tasks performed instead of simply the completion of the tasks outlined in the rules (Pelletier and Kneebone 2016). Some argue that simulation provides an opportunity to dissect process (Murray 1997, in Pelletier and Kneebone 2016) and in this way it leans towards the trial and error or the player's ability to question realities and activities that are possible in play (as opposed to serious games).

Likewise, an activity may be considered a 'simulation' if it gives the player/ learner an opportunity to be fully immersed in the game and, in addition to being able to work within rules, towards a goal; the player/learner can also engage with what doing this activity 'feels like' (Hamari and Koivisto 2014). The immersive experience, and hence 'flow', that a simulation creates means that we can start to see the activity as a 'cultural practice' which is about build-ing relationships in addition to knowledge delivery or outcomes (Pelletier and Kneebone 2016). The use of fictional scenarios provides the moderator with the opportunity to guide what is learned by players (Pelletier and Kneebone 2016). Video games – as simulation or 'serious play' – have been used by military and political bodies for decades. (Typical examples of a serious game used for training are *America's Army* and *Full Spectrum Command* (Wray et al. 2004).) This leads to more intense gameplay, higher levels of pleasure and, at the same time, more opportunities for learning.

Gamification

There are several definitions of gamification; however, the most established one is provided by Deterding, who defines gamification as using game ele-ments in non-gaming contexts (Deterding 2012, 2015; Deterding et al. 2011). Another popular definition of gamification was provided by Zichermann and Cunningham (2011) and Zichermann and Linder (2010), and states that gami-fication is the use of game mechanics and 'thinking' to motivate individuals to perform an action, which could be workers solving tasks or customers engaging

Table 1.1   *Most commonly used gamification elements*

Term	Definition	Alternatives
Points	Numerical units indicating progress	Experience points, score
Badges	Visual icons signifying achievements	Trophies
Leader boards	Display of ranks for comparison	Rankings, scoreboard
Progression	Milestones indicating progress	Levelling, level up
Status	Textual monikers indicating progress	Title, ranks
Levels	Increasingly difficult environments	Stage, area, world
Rewards	Tangible, desirable items	Incentives, prizes, gifts
Roles	Role-playing elements of character	Class, character

Source: Andrews et al. (2017); Lameras et al. (2017); Shi et al. (2017).

with products or services. The common denominator of these definitions is the 'use of game mechanics'.

The different variety of games and elements associated with them makes the creation of a detailed list of the elements/mechanics that form the content of games impossible (Dorling and McCaffery 2012; Downes-Le Guin et al. 2012; Andrews et al. 2017; Shi et al. 2017). Nevertheless, there is a selection of game elements that are commonly used with gamified applications such as points, badges, leader boards, levels, progress and rewards (Table 1.1).

The application of game content and mechanics within non-game contexts provides benefits unachievable using traditional learning approaches.

On engagement, the application of gamification can increase the engagement of the participants due to the strong relationship created between participant and content. This is linked with Csikszentmihalyi's (1990) theory of 'flow' (Csikszentmihalyi 1975; Csikszentmihalyi and Kubey 1981). As discussed previously, 'flow' is the optimum state that players of games experience, and it occurs when the content and mechanics of games are perfectly balanced with the players' skills and their potential to progress through the game's challenges, objectives or goals (Terlutter and Capella 2013; Liu et al. 2011). Gamification tries to create an emotional link between the participant and the context, in order to result in an emotional response. Gamification applications aim to exploit this state in contexts not associated with games, resulting in higher engagement of the participants. Therefore, in the classroom, gamification leads to higher engagement – we have the students' attention, they are ready and eager to learn, and are in a position to realise their goals.

Gamification can also increase the motivation of the participants through the potential rewards that the user can get through the application (Andrews et al. 2017; Shi et al. 2017). According to the literature, motivation can be divided into intrinsic and extrinsic motivation (Yu-kai Chou 2015). Intrinsic motivation occurs when the output is a direct consequence of performance and action. A typical example of intrinsic motivation is an athlete who plays basketball for the experience rather than the reward. So this action is driven by hedonic motives: the action is done simply for the enjoyment of doing (i.e. playing basketball). An extrinsic motivation refers to our tendency to perform actions/ activities for the external rewards, whether they are tangible (i.e. money or grades) or psychological in nature. For example, taking part in online competitions with the sole purpose of winning is an extrinsic motivation. This is driven by our pleasure maximisation motives and depends upon the use or value of the outcome or the action (Malone 1981; Malone and Lepper 1987). Related to the above, game elements such as points, badges and leader boards could be extrinsic motivators, whilst the challenge of progressing through levels or the fantasy of taking on different roles would be intrinsically motivating.

Increased levels of engagement, enjoyment and motivation are all benefits that can build towards increased levels of performance associated with the flow state, due to increased immersion and concentration in an activity (Eickhoff et al. 2012; Hamari and Koivisto 2014; Long and Aleven 2014). Based upon its potential in contexts not normally associated with games, it is unsurprising to find that gamification has a wide range of applications (Roth et al. 2015). Gamification has been implemented in the following contexts: work training, education, crowdsourcing, data collection, health, marketing, social networks and environmental protection (Michael Sailer et al. 2017). Differentiating aspects of these applications can be related to the specificity of the approaches taken and who would benefit from them. Overall, general applications of gamification incorporate extrinsic motivators, whilst specific applications employ a complex combination of intrinsic and extrinsic motivators.

CONCLUSIONS

From an evolutionary standpoint, we have a 'need' to grow as a person. Play, and games in particular, gives us the opportunity to achieve goals, which in turn releases dopamine, making us happy. We come back for more of that happy feeling and in the process practise a skill. We grow. The more 'flow' we feel, the more we practise and the more we grow.

It is this growth through pleasure creation that playful and games-based pedagogy harnesses. As computers advance and the popularity of certain games (i.e. video games) increases, the more obvious a choice for pedagogical approach this becomes. We want students to increase their engagement with and enjoyment of their learning. We want students to be motivated to practise. Play, games, simulation and gamification are ideal ways of creating this kind of learning environment and ultimately improving performance.

REFERENCES

Abt, C.C. (1970) *Serious Games*. New York, NY: Viking Press, New York.

Alvarez, J., J.-P. Jessel, O. Rampnoux and D. Djaouti (2011). Origins of Serious Games. In *Serious Games and Edutainment Applications*, ed. M. Ma, A. Oikonomou and L. Jain. London: Springer, 25–43.

Andrews, D., P. Petridis, T. Baines, A. Bigeli, Victor Guang Shi, J. Baldwin and Keith Ridgway (2017). Gamification to Engage Manufacturers with Servitization. 15th International Conference on Manufacturing Research ICMR 2017.

Anette Braun, A. M., Fabian Mertens and Annerose Nisser (2020). Rethinking Education in the Digital Age. European Parliamentary Research Service.

Bankmycell (2020). How Many Smartphones Are in the World? Retrieved 23 September 2020 from https://www.bankmycell.com/blog/how-many-phones-are-in-the-world

Bateson, G. (1976). A Theory of Play and Fantasy. In *Ritual, Play and Performance: Readings in the Social Sciences/Theatre*, ed. R. Schechner and M. Schuman. New York: Seabury Press.

Bogost, I. (ed.) (2007). Persuasive Games – The Expressive Power of Videogames. Cambridge, MA: The MIT Press.

Coen Teulings, T. v. R. (2008). Education, Growth, and Income Inequality. *The Review of Economics and Statistics* 90(1): 89–104.

Csikszentmihalyi, M. (1975). *Beyond Boredom and Anxiety: Enjoyment and Intrinsic Motivation*. London: Jossey-Bass Inc.

Csikszentmihalyi, M. and R. Kubey (1981). Television and the Rest of Life: A Systematic Comparison of Subjective Experience. *Public Opinion Quarterly* 45(3): 17–328.

Csikszentmihalyi, M. (1990). *Flow: The Psychology of Optimal Experience*. New York, NY: Harper and Row.

Deterding, S. (2012). Gamification: Designing for Motivation. *interactions* 19(4): 14–17.

Deterding, S. (2015). The Lens of Intrinsic Skill Atoms: A Method for Gameful Design. *Human–Computer Interaction* 30: 294–335.

Deterding, S. et al. (2011). Gamification: Towards a Definition. CHI.

Dorling, A. and F. McCaffery (2012). The Gamification of SPICE. In *Proceedings of the 12th International Conference on Software Process Improvement and Capability Determination*, Palma.

Downes-Le Guin, T., R. Baker, J. Mechling and E. Ruyle (2012). Myths and Realities of Respondent Engagement in Online Surveys. *International Journal of Market Research* 54: 613–633.

Eickhoff, C., C. G. Harris, A. P. De Vries and P. Srinivasan (2012). Quality through Flow and Immersion: Gamifying Crowdsourced Relevance Assessments. In *Proceedings of the International ACM SIGIR Conference on Research and Development in Information Retrieval*. Presented at the SIGIR '12: 871–880.

Ejinsight (2020). Video Game Industry Silently Taking Over Entertainment World. Retrieved 21 September 2020 from https://www.ejinsight.com/eji/article/id/2280405/20191022-video-game-industry-silently-taking-over-entertainment-world

Frasca, G. (2003). Simulation versus Narrative. In *The Video Game Theory*, ed. M. Wolf and B. Perron. London: Routledge, 221–235.

Freitas, S. de and T. Neumann (2011). Game for Change. *Nature* 470(7334): 330–331.

Garris, R., R. Ahlers and J. E. Driskell (2002). Games, Motivation, and Learning: A Research and Practice Model. *Simulation Gaming* 33(4): 441–467.

Gottfried, J. A. (2011). What Can Different Brains Do with Reward? In *Neurobiology of Sensation and Reward*. Boca Raton, FL: CRC Press.

Hamari, J. and J. Koivisto (2014). Measuring Flow in Gamification: Dispositional Flow Scale-2. *Computers in Human Behavior* 40: 133–143.

Huizinga, J. (2016). *Homo Ludens: A Study of the Play-Element in Culture*. Kettering, OH: Angelico Press.

Isfe (2010). Retrieved from http://www.isfe.eu/objects/education

Lameras, P., S. Arnab, C. Stewart, S. Clarke and P. Petridis (2017). Essential Features of Serious Games Design in Higher Education: Linking Learning Attributes to Game Mechanics. *British Journal of Educational Technology* 48(4): 972–994.

Liu, Y., T. Alexandrova and T. Nakajima (2011). Gamifying Intelligent Environments. In *Proceedings of the 2011 ACM Multimedia Conference and Co-Located Workshops*. Presented at the Ubi-MUI '11.

Long, Y. and V. Aleven (2014). Gamification of Joint Student/System Control over Problem Selection in a Linear Equation Tutor. In *Proceedings of the 12th International Conference on Intelligent Tutoring* Systems, *Lecture Notes in Computer Science*. Presented at the ITS 2014. Honolulu, HI: Springer Verlag.

Malone, T. W. (1981). Toward a Theory of Intrinsically Motivating Instruction. *Cognitive Science* 5(4): 333–369.

Malone, T. W. and M. R. Lepper (1987). Making Learning Fun: A Taxonomy of Intrinsic Motivations for Learning. In *Aptitude, Learning and Instruction: III. Conative and Affective Process Analyses*, ed. F. J. Snow and R. E. Erlbaum. London: Routledge, 223–253.

Maslow, A. H. (1954). *Motivation and Personality*. New York: Harper and Row.

Mautone, T., V. Spiker and D. Karp (2008). Using Serious Game Technology to Improve Aircrew Training. In *Proceedings of I/ITSEC 2008*.

Michael Sailer, J. U. H., Sarah Katharina Mayr and Heinz Mandl (2017). How Gamification Motivates: An Experimental Study of the Effects of Specific Game Design Elements on Psychological Need Satisfaction. *Computers in Human Behavior* 69: 371–380.

Panzoli, D., C. Peters, I. Dunwell, S. Sanchez, P. Petridis, A. Protopsaltis, V. Scesa and S. de Freitas (2010). A Level of Interaction Framework for Exploratory Learning with Characters in Virtual Environments. In *Intelligent Computer Graphics*, ed. D. Plemenos and G. Miaoulis. Berlin: Springer Berlin/Heidelberg, 123–143.

Pelletier, C. and R. Kneebone (2016). Playful Simulations Rather than Serious Games: Medical Simulation as a Cultural Practice. *Games and Culture* 11(4): 365–389.

Perez, M. (2020). US Video Games Sales Set Record Second Quarter, Spurred by Pandemic. Retrieved 23 September 2020 from https://www.forbes.com/sites/mattperez/2020/08/10/video-games-set-record-second-quarter-spurred-by-pandemic-sales/#3dd179966f4e

Petridis, P., K. Hadjicosta, Victor Shi Guang, I. Dunwell, T. Baines, A. Bigdeli, Oscar F. Bustinza and V. Uren (2015). State-of-the-art in Business Games. *International Journal of Serious Games* 2(1).

Roth, S., D. Schneckenberg and C.-W. Tsai (2015). The Ludic Drive as Innovation Driver: Introduction to the Gamification of Innovation. *Creativity and Innovation Management* 24: 300–306.

Shi, V., T. Baines, J. Baldwin, K. Ridgway, P. Petridis, A. Ziaee Bigdeli, V. Uren and D. Andrews (2017). Using Gamification to Transform the Adoption of Servitization. *Industrial Marketing Management*.

Sicart, M. (2014). *Play Matters*. Cambridge, MA: The MIT Press.

Stéphanie Philippe, A. D. S., Petros Lameras, Panagiotis Petridis, Julien Caporal, Gildas Coldeboeuf and Hadrien Duzan (2020). Multimodal Teaching, Learning and Training in Virtual Reality: A Review and Case Study. *Virtual Reality & Intelligent Hardware* 2(5), 421–442.

Terlutter, R. and M. L. Capella (2013). The Gamification of Advertising: Analysis and Research Directions of In-game Advertising, Advergames, and Advertising in Social Network Games. *Journal of Advertising* 42: 95–112.

Unterhalter, E. (2003). Education, Capabilities and Social Justice. UNESCO EFA Monitoring Report.

Whitton, N. and A. Moseley (2019). Play and Learning in Adulthood. In *Playful Learning Events and Activities to Engage Adults*, ed. N. Whitton and A. Moseley. New York: Routledge, 11–24.

Wired Magazine (1996). Go with the Flow. Retrieved 21 September 2020 from https://www.wired.com/1996/09/czik/

Wray, R., J. E. Laird, A. Nuxoll, D. Stokes and A. Kerfoot (2004). Synthetic Adversaries for Urban Combat Training. *Proceedings of the 2004 Innovative Applications of Artificial Intelligence Conference*, San Jose, CA.

Yu-kai Chou (2015). Actionable Gamification: Beyond Points, Badges and Leaderboards. CreateSpace Independent Publishing Platform.

Zichermann, G. L. and C. Cunningham (2011). *Gamification by Design: Implementing Game Mechanics in Web and Mobile Apps*. Sebastopol, CA: O'Reilly Media.

Zichermann, G. L. and J. Linder (2010). *Game-Based Marketing: Inspire Customer Loyalty Through Rewards, Challenges, and Contests*. Wiley.

Zyda, M. (2005). From Visual Simulation to Virtual Reality to Games. IEEE Computer.

2. The use of games to teach corporate social responsibility and sustainability

Maria Kozlovskaya

THE GROWING IMPORTANCE OF SUSTAINABILITY EDUCATION

Corporate social responsibility (CSR) is the duty of business to protect the environment, their workers and society. Corporations were not always expected to guard such broad interests. According to the traditional view, the only duty of a business is to maximise profit for its shareholders, while workers', consumer and environmental rights should be protected by government laws and regulations. This view has recently fallen out of favour, and businesses are now expected to care about other stakeholders' interests too. The reasons behind this shift include a recognition that governments can fail in their protection duty (due to corruption, inefficiency or limited territoriality of jurisdiction), as well as the emergence of post-materialist values and greater public awareness of environmental effects of large corporations (Bénabou and Tirole, 2010). As a response to these societal demands, many businesses are taking a pre-emptive approach by actively engaging in CSR and using it to advance their marketing, HR and operational goals. Indeed, being sustainable (or at least being viewed as such) often helps increase sales, motivate staff and cut material and energy expenses.

The growing importance of corporate social responsibility, both as a political ideology and as a business practice, made it an essential component of business education. All major accreditation bodies want to see CSR embedded into the programmes they approve. According to one of the leaders in the field – AACSB – "sustainability, ethics, and corporate social responsibility relate to everything that is taught and should be taught in a business degree" (Weybrecht, 2017). In their turn, accredited business schools require their lecturers to outline the 'sustainability dimension' of every course during the annual module approval process. Last but not least, many educators consider it their moral duty to help students become socially responsible and ethical business leaders (Persons, 2012).

CHALLENGES OF TEACHING CSR TO BUSINESS SCHOOL STUDENTS

Business and Economics students seem less enthusiastic about corporate social responsibility than quality assurance associations and programme offices. When I was teaching a compulsory module on CSR to a cohort of 1000 – the biggest module in the year – students were surprised they were required to take it. "The module provided good background knowledge but I do not understand why it is compulsory" was a very common comment in annual teaching evaluations. Students found it hard to connect CSR to other modules on their degree, as well as to apply the technical tools we had taught them before to the problems of sustainability and responsibility. I attribute it to the fact that most Business-related modules take the perspective of a firm, while Economics-related modules rely on the principle of individual rationality. It is not surprising that, after two years of learning how to maximise profit and minimise costs, some students struggle to analyse scenarios where there is a conflict between achieving business efficiency and preserving societal assets. This gap between the business-oriented approach and the sustainability approach cannot be easily closed by a lecturer's teaching style alone. Over the years, the module in question has been taught by a great number of academics at my university. Their research specialisms ranged from Sociology through Entrepreneurship to Behavioural Economics, so there was a spectrum of perspectives and viewpoints. However, regardless of the instructor, a balanced way to teach the subject still inevitably looked 'anti-business' compared to other modules on Business and Economics degrees. It is not just what we teach our Business School students, but also how we treat them which makes the module on corporate social responsibility the cuckoo in the nest. According to Cornelius et al. (2007), commercialisation of universities has compromised the effectiveness of CSR education. We view our students as customers and focus the marketing of Business degrees on salary enhancement. This approach is much more likely to promote careerist egoism, rather than the sense of civic duty, in our students – the business leaders of tomorrow.

In addition, the political and even moral undertones of the sustainability debate can alienate some learners from the subject, even if they appeal to those students who feel strongly about environmental and social problems. This polarisation can ignite some heated classroom debates, but on balance it is undesirable if we want all students to be equally involved in the learning process. In my experience, Business and Economics students find concepts such as a 'moral duty' (of a corporation, a manager or a consumer) vague and patronising. One example is a poll I held in a lecture, asking students if they would be happy to pay more for eggs coming from a farm with better animal welfare standards. The overwhelming majority of responses were negative, in sharp contrast to the actual consumer behaviour in the UK, where most sold eggs are free range.[1] While students may be on tighter budgets than the general population, I suspect some of the responses were a protest vote, objecting to what they perceived was a 'morally right' answer imposed on them by force. In technical terms, some of the analysis in a CSR module is prescriptive, whereas students in the Business School are more used to a descriptive approach entirely free of value judgements.

A GAME AS A UNIVERSAL LANGUAGE OF LEARNING

Introducing games into a module on corporate social responsibility can help with the problems outlined above. In my experience, short classroom games successfully engage Business School students, who are used to the following analytical tools:

- quantitative methods;
- strategic reasoning;
- the business viewpoint (this is related to the principle of individual rationality in Economics);
- a positive (descriptive), rather than a normative (prescriptive), approach.

Importantly, by a 'game' I mean a structured activity in a game-theoretic sense of the word. In particular, in a game:

1. Every participant chooses one of several available actions (those actions can depend on the opponents' previous actions in more complex games).
2. Once all participants have decided on their actions, an outcome is determined from a pre-specified rule. The rule describes which outcome follows each possible combination of players' chosen actions.
3. The outcome implies a pay-off (that is, a result) for every participant, and this result is measurable. That is, all possible pay-offs (results) can be ordered by how preferable they are.

This may sound like a very restrictive definition of a game, but in fact it fits all games in the everyday sense of the word. For example, in the game of chess, each player selects a series of moves (some of which are conditional on the opponent's previous moves – this is allowed by the definition), and the outcome is either a checkmate by one of the players, or a stalemate. The pay-off for each player is one of the three options: a win, a draw or a loss. Note that the pay-off here is measurable: a win is better than a draw, which is in its turn better than a loss.

Playing a game utilises all of the previously discussed analytical tools familiar to Business and Economics students. First, assuming the role of a player and trying to win satisfies the principle of individual rationality (or 'business viewpoint', if the student plays the role of a firm). Second, the game requires one to predict and optimally respond to the moves of the opponents, i.e. to employ strategic reasoning. Finally, the measurability of pay-offs makes quantitative analysis of the game possible and facilitates a descriptive, rather than a prescriptive, evaluation of players' actions. For example, by playing a game where businesses decide on their use of a shared resource, students can see for themselves that overusing the resource will result in its depletion and eventually every business will lose out (descriptive approach). Experiencing this outcome first-hand helps students appreciate the importance of sustainability better than if they were simply told that overusing resources is not a responsible thing to do (prescriptive approach).

I will now expand on how these principles can be put to practice by introducing two classroom games I used in my Corporate Social Responsibility course. Both are based on a game-theoretic model of the Tragedy of the Commons, which illustrates the conflict between individually rational and socially optimal actions. In these games, students in the class jointly own a common pool of resources, and decide how much of the resource to harvest. Keeping other participants' harvesting decision fixed, each player is better off harvesting more of the resource. However, once the sum of harvesting decisions exceeds the capacity, the resource gets depleted and all players make a loss. The model was first adapted to a classroom environment by Hazlett (1997), who used a plate of M&Ms from which students could physically 'harvest' chocolates. The use of treats certainly helps students directly experience Economics incentives. However, in my view, this game is most conveniently run in a spreadsheet, where the instructor enters players' harvesting decisions, and pay-offs are automatically calculated. You can download Excel spreadsheets for both games from my personal website: www.mariakozlovskaya.com

THE MILK FARM GAME

This game requires at least three players, but is optimally played with 5–30 participants. As an Economics game, it involves variables such as the price of milk and the cost of buying a cow. In the description below I will suggest concrete numbers for those variables – they are approximate, but they are realistic in terms of order of magnitude. You can use other figures in place of those, but make sure to check that the players can make a profit when each farmer owns a moderate number of cows and will make a loss (because of overgrazing) when the farmers own a maximum permissible number of cows.

In The Milk Farm Game, students take the roles of farmers. Each farmer needs to decide how many cows they would like to keep (from 1 to 5) – in the game-theoretic parlance introduced above, this is the *action* the players choose. The cows feed at the common grazing field, which has the amount of grass equal to ten times the number of players. The more cows graze on the field, the less grass each of them consumes, and the less milk each cow gives as a result. In particular, a cow produces 1600 litres of milk a year, for each tonne of grass consumed.[2] Each farmer's total milk yield then equals the number of cows they have times the amount of milk each cow gave. The farmers' *pay-off* in the game is the amount of profit they earn. Profit is their milk sales (calculated as total milk yield times the wholesale price of milk, which I took to equal 30p[3]) less their cost of buying cows (calculated as the number of cows they own times the price of a cow, which I set to £1200[4]).

Mathematically, a player's profit equals revenue from selling milk minus the cost of the herd:

$$\text{PROFIT} = .3 * x * 1600 * \left(\frac{10n}{X}\right) - 1200x$$

where x is the number of cows the player has chosen, X is the total number of cows on the field and n is the number of players.

If every farmer chooses to keep one cow only (if $x = 1$ and hence $X = n$), they make a profit of £3600 each:

$$\text{PROFIT} = .3 * 1 * 1600 * \left(\frac{10n}{n}\right) - 1200 = 4800 - 1200 = 3600$$

Now imagine that, in a game with five farmers, one business-minded player decides to keep two cows while everyone else sticks to one (hence $x = 2$ and $X = 4*1 + 1*2 = 6$). The business-minded farmer's profit will go up to £5600:

$$\text{PROFIT} = .3 * 2 * 1600 * \left(\frac{10*5}{6}\right) - 2*1200 = 8000 - 2400 = 5600$$

However, the total number of cows on the field has just increased, implying less grass per cow and hence less milk produced by each cow. This means that everyone else's profit will go down to £2800:

$$\text{PROFIT} = .3 * 1 * 1600 * \left(\frac{10*5}{6}\right) - 1200 = 4000 - 1200 = 2800$$

It is easy to check, using the formula above, that an individual farmer's profit will be even higher with three cows (and higher still with four cows, etc.) Indeed, choosing to have more cows while others keep their herds constant increases an individual farmer's profit (at the expense of decreasing everyone else's pay-off – a phenomenon known as negative externality in Economics).[5] The catch, of course, is that others' herds are not going to stay constant. The rest of the farmers are likely to follow suit and also increase the number of cows. Now, if everyone decides to keep two cows (hence $x = 2$ and $X = 2n$), then each farmer's individual profit will be equal to £2400 (less than what each player was getting in the scenario with one cow per farmer):

$$\text{PROFIT} = .3 * 2 * 1600 * \left(\frac{10n}{2n} \right) - 2 * 1200 = 4800 - 2400 = 2400$$

You can use the formula to check that individual profits will keep falling as everyone increases their herds. With three cows per person, each farmer is only earning £1500 in profit, going down to 0 with four cows per person and a loss of £500 with five cows per person! As people choose to have more cows, the shared field gets overgrazed, culminating in a loss for each farmer under the maximum herd size!

When running the game in the classroom, I found it works best if students choose the number of cows intuitively, without undertaking any formal calculations (after all, they would not be able to perfectly predict their profit as it depends on other players' choices, which they do not know). Hence I usually run the game by briefly explaining how it works (you can use the second paragraph in this section for that), then asking each student to pick the number of cows they would like to keep (1 to 5), and then entering their choices in a spreadsheet with pre-set formulas. We then look at everyone's pay-offs in the spreadsheet and it becomes evident that farmers with more cows earn higher profit. I suggest first having a practice round to let students familiarise themselves with how the game works and how profit is calculated. I then ask them to submit their choices again. Typically, after seeing that pay-off is directly proportional to herd size, students choose a greater number of cows the second time round. However, as we saw above, it leads to average profits falling! This result already provides a basis for discussion, but if you have time I suggest finishing the game by demonstrating what everyone's profit would have been if they all picked just one cow (which would be higher than the profit they actually earned in the game).

Once the game is completed, we discuss its implications for corporate social responsibility. A market economy consisting of independent producers (such as farmers in this example) will lead to over-exploitation and depletion of limited resources. This is why we need the government and international organisations to regulate resource use, either by imposing limits or by taxing producers. The same applies to pollution: factories 'use' air to dump their emissions in, and air is also a limited resource, just like grazing land.

THE FISHERY GAME

This game is similar to The Milk Farm Game, but with students now playing the role of fishermen rather than farmers. The main difference between the two games is that the common resource in The Fishery Game is renewable; however, a viable population needs to remain after harvesting in order for the stocks to replenish. The game is played across several rounds, which helps highlight the importance of sustaining a viable stock of the resource. I found it easier to run this game with a smaller number of players (3–10), because every student's decision needs to be recorded and processed several times, corresponding to the number of rounds. Similarly to The Milk Farm Game, I suggest some concrete numbers below, but you can use your own.

The fishermen jointly own a fishing pool with the number of fish equal to ten times the number of players. Every fisherman decides how many fish to catch; this can be any number between 0 and the total number of fish in the pool. If the total desired catch exceeds the number of fish in the pool, then all fish are distributed between players proportionally to their harvesting decisions; otherwise each player obtains their desired catch. If there are at least two fish left in the pool, they reproduce, increasing the total number of fish in the pool by a factor of two. The next round then begins where fishermen make new harvesting decisions. If there are fewer than two fish in the pool, the game ends.

If you wish, you can increase the viable limit of fish in the pool to reflect the role of biodiversity in reproduction of ecological systems. Another option is to cap the maximum number of fish in the pool after a reproduction cycle. Both modifications can be easily made in the game spreadsheet available at www.mariakozlovskaya.com

Each player's pay-off in the game is the total catch across all rounds. Since no profit calculations are involved, The Fishery Game is very intuitive and students need less time to get to grips with the rules, compared to The Milk Farm Game. For this reason, I do not usually run a practice round of The Fishery Game. The spreadsheet I use is pre-set for three rounds – in my experience, fish stocks usually get depleted earlier. If your students are unusually responsible in their harvesting decisions, you can copy the number of fish left in the pool after the third round and paste it into the 'starting fish level' cell, to play three more rounds.

When playing the game students quickly realise that it is in each fisherman's interest to catch more fish than their competitors. This individually rational behaviour results in overfishing and depletion of a common resource. We discuss this social dilemma with students and then link it to policies imposing fishing limits (such as the EU's 'total allowable catches') and their role in preserving the population of fish. These post-game discussions help students integrate personal playing experience into the course content and hence facilitate deep learning.

It is easy to see that both games above share the same underlying structure: players, actions (how many units of a shared resource to exploit) and pay-offs (how much benefit one extracts from the resource, given everyone's decision about its use). In fact, this structure is context-free, which makes it applicable to any other business scenario involving a common resource pool. For example, you can replace the decision on the 'number of fish' with the 'amount of pollution' (and 'fishery' with 'fresh air'), and use the game to teach students about the social benefits of green technologies. The same game structure can even be applied to the problem of antibiotic resistance, where players assume the role of doctors deciding on which medicine to use to treat a bacterial infection. Naturally, doctors are concerned about their patients' well-being (and, in extreme cases, survival), which makes it individually rational for them to prescribe antibiotics. However, in the long term this practice leads to the emergence of 'superbugs' undermining the effectiveness of existing treatments and hence threatening every patient's survival.

OTHER BENEFITS OF CLASSROOM GAMES

I have shown how the use of a classroom game can 'translate' the dilemmas of corporate social responsibility into the analytical language familiar to Business School students, namely, quantitative methods, strategic reasoning, individual rationality and descriptive approach. However, the benefits of using classroom games extend far beyond 'businessifying' your classroom. Games have been shown to increase student engagement, cater for different learning styles and help students develop a range of transferable skills, including learning-by-doing and teamwork (Guest et al., 2019). Moreover, student attainment can also be improved by using classroom games (Emerson and English, 2016). Finally, using games to teach corporate social responsibility goes in line with the goal of using proactive sustainability education (Cornelius et al., 2007). Unlike reactive CSR education (merely informing students about legal and regulatory requirements), the proactive approach encourages future business leaders to develop moral courage and flexible sustainable thinking.

NOTES

1. Data from the official United Kingdom Egg Statistics for 2018: https://assets
    .publishing.service.gov.uk/government/uploads/system/uploads/attachment_data/
    file/752939/eggs-statsnotice-02aug18.pdf
2. This number is derived from the known facts that a typical cow eats 5 tonnes
    of grass a year (source: https://www.irishexaminer.com/farming/arid-20283789
    .html) and produces 8000 litres of milk a year (source: https://ahdb.org.uk/dairy/
    uk-milk-yield), but the linear relationship between grass consumption and milk
    production is of course a simplification.
3. According to the Agriculture and Horticulture Development Board, farmgate milk
    price in the UK was 27.56p per litre in July 2020: https://ahdb.org.uk/dairy/uk
    -farmgate-milk-prices
4. According to the Agriculture and Horticulture Development Board, the average
    price of a milk cow in the UK was £1214 in August 2020: https://ahdb.org.uk/cow
    -heifer-prices
5. This only works if the field is already overgrazed. If four out of five players keep
    four cows each, the optimal number of cows for the fifth player is three.

REFERENCES

Bénabou, R. and Tirole, J., 2010. Individual and corporate social responsibility. *Economica*, *77*(305), pp. 1–19.

Cornelius, N., Wallace, J. and Tassabehji, R., 2007. An analysis of corporate social responsibility, corporate identity and ethics teaching in business schools. *Journal of Business Ethics*, *76*(1), pp. 117–135.

Emerson, T. and English, L., 2016. Classroom experiments: Teaching specific topics or promoting the economic way of thinking. *Journal of Economic Education*, *47*, pp. 288–299.

Guest, J., Kozlovskaya, M. and Olczak, M., 2019. The use of short in-class games. In *Learning and Teaching in Higher Education*, ed. K. Daniels, C. Elliott, S. Finley and C. Chapman. Cheltenham, UK and Northampton, MA, USA: Edward Elgar Publishing.

Hazlett, D., 1997. A common property experiment with a renewable resource. *Economic Inquiry*, *35*(4), pp. 858–861.

Persons, O., 2012. Incorporating corporate social responsibility and sustainability into a business course: A shared experience. *Journal of Education for Business*, *87*(2), pp. 63–72.

Weybrecht, G., 2017. How We Talk About Responsible Management Education. *AACSB Blog*. Available at https://www.aacsb.edu/blog/2017/june/how-we-talk -about-responsible-management-education

3. Why so serious? The role of non-serious games in sparking educational curiosity: a reflection

David Yates

1. INTRODUCTION

Part of my personal interest in business and organisations stemmed from playing business-themed strategy computer games from a relatively early stage in my life. Having no option to study business-related courses until the age of 16, my first experience of attempting to manage businesses and learn about how they might run came through the surreal fantasy worlds provided by these computer games.

After returning to these games, having completed various accounting-related qualifications, I have since been able to apply the arguably more theoretical-based models and tools to the environment of these games, with some success. This opportunity to practise what I had learned in the classroom and utilise this to conquer games previously deemed impossible has given me some satisfaction, but also led me to think as to how these games could be used in an educational context, either as a supplement to, or as part of, an academic curriculum. With a drive towards more innovative practices in UKHE, and the increased deployment of simulations and related exercises, a consideration of the potential role of non-serious games in business education is warranted.

In section two, I provide a brief discussion of the value of games in education. In section three, I offer a description of three computer games (each with business elements) that I feel have contributed towards my interest in business, and that I believe *could* hold educational value at different stages in an individual's business education. In section four there is a discussion regarding the business elements of the games selected, with section five taking this discussion further with respect to educational value in business-related disciplines. Section six contains my personal views regarding the potential pitfalls associated with gaming and, in particular, 'prescribing' gaming within the educational context. I conclude the chapter in section seven, hoping to inspire further thought and enquiry.

2.   GAMES AND EDUCATION

The educational value of games is not a new concept. Indeed, games form part of the early learning and development of children, assisting in the development of cognitive and motor skills. As the child develops, games become more sophisticated, and engage with themes associated with part of 'growing up' and becoming an adult. For example, board games increase in difficulty and sophistication with recommended age ranges.

Computer games, although an unlikely educational tool, have also been recognised as promoting learning (Linderoth, Lindström & Alexandersson, 2004). As a subset of games in general, computer games, such as the *Total War* series (SEGA, The Creative Assembly) for example, have fused educational subjects (in this case history) with strategic gaming. The records of military units[1] and digital recreations as such allow for the user to immerse themselves in another time and place, and to experience a representation of what it would be like to command and govern in different historical ages.

Although arguably dominated by the strategy genre, many computer games possess business and economic themed elements. Sports games such as the *FIFA* and *Madden* series (Electronic Arts) have 'career'/'franchise' management modes, requiring the player to manage their team's personnel, finances and marketing. Role-playing games (RPGs) often have a personal finance element, and in-game currency, and games such as *The Sims* (Maxis, 2000) require the player to manage their personal finances, and prioritise their spending on various consumer goods, food items and leisure activities.

Within more business-related fields, however, many simulation games exist. In terms of education, the computer game *Capitalism* (Enlight Software, 1995) has been utilised on business programmes at both Harvard and Stanford universities. Various PC gaming magazines likened it to 'an MBA in a box'. Mahboubian (2010) provides an endorsement of the educational features of the sequel, *Capitalism 2* (Enlight Software, 2001), in their discussion of business simulation software.

3.   THE GAMES

For the purposes of this chapter, I have chosen to focus on three computer games that I have played extensively, and therefore ones that I am familiar with. These three games were released in the late 1990s, and are showing their age in the current climate. However, the business strategy genre was very strong at this time, and the games are still available now, possessing a retro appeal. One of the games has been remastered, while others have warranted sequels and more contemporary games based on these earlier trailblazers.[2]

3.1 *Constructor*

Constructor (System 3, 1997) is a surreal business strategy game. It places the user in the role of a developer, with the aim being to build houses and additional support buildings in order to make a profit from tenants, and doing so against (up to three) computer-based opponents. Victory conditions include building a bank balance of £1,000,000, constructing 'special commission' buildings, and achieving 90% average tenant happiness. Computer opponents try to prevent the player achieving their objectives, while building up their own, competing businesses. The game was remastered and re-released in 2017, with a sequel, *Constructor Plus*, released in 2019.

3.2 *Theme Hospital*

Theme Hospital (Bulfrog Productions, 1997) places the player in the role of a private sector hospital manager, with the objective of completing scenarios at different fictional locations and levels. Players recruit staff with different skills (surgeons, psychiatrists, nurses, etc.) and build a hospital for them to work in, treating patients and earning money as a result. The game sold over four million copies worldwide, and is still available via retro gaming websites.

Scenario completion criteria will often involve financial targets, as well as achieving a number of cures and a 'patients treated percentage'. There is also a hospital reputation scale (from 1 to 999) which rises with cures and award wins, and decreases with deaths, public exposure of poor practice and 'negative awards'. The game is lost when reputation falls too low, too many deaths occur, or a certain limit of financial debt is breached (varying from scenario to scenario).

3.3 *Railroad Tycoon II*

Railroad Tycoon II (PopTop, 1998) is the sequel to the initial offering in railroad simulation: *Sid Meier's Railroad Tycoon* (MPS Labs, 1990). The game puts the user in the shoes of a historically important railroad entrepreneur (e.g. Isambard Kingdom Brunel, Cornelius Vanderbilt), with the aim of completing scenarios similar to those faced by the individual they have assumed the identity of. The game also features pioneers of engineering, who can be hired as company managers, granting specific benefits to the player based on their historical achievements (for example, hiring Thomas Crampton will give the player a bonus on steam locomotive acceleration). The aim of the game is to complete objectives set in each scenario, such as inter alia: achieving a target personal net wealth before the game reaches a certain date, connecting two cities, achieving a certain 'company book value', or being the last surviving railroad company in the scenario. Mullgardt (2014) discusses the educational value and shortcomings of the successor to the game, *Railroad Tycoon 3* (PopTop, 2003), when deployed in an educational setting, and proposes that using games in this way could provide a substitute for more traditional teaching and learning mechanisms.

4.   FINANCIAL FEATURES

As an accounting lecturer, I feel it necessary to focus on the financial aspects of the games for the purposes of this chapter, reflecting on my core area of expertise. This does not mean that the games are limited to financial education; in fact, they contain elements that could be applicable to wider business education in general.

4.1   Accounting

Most games of this type feature income and expense accounts, with accounting automatically computed by the game on a cash basis. For example, *Constructor* provides a year-on-year statement of income and expenses. *Theme Hospital* provides the user with a similar income and expense approach, again based on cash accounting, presented in the graphical form of a bank statement, with the date of each transaction.

Opportunities to use such computer games to offer students a chance to play, and then engage with the financial reporting associated with these financial statements, could be one method of 'bolting on' technical aspects of accounting to the gaming experience. This could be possible with the figures generated from *Constructor* and *Theme Hospital* with some instructor guidance. A trial balance could be generated taking data from the statements given and put into a spreadsheet format. This presents opportunities to use the numbers for preparation of financial statements, and thus a personalised learning opportunity stemming from playing the game.

In *Railroad Tycoon II*, three key financial points of reference exist, including a balance sheet, income statement for the year, and statement of personal wealth for the player. The balance sheet goes into significant detail regarding the assets, liabilities and equity of each company in the game. Policies such as depreciation, however, are not disclosed to the player. The level of information disclosed makes the compilation of financial statements somewhat of a formality, so the potential exercises from this could be more aligned with the interpretation of financial statements, and producing recommendations for the companies in the game.

4.2   Finance

4.2.1   Debt management

In *Constructor*, debt is available to the player via a simple loan system, where the player can borrow in £5,000 increments up to a maximum of £50,000 from each lender, repayable at the player's leisure. The two lenders that are available are:

- The Bank – which lends £5,000 at a £50 monthly interest fee (12.0% per annum).
- The Mafia – which lends £5,000 at a £400 monthly interest fee (96.0% per annum), designed to be used when the player has exceeded their credit limit with the bank.

Theme Hospital allows the player to borrow in £5,000 increments, with the interest rate varying depending on the difficulty of the level. Again, debt can be repaid at the leisure of the player; however, it counts negative against their cash total when calculating win criteria.

In *Railroad Tycoon II*, players can issue bonds in $500k increments. Interest rates vary depending on the credit rating of the company, with credit rating decreasing with each bond issued, and increasing with strong financial performance. The state of the economy at the time of the bond issue also affects the interest rate granted. Unlike the other previous two games, these bonds have a maturity date of 30 years from issue. When playing, I found that I repaid these early, incurring a 2% fee, but avoiding future coupon payments. The parallels with real-world debt (early repayment penalties on mortgages for example) may provide students with a level of familiarity useful for the future.

All three of these games present the user with a decision as to when to issue debt and utilise this to invest in potentially profit-making operations. When playing these games as a child, taking out loans was always to be avoided, and a sure sign of imminent scenario failure. However, mentally, the player can calculate a rate of return, or at least absolute values of profit that can be made from investing in new activities, with the notion that if these exceed the interest payment, then taking on debt becomes a rational course of action.

4.2.2   Buying and trading stock

Perhaps one of the most sophisticated features of *Railroad Tycoon II* is that of the in-game stock market. The player may personally purchase and sell stock of other companies that they are in competition with. In purchasing this stock, they may also purchase stock on margin and short sell stock. This makes for an interesting experience for the player, as manipulating the stock market can hold the key to victory where increasing personal net worth is a victory condition.

Companies in *Railroad Tycoon II* can also raise finance by issuing stock, which again allows the player to experience a level of financial realism in this regard, with brokerage fees applied to share issues. Issuing stock forces stock prices down, and raises low levels of finance when compared to issuing bonds. The player can also set the dividend for the company, resulting in the agency problem being exacerbated (see later in this chapter).

4.3   Other Features

4.3.1   Human resource management
Within *Theme Hospital*, the player faces the prospect of managing their staff, skill levels, qualifications and financial cost to the business. The player is responsible for recruiting staff who they feel will best serve their organisation, with lower-skilled staff moving slower, and providing a poorer service, e.g. doctors taking longer to diagnose conditions. Should the player create an undesirable work environment (reflected in the physical structure of the hospital, objects in the hospital environment and general working conditions) staff will respond by demanding an increase in wages (monthly salary). The player then must make cost–benefit decisions of either giving in to the wage demands or firing the employee. This can put players in a quandary if they have built up an attachment to their favourite staff members, or such staff members possess skills unlikely to be replaced via the in-game labour market (surgeons are notably hard to come by). The player is also responsible for training doctors, increasing their skill level and specialisms.

4.3.2   Supply chain/recognising opportunity
In order to make profit in *Railroad Tycoon II*, players must ship various cargo from one location to another via their railway. Raw materials industries will supply cargo, which, when the player builds a station nearby (each station has a catchment area), can be collected and shipped to manufacturers or to consumers (via building a station near another industry or a town). On higher difficulty settings, players can also purchase industries, providing an ancillary revenue stream. Occasionally this feature will form one of the victory conditions for a particular scenario.

Perhaps of greater value may have been what I experienced and conceptualised as 'recognising opportunity' while playing the game. For example, detailed studying of the map allowed me to see if industries within the same supply chain were within feasible distance of one another, and whether towns had industries attached to them that would make building a station worthwhile. Such cost–benefit decisions that the player needs to make quickly in order to maintain an advantage against competitors can contribute towards the development of an entrepreneurial mentality.

4.3.3 Social responsibility/irresponsibility

Social responsibility forms one of the key aspects of business curricula in the current age (Collison, Ferguson & Stevenson, 2014). In *Theme Hospital*, players can guess at a cure when diagnosis fails, conduct autopsies on living patients and attempt to cover up 'epidemics' should they occur in their hospital. Guessing at a cure usually results in the patient's death, while if the public learns of the autopsy process the hospital reputation takes a hit and the patient involved will also die. Covering up epidemics requires the player to cure all infected patients before the Minister of Health becomes aware of the epidemic, visiting the hospital and issuing a fine if all patients are not cured, or government compensation if there is no evidence of the epidemic (i.e. the player successfully executed a 'cover-up').

Constructor allows the player to build various buildings harbouring what the game refers to as 'undesirables'. These include characters such as a thief, a clown, a hippy, a cowboy repairman, a group of thugs, a ghost and a psychopath. There is also the option to enlist a stereotypical mafia character, not strictly classed by the game as an 'undesirable', but having much of the same effect. The player may then use these characters to commit illegal (in wider society) activities against opposition players that will hinder them, and in some cases assist the player (theft for example on the part of the thief means the player gains resources at the expense of their chosen victim). Activities that the player can inflict on opponents include inter alia: theft, vandalism, harassment, murder of a character, arson, squatting and picketing.

In *Railroad Tycoon II*, the game takes place in a much less surreal environment in terms of the humorous elements added by developers, and therefore less potential for irresponsible behaviour is contained within the game. However, the player can manipulate the game itself in order to gain advantages over opponents. Artificially manipulating share prices to increase personal wealth or gain an advantage over opponents is one example of how the player is arguably encouraged by the victory requirements in each scenario to undertake such illicit activity. Stock buybacks are but one method by which the player can do this, somewhat mirroring current controversies associated with this practice.[3]

The agency problem is also present in full force, with the player both controlling the company and owning a share in it. Issuing bonds in order to pay large dividends from the company to the player is but one example of financial skulduggery the player is capable of through this feature of the game.[4] The player can also set high dividend levels to funnel cash from the company to their personal account. This action can be executed by the player, with little restriction.

5.   USING THE GAMES IN AN EDUCATIONAL CONTEXT – FEATURES OVER FORM?

The million-dollar question that ensues from the above discussion is whether these games have any educational value, or are they so far removed from the business environment that they provide little in this regard? These games were never meant to be perfect reflections of 'apparent reality'. They may resemble it in some way, but are limited to their media in terms of symbolic representation (Lacan, 1977), through graphics, algorithms, language and mechanics. But even if the surreal context is not the most important feature of the game in terms of educational value, it still has a role to play in encouraging engagement and associated learning. It may be that the surreal environment is seen as an enabling force, something that encourages the fun aspect of gaming and maintains the separation between the game and 'the real' as we know it in everyday life (Huizinga, 1955). The surreal theming enables humour, and offers a 'cloaking' (MacCallum-Stewart, 2011; Sharp, 2012) of the underlying business features that may carry some educational value. Without this, the games are likely to be bland simulations, offering little enjoyment or replay-ability potential past a single experience.

Beyond the representations provided in the games, the business-related features have some applicability to wider business education. Playing *Railroad Tycoon II* provided me with a foundational understanding of shares and bonds long before I began my academic business education and could assist other students at an introductory level. The chance to experience business features such as those mentioned in section 4 of this chapter could also whet the appetite and allow a curiosity for business to take root.

6.   GAMER BEWARE – WIDER IMPLICATIONS FOR EDUCATION

The debate on whether behaviour in gaming is replicated in real life still rumbles on in popular circles. Media accounts of mass shootings rarely fail to recognise violent computer games as a contributing factor. The emotions involved with gaming have the potential for powerful emotions and feelings to be experienced by the player (Squire, 2003). The presences of a link between what the layman may refer to as 'real life' and what takes place within the notion of reality that the player experiences when playing computer games is open for debate (Nutt & Railton, 2003). Whether this acts upon the player, or the player interprets this with reference to their own personal context remains contested (see Anderson & Dill, 2000; DeVane & Squire, 2008). What can be said with reasonable certainty, however, is that games are influential on those who play them.

The movement to make games as realistic as possible, through improved graphics, voice acting and more realistic artificial intelligence, has led to games offering a potentially different level of experience and realism than before. The player experiences a new world, one that is becoming more immersive with each technological advance, proposing a new form of subjectivity for the player while playing, and potentially influencing that which is experienced and enacted outside of the game environment. Behind this apparent realism, however, lie algorithms, code and mathematical calculation, encouraging the user to become better at the game based on the parameters dictated by these mathematical functions. At what point do games and simulations become so graphically realistic that they implicitly 'reflect' a life that can be led outside of games, but mistakenly dictated by imagined algorithms and rules?

Relating this more to business-themed games and the business environment – is there a chance that these such games can reinforce forces of violence outside the realm of the physical, such as symbolic, economic and systemic violence (see Žižek, 2009)? Does the widespread playing of such economic-based games reinforce hegemonic forces associated with capitalist forms of society? If we are to believe that journeying into such games creates a new sense of the Lacanian 'real' for the player, then we cannot ignore the power of games to influence the world experienced by others. A more comprehensive consideration of this debate sits outside the scope of this chapter; however, as socially responsible educators we should be aware of this when selecting and deploying gaming/simulation software to our students.

One of the necessities for the creation and execution of computer games is quantification. This allows the player to execute supposedly rational judgements, quickly, and based on the information given. Within these business-themed games, this is relatively limited. However, staff in *Theme Hospital* are all rated on a skill bar, with an additional 'attention to detail' rating somewhat hidden in their staff profile. Company managers recruited in *Railroad Tycoon II* bring clearly quantified costs and benefits, fitting their historical profile. In other computer games, 'virtual' people in particular are rated on their skills. Sports games quantify everything down to the last detail, determining a (virtual) player's value to the user. Thinking of the wider impact of computer games, what implications does this carry for our interactions with others and how we manage people when the opportunity arises? Is there at least potential for the promotion of seeing others simply as ways to get us to the 'next level', be that a promotion, pay rise or success measured in other ways? Should this be the case, then the ethical implications of gaming on other aspects of life and society should not be ignored. Games/simulations are not literal reflections of society and should never be promoted as such.

7.   CONCLUSION

This chapter has been enjoyable to write, and I admit that I may have fallen victim to nostalgia somewhat while renewing my interest with these games, and recalling memories from my childhood. I cannot give these games justice through a book chapter alone, and I encourage the reader, should they desire, to experience the games first-hand and share the experiences that I have enjoyed once again.

Playing games (whether computerised or not) can allow us to experience a different notion of subjectivity to the one we must 'wear' in everyday life. The escapism they offer not only allows the opportunity to temporarily leave the life we lead and the toils that it brings, but also allows for us to become someone else, in a different world, if only through the game. The experiences that we can encounter through this escape into the surreal allow for the practice of our skills and knowledge in a new field, one that we are never likely to experience in life outside of games. This opportunity to apply skills previously taught in more traditional ways allows for a different style of learning to be enacted, and potentially greater effectiveness in this regard. In this chapter I have outlined three non-serious computer games aimed at the retail market when they were first released, and highlighted their educational potential within both financial and wider business contexts.

Non-serious games (and serious games/simulations) should be deployed with caution, however. In recognising that student cohorts are becoming more diverse in HE, there is greater scope for the individual learner to find it hard to relate to such games, topics or elements of the game that the user does not warm to (see Koivisto & Hamari, 2014). Barnett (2009) warns that 'unconvincing and trivial games can undermine the learning process' (p. 414). Should the learner judge the non-serious game in either of these two ways then engagement is unlikely. The aforementioned quantification of everything involved with computer games makes for a grim reflection of society, a reflection that, at least in part, simulation games attempt to achieve in their design.

As a final note, I would be betraying my true feelings if I thought that games, be they serious or non-serious, could ever replace traditional scholarship. One of my observations from working in academia is the move away from more traditional methods, towards different ways of learning, often presented under the guise of innovation. Games can be fun, collaborative, competitive, and are often enjoyed by students. However, as educators we need to be aware of becoming slaves to quantification of performance ourselves, and giving in to the potential to 'over-innovate' as a tokenistic, personal point-scoring gesture.

Traditional scholarship activities and elements, such as research, reading, theory, philosophy and reflection, all must endure within the university degree. These elements give a degree of rigour, challenge and prestige. They contribute towards making the institution a place where philosophy is encouraged, and a place where high-quality staff desire to work. These aspects of a degree are often not fun, and may not result in high student satisfaction scores, an aspect of UKHE that is increasingly dominating the agenda (Gebreiter & Hidayah, 2019). I am yet to witness a game (serious or non-serious) take me to a place where these elements of thinking and associated reflective interaction have done so. The UKHE environment is littered with numbers and KPIs, with rewards attached for achievements, much like in a game itself (Toyama, 2015). If we as educators become caught up in playing to numbers prescribed to us (Hoskin, 1996), then the question arises: are we providing quality education, or are we simply characters in someone else's game?

ACKNOWLEDGEMENT

Thank you to Professor Ivo de Loo for his comments on an early draft of this chapter.

NOTES

1. *Empire: Total War* specifically references the Royal Maritime Museum as a reference for the naval vessels featured in the game.
2. *Two-Point Hospital* was released in 2018 and has been heralded as a spiritual successor to *Theme Hospital*, being developed by some staff involved with the design and development of *Theme Hospital*.
3. The US aviation sector has recently attracted attention on this subject.
4. Again, parallels with 'real-world' cases such as the British Home Stores scandal can be drawn.

REFERENCES

Abt, C. C. (1970). *Serious Games*. New York: The Viking Press.
Anderson, C. A. & Dill, K. E. (2000). Video games and aggressive thoughts, feelings, and behavior in the laboratory and in life. *Journal of Personality and Social Psychology, 78*(4), 772.
Barnett, L. (2009). Key aspects of learning and teaching in economics. In H. Fry, S. Ketteridge & S. Marshall (eds), *A Handbook for Teaching and Learning in Higher Education: Enhancing Academic Practice* (3rd edn, pp. 404–423). New York: Routledge.
Bulfrog Productions. (1997). *Theme Hospital*. Redwood City, CA: Electronic Arts.
Collison, D., Ferguson, J. & Stevenson, L. (2014). Sustainability accounting and education. In J. Bebbington, J. Unerman & B. O'Dwyer (eds), *Sustainability, Accounting and Accountability* (pp. 30–47). London: Routledge.

DeVane, B. & Squire, K. D. (2008). The meaning of race and violence in *Grand Theft Auto: San Andreas. Games and Culture, 3*(3–4), 264–285.

Enlight Software. (1995). *Capitalism.* North Carolina: Interactive Magic.

Enlight Software. (2001). *Capitalism II.* San Francisco, CA: Ubisoft.

Gebreiter, F. & Hidayah, N. N. (2019). Indivdual responses to competing account-ability pressures in hybrid organisations: the case of an English business school. *Accounting, Auditing & Accountability Journal, 32*(3), 727–749.

Hoskin, K. W. (1996). The 'awful idea of accountability': inscribing people into the measurement of objects. In R. Munro & J. Mouritsen (eds), *Accountability: Power, Ethos & the Technologies of Managing.* London: Thompson.

Huizinga, J. (1955). *Homo Ludens: A Study of the Play Element in Culture.* Boston, MA: Beacon Press.

Koivisto, J. & Hamari, J. (2014). Demographic differences in perceived benefits from gamification. *Computers in Human Behavior, 35,* 179–188.

Lacan, J. (1977). *Ecrits.* Trans. A. Sheridan. London: Tavistock.

Linderoth, J., Lindström, B. & Alexandersson, M. (2004). Learning with computer games. In J. Goldstein, D. Buckingham & G. Brougere (eds), *Toys, Games, and Media* (pp. 157–176). Mahwah, NJ: Lawrence Erlbaum Associates.

MacCallum-Stewart, E. (2011). Stealth learning in online games. In S. de Freitas & P. Maharg (eds), *Digital Games and Learning* (pp. 107–128). London: Continuum.

Mahboubian, M. (2010). Educational aspects of business simulation softwares. *Procedia Social and Behavioral Sciences, 2,* 5403–5407.

Maxis. (2000). *The Sims.* Redwood City, CA: Electronic Arts.

MPS Labs. (1990). *Sid Meier's Railroad Tycoon.* Hunt Valley, MD: Micropose.

Mullgardt, B. (2014). Gaming in the gilded age. *The Councilor: A Journal of the Social Studies, 75*(1), 2.

Nutt, D. & Railton, D. (2003). *The Sims*: real life as genre. *Information Communication & Society, 6*(4), 577–592.

PopTop. (1998). *Railroad Tycoon II.* New York: Gathering of Developers.

PopTop. (2003). *Railroad Tycoon 3.* New York: Gathering of Developers.

Sharp, L. A. (2012). Stealth learning: unexpected learning opportunities through games. *Journal of Instructional Research, 1,* 42–48.

Squire, K. (2003). Video games in education. *International Journal of Intelligent Games & Simulation, 2*(1), 49–62.

System 3. (1997). Constructor. New York: Acclaim Entertainment.

Toyama, K. (2015). The Looming Gamification of Higher Ed. *The Chronicle of Higher Education, 62*(10), 10–17.

Žižek, S. (2009). *Violence: Six Sideways Reflections.* London: Profile Books.

4. Creating a monster: developing a mobile digital game application for accounting courses

Matt Davies, David Yates, Martin Potts and Frances Rosairo

1. INTRODUCTION

In this chapter we provide detail regarding the development of an accounting-themed mobile digital business game application: *Count FEFE*.[1] This was the main output of the Financial Education for Future Entrepreneurs (FEFE) Project, which was funded by the Erasmus+ Programme. The project ran from October 2016 to September 2018 and was led by Aston Business School. The *Count FEFE* application allows users to develop introductory accounting and finance skills for business, and while primarily aimed at learners in the 16–23 age range who are studying accounting as part of a vocational or higher education programme, it is potentially relevant to anyone wishing to improve their financial literacy.

2. THE INITIAL IDEA

Smartphone use is at an all-time high (Elhai, Levine, Dvorak, & Hall, 2017). At the same time, declining student engagement is also an issue in higher education (Lindon & Butler, 2019). This presents both a potential threat and an opportunity for education. Mobile phones (essentially personal computers) constitute a distraction in classroom-based environments, and another, easy-to-hand distraction outside of the classroom for students focusing on self-study and exam revision. Yet, the possibilities for the use of such devices within education also exist.

While travelling on a train, one of us noticed that many of the commuters had their attentions fixed on their mobile phones, with many playing games. The question of whether this time could be used productively was one that inspired the creation of the application. Other sources of inspiration came from accounting itself. Accounting is effectively a language, symbolically representing objects and subjects,[2] creating and maintaining specific aspects of meaning to those versed in it (Bassnet, Frandsen, & Hoskin, 2018; Ezzamel & Hoskin, 2002; Hoskin & Macve, 1994) and prohibiting those who are not. This symbolic representation of objects, subjects and events through accounting forms part of the symbolic order (Lacan, 1977) that supports the organisation of institutions and wider society. With this consideration, inspiration was drawn from linguistic educational applications and software (particularly *Duolingo*, which utilises gamification principles), in addition to computer games. In the following section, we outline the development process for the mobile phone application.

3.   STEALTH LEARNING

The pedagogical foundations of the application lie within the concept of stealth learning.

Sharp (2012, p. 42) defines stealth learning as:

> when an instructor uses clever, disguised ways to introduce learning objectives through non-traditional tools, such as games, to encourage students to have fun and learn. Students think they are merely playing, but they are simultaneously learning.

The potential for games to promote stealth learning is therefore apparent. Games are designed to encourage fun and competition, and to provide the rules for play to function (Huizinga, 1955). Education therefore is a secondary or ancillary trait of some games. The idea of educational games is not new. As early as 1832, *Mansions of Happiness* was created to re-enforce cultural axioms and was one of the first games to be manufactured in the USA (Bracey, 2019). The educational value of other games has also been recognised; *Monopoly* for instance has been utilised in teaching double-entry bookkeeping (Albrecht, 1995; Shanklin & Ehlen, 2007), and video games such as *Capitalism* (Enlight Software, 1995) have been utilised in USHE.

The fun and competitive aspects of the game therefore need to be present, and felt by the learner, to encourage continued engagement. In addition, gamification tools such as achievements also contribute towards this, as the user attempts to obtain the next symbolic achievement available, e.g. a medal or badge. These immersive elements have the potential to mask learning, so that the user may be oblivious to the educational aspects of the game, yet still be engaging and learning with them (MacCallum-Stewart, 2011).

From the outset, therefore, it was clear that we would need to build in a 'theme' to the game, both complementing (via providing context) and masking the accounting material contained therein. This would be one of the key considerations related to the project, and is covered in the next section of this chapter.

4. DEVELOPMENT

The game was developed through a collaborative partnership between two of the FEFE project partners: Aston Business School (ABS) and ELearning Studios (ELS).

4.1 Initial Design

We envisaged a game which would be free to download and play, and which would be available on mobile devices such as smartphones. In order to promote the stealth learning approach, the game would also require an eye-catching, appealing and functional user-friendly interface (Adobor & Daneshfar, 2006), while still placing emphasis on the use of financial information for decision making. A system for rewards and feedback would also be required, as part of the gamification process (Nicholson, 2015), in line with the stealth learning approach adopted.

The design of the game was informed by principles, as proposed by Rucker (2003):

- the game needs a good interface
- the user should get instant visual game feedback from game actions
- the user should have a score or some other way of tracking performance
- there should be clear goals and a clear termination point
- there have to be advances and setbacks
- doing well should involve strategy
- things should happen at a 'human' pace; not too fast/slow.

The ability to incorporate these principles into the application would influence the success of the project. The audio/visual context in particular would be important in establishing and maintaining interest from the target audience (Moncada & Moncada, 2014).

4.2 The Game Context and Objectives

Initially, 'success' in the game would require the demonstration of accounting and finance competence by achieving two performance targets: one related to the performance of the user's business, and one related to the user's performance in challenges which tested specific accounting and finance knowledge and skills. This would help maintain the educational focus throughout the design of the game.

The objective of the game was to provide context that would allow users to consider key business transactions of an entity. To achieve this, the context needed a business that sold a product, in order to incorporate fluctuations in inventory levels. We settled on a retail business and we wanted to avoid the complexities of having to account for high-volume transactions and detailed manufacturing production costs. Whilst initial product ideas included cars and jewellery, we eventually settled on something that we felt was more aligned with the theme for the game, as explained below.

4.3   The Vampire Theme

Early in the development process it became apparent that a theme for the game was required to enable the graphic designers to be able to make progress with the graphics and characters. We desired something that would appeal to learners in the target age range and that carried some surreal elements (and humour), in order to facilitate stealth learning. The vampire theme was agreed, mobilising a play on words: count/accounting. This led to the creation of cartoon, gothic horror-inspired graphics and characters, and provided a theme for the game content.[3]

Figure 4.1   The Count FEFE main menu

4.4 The Accounting System

The requirement that the game would provide the user with financial statements that represented the transactions for their simulated business meant that we would need to build an accounting system for the game. This was vital if the user was to be able to make connections between the decisions they made in the game and the impact of these decisions on their business's financial statements.

Though the bookkeeping element of the game was an optional feature, this was the part of the game that was developed first as it was seen as an area for the ELS team to begin. We had previously experienced other computerised accounting games that required the user to manually type the accounting entry for transactions, but found this approach to be cumbersome when attempted on touch-screen mobile devices. The approach the ELS team developed involved users being presented with a 'transaction card' which summarised a particular transaction, and then having to identify the correct 'accounts' for each of the debit and credit entries. Users achieve this by activating a 'gem' (green gems for the debit or red gems for the credit) which is attached to the transaction card, and then clicking through the ledgers in order to find the correct account.

4.5 Business Decisions

Whilst we had created a system for recording business transactions, we still did not have the means through which those transactions would occur. So the next stage of the development was to create the 'Business Decisions' feature. We felt it was important that there were a sufficient number of decisions to assist in user engagement, though we also recognised too many decisions and the game might become too slow to play and too complex, not only for the user but also from a development perspective. In the end, we settled on just two decisions being required of the user, with all other transactions at that stage being predetermined. The two decisions required were, first, the number of units of inventory to purchase and, second, the number of sales staff to employ, both of which affected the capacity to meet expected customer demand.

Developing the 'Business Decisions' feature of the game proved to be a catalyst for refining the game's scoring system and performance targets. We introduced the idea that the level of demand for the product would act as a scoring system, which would link to financial performance. So, for example, for every quiz question answered correctly, customer demand would increase by one unit. In this way, the performance of the user's business was linked to the user's accounting and finance literacy.

4.6   Financial Data

To assist the ELS programmers in creating a system which ensured the financial statements correctly reflected the effect of each transaction, the Aston team built a spreadsheet showing how each different transaction simultaneously impacts on the three main financial statements: the statement of profit or loss, the statement of financial position, and the statement of cash flows.

This spreadsheet was also used to show how year-end accounting processes worked in addition to how the start of the following year statement of profit or loss accounts (income and expenses) were re-set to zero, but account balances for statement of financial position accounts (assets, liabilities and equity) are brought forward from the previous year.

4.7   Monthly Quiz Questions

The 'Monthly Quiz' feature provided the main mechanism for testing and giving instant feedback on the user's accounting and finance knowledge and skills. The Aston team created a database of multiple-choice questions that required the user to choose the correct response from four potential answers. The user interface for this feature required the user to drag the question and then drop it on their preferred answer. Three hundred and ten questions were created covering a range of introductory financial accounting topics.

Although the Aston team had considerable experience of writing multiple-choice questions, the process proved more difficult and time-consuming than we had expected. The small size of smartphone screens meant that considerable care was needed in the creation of suitably worded questions and answers to avoid the text being so small that it would be difficult to read. There were also issues with formatting and making sure the text appeared as we had intended, and fixing these took much longer than we had anticipated.

One of the difficulties accounting students experience is being able to navigate their way through a set of financial statements to find the information they need. We therefore built a second type of quiz that requires users to find the correct values of various items found within their financial statements. We decided to frame this quiz as a quarterly meeting with the Bank Manager, and the user's score on these quizzes influenced the rate of interest payable on any subsequent bank loans secured by the user for their business. Both types of quiz were initially given a time limit of 60 seconds, which was increased to 100 seconds following tester feedback.

4.8   Event Cards

Partly inspired by 'Chance' cards in the *Monopoly* board game, we introduced the idea of a monthly 'Event Card', some of which were programmed to appear at a particular point in the game and others that were random. Event Cards were developed to introduce new concepts and business features, and to keep the user experience fresh, with new business circumstances to tackle with each card. We decided that the Event Card would appear at the start of each month and would require a user response. Similar to 'Chance Cards' in *Monopoly*, many of the events can have either positive or negative outcomes, but for some events the outcome depends on whether the user chooses the appropriate response to the challenge arising.

As well as introducing variety, we also realised that the Event Cards would allow us to gradually introduce more complexity into the game in line with the new features arising as the user unlocked new game levels. For example, at the start of Level 1 an Event Card reveals that the user's business will purchase non-current assets that month and the user is required to calculate the amount of monthly depreciation arising. As another example, at Level 3 an Event Card reveals that new shares will be issued and the user is required to identify how to account for this in the financial statements.

4.9   The 'Wheel of Fate'

The 'Wheel of Fate' appears in each decision round and adds a +/− modifier to the demand level for the period. Without this feature, users would always be able to purchase exactly the right number of units to meet demand and the business would not carry any inventory. The absence of inventory would be a significant limitation of the game as a tool for developing introductory accounting skills. The user taps the screen to spin the wheel and then taps the screen again for the wheel to slow. Eventually the wheel settles on a segment, determining the particular adjustment to the level of customer demand that was predicted for the month. This introduction of a random element carries similarities with dice rolling in other games and has been shown to contribute to maintaining user interest (Knechel, 1989; Shanklin & Ehlen, 2007).

5.   PLAYING THE GAME – HOW THE GAME WORKS

The premise behind the game is that accounting and finance literacy is a key entrepreneurship skill and to successfully complete the game the user is required to demonstrate their accounting and finance competence.

The game puts the user in the role of the owner-manager of a retail start-up business, buying and selling coffin-shaped musical instruments. The user chooses their character for the game to be either Count or Countess FEFE, a vampire who has inherited 100,000 Vampire Dollars (V\$) with which to establish a retail business. The object of the game is to grow this business, unlocking new levels along the way. Eventually, by completing the final level of the game (Level 3), there is the chance to float the business on the 'Transylvanian Stock Exchange'. There are a maximum of eight simulated years to complete the game, with each simulated month representing a separate 'decision round'. Each simulated month takes about five minutes to complete with bookkeeping set to manual or about three minutes if set to automatic.

To grow the business, the user needs to increase customer demand and make appropriate decisions to increase capacity in order to meet that demand. Increasing customer demand is primarily achieved through successfully answering accounting and finance quiz questions and through making appropriate responses to the 'events' which occur at the start of each simulated month.

5.1   Level Objectives

Beyond the initial level (Level 0, which is effectively a 'training level' for the user to become familiar with the game), to successfully complete each level of the game, the user is required to achieve two annual performance targets:

1. a minimum score of 80% in the 12 end-of-month Financial Competence Quizzes
2. an annual financial target for their business which is linked to a progressively more sophisticated measure of financial performance:
    Level 0: to end Year 1 of the game with a positive cash balance
    Level 1: to achieve an annual Revenue target of over V\$3.6m
    Level 2: to achieve an annual Profit target of over V\$0.75m
    Level 3: to achieve an annual Return on Capital Employed of over 20%.

If the game is played with the bookkeeping mode set to 'manual', then the user is also required to achieve an additional annual performance target:

3. a minimum score of 80% for recording the business's transactions with the correct debit and credit entries.

5.2   The Game Levels

As the user advances to new levels, this not only unlocks new accounting and finance questions and challenges, but there is also an evolution in the business structure, business features, business decisions required and financial data provided. This evolution was partly intended to help support learning, in that the complexity of the challenge increases once students have mastered the lower-level requirements but also to ensure sufficient variety to maintain the user's interest (Koster, 2004). This is summarised in Table 4.1.

Table 4.1   Game levels and events

Year	Business structure	Business features	Business decisions	Financial data provided
0	Sole trader	Cash transactions only. Store is rented. Drawings paid to the owner.	Number of units of inventory to purchase. Number of sales staff to employ.	Statement of profit or loss. Statement of financial position. General ledger (if bookkeeping mode set to manual).
1	Sole trader	Purchase of fixtures and fittings for store.		Asset register (if bookkeeping mode set to manual).
2	Sole trader	Credit transactions introduced. Loan issued to finance the purchase of the store.		Financial metrics and ratios.
3	Limited company	Share issue. The purchase of a website. Bad debts. Dividends paid to shareholders.	Whether to purchase new stores. How to finance the purchase of new stores.	Statement of cash flows.

5.3   The Game Process

The game process largely comprises a monthly cycle of activities, with each month equivalent to a 'decision round'. This process involves the following sequence of activities that we explain in the following subsections.

5.3.1   Respond to an event

At the start of each month the user is confronted with an 'Event Card' and must decide how to respond based on the alternative options available. The Event Cards cover a wide range of business and accounting topics (such as accounting calculations, commercial opportunities, customer complaints, personnel issues, etc.). This adds some 'on the spot' decision making to the application and assists the learning of more general business competencies.

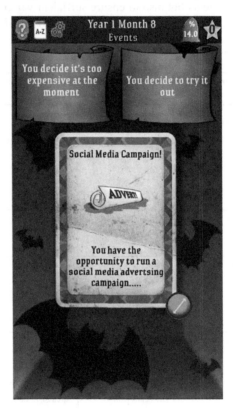

Figure 4.2   Responding to an Event Card

5.3.2   Make decisions for the business based on predicted customer demand

The user must decide on the number of units of inventory to purchase and the number of sales staff to employ in order to be able to sell sufficient units to meet customer demand. This is tailored to setting appropriate purchase quantities (in line with leaner business practices), and embedding an element of risk of lost sales when combined with the 'Wheel of Fate' feature (see subsection 4.9).

Figure 4.3   Inventory purchase and sales staffing screen

5.3.3   Spin the 'Wheel of Fate'

The user spins the 'Wheel of Fate', which can lead to an increase/decrease in the actual level of customer demand from that predicted.

Figure 4.4   The 'Wheel of Fate'

5.3.4 Record the transactions for the business (if bookkeeping mode is set to manual) or review the transactions for the business (if bookkeeping mode is set to automatic)

Stage four varies according to which bookkeeping mode has been selected. If the bookkeeping mode is set to manual then the user is required to perform the double entry bookkeeping for the business transactions that month. We introduced an optional 'skip' feature so that once the user had proved they were able to perform the bookkeeping correctly for a transaction for two consecutive months, in the next month they had the chance to skip to the next transaction. To ensure that bookkeeping skills previously mastered were not lost through lack of practice, the 'skip' feature can reset at any time (based on a random number generator).

Figure 4.5   A double entry bookkeeping transaction

If the bookkeeping mode is set to automatic, then the user is able to review a summary of the transactions, and their effect on the five main elements of the financial statements (assets, liabilities, equity, income and expenses).

Transaction Summary		
Pay Staff		V$8,000
Dr Staff Costs	Expenses	Increase
Cr Cash at Bank	Assets	Decrease
Inventory Purchases for Cash		V$80,000
Dr Inventory	Assets	Increase
Cr Cash at Bank	Assets	Decrease
Inventory Sales: Revenue for Cash		V$112,000
Dr Cash at Bank	Assets	Increase
Cr Revenue	Income	Increase
Next		

Figure 4.6   Transaction summary

5.3.5 Review financial data for the business

The user is presented with financial data for their business for the month ended. This takes the form of a statement of profit or loss and statement of financial position, with other information presented as the game progresses (see Table 4.1).

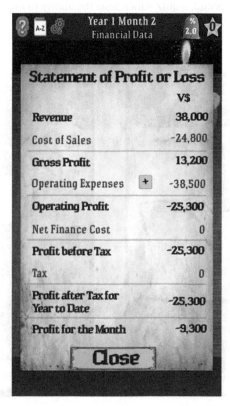

Figure 4.7   Financial data – statement of profit or loss

5.3.6   Complete a financial competence quiz

The final activity at the end of each simulated month requires the user to complete a timed multiple-choice quiz which has two different formats: first, a quiz that tests the user's accounting and finance knowledge and skills that appears at the end of eight months of the year (months 1, 2, 4, 5, 7, 8, 10 and 11 respectively); second, a quiz which tests the ability to locate specific values in the financial data provided at the end of each quarter (months 3, 6, 9 and 12 respectively).

Figure 4.8   End-of-month quizzes

Success in the quizzes results in benefits such as lower financing costs and increased demand, therefore linking technical competence to future success within the game.

6. NEXT STEPS

6.1 Final Enhancements Prior to Launch

In the six months prior to the launch of *Count FEFE*, testing was undertaken by both students and educators. The feedback we received from this final testing phase allowed us to make a number of important enhancements to the game prior to its launch in October 2018. The most significant enhancement was to introduce a 'training level' for the game in response to feedback that suggested that some users found the initial level of the game too difficult. We therefore developed a new tutorial level, 'Level 0', in which the user receives guidance on the business decisions they make and for which the performance target is relatively easy to achieve. This means that users (usually) enjoy a successful first year for their simulated business. We felt that experiencing early success in the game would encourage users to engage with the progressively more difficult challenges at Level 1 and beyond. We also introduced other changes that focused on improving the educational value of the game. These changes related to the ways in which feedback to users for incorrect answers worked within the game.

For the monthly quizzes, the prototype allowed users to skip to the next month without reviewing the correct answers to those questions they had answered incorrectly. We changed the navigation route through the game so that the user was automatically provided with the screen that allowed them to review their performance in the monthly multiple-choice quizzes.

The prototype bookkeeping feature involved the user receiving immediate feedback regarding whether their selected bookkeeping entries were correct, but the user was not provided with solutions where errors were made. We therefore developed a new feedback mechanism for the bookkeeping feature so that if the user selected the wrong account for a particular bookkeeping entry, they would be immediately shown the correct solution and would need to confirm the solution before proceeding to the next part of the game.

6.2 Further Development and Aspirations

We have continued to work with ELS on '*Count FEFE* Phase 2', which has involved some further enhancements to the game. The following enhancements were also added, based on feedback from tutors and students.

Accountants use two primary bookkeeping inventory systems. The original *Count FEFE* game was based on the 'Perpetual' system, which was the easier of the two systems for us to implement and which is also increasingly used in practice within contemporary accounting software (e.g. *Xero*). There are many tutors, however, who continue to teach double entry bookkeeping based on the more traditional 'Periodic' inventory system. Therefore, we introduced a 'Periodic Inventory' option so that tutors could align the game to their course requirements.

Other changes included introducing the option to change the time limit on quiz questions, in order to adjust this element of difficulty. This was following feedback from students for whom English was not their first language. The scoring system was also made more transparent, with detail provided for the four areas that determined a user's score:

- customer demand
- monthly quiz results
- quarterly bank manager meeting quiz results
- bookkeeping accuracy (if selected).

We also introduced a 'speed bonus' which means that correct answers gain double points if the shorter time period is selected.

The most significant development was the introduction of a new online tutor platform. The platform allows the tutor to customise the monthly quiz questions to the specific requirements of their course. To enhance this feature, we added additional questions and widened the scope of these to new accounting and finance topics. Therefore, while the original game had 310 questions focused on financial accounting, there are now 650 questions to choose from, including questions on management accounting and financial management. Using the platform, the tutor is now able to select which 256 questions appear in the game and at which level, increasing the customisation options for the tutor in line with their course requirements. The new 'Learner Analytics' feature allows the tutor to track the performance of their students in the game, and to identify which questions students have answered least well and provide additional support as appropriate.

7.   CONCLUSION

In this chapter we have outlined the development of an accounting-themed educational mobile application. We have shown how the audio/visual theming of the game was designed around the principles of stealth learning, and also discussed how key educational aspects of accounting were worked into the game application. We also emphasised the importance of feedback in developing the application further.

One thing is certain: mobile communication devices are here to stay. The ability to work 'on the go' ties in with trends towards even busier lifestyles and the need to be contactable at almost any time. Therefore, this medium offers a method in which education can be accessed at a user's leisure, in a user-friendly and fun way. It is with the use of this medium that we hope to provide support to accounting courses and skills for both students and those in the wider business world.

NOTES

1. *Count FEFE* is available on both iPhone and Android operating systems. Please visit the App Store/Google Play to download: https://apps.apple.com/gb/app/count-fefe/id1256566061 and https://play.google.com/store/apps/details?id=com.els.countfefe&hl=en_GB
2. For example, buildings become 'property, plant and equipment' (non-current assets), repayable loans become (long-term) liabilities etc.
3. For example, the ultimate aim of the game is for the user to achieve a listing for their business on the Transylvanian Stock Market, and the currency used in the game became Vampire Dollars ('V$s').

REFERENCES

Adobor, H., & Daneshfar, A. (2006). Management simulations: determining their effectiveness. *Journal of Management Development, 25*(2), 151–168.

Albrecht, W. D. (1995). A financial accounting and investment simulation game. *Issues in Accounting Education, 10*(1), 127.

Bassnet, S., Frandsen, A. C., & Hoskin, K. W. (2018). The unspeakable truth of accounting: on the genesis and consequences of the first 'non-glottographic' statement form. *Accounting, Auditing & Accountability Journal, 31*(7), 2083–2107.

Bracey, R. (2019). *Playing With Money*. London: Spink Books.

Elhai, J. D., Levine, J. C., Dvorak, R. D., & Hall, B. J. (2017). Non-social features of smartphone use are most related to depression, anxiety and problematic smartphone use. *Computers in Human Behavior, 69*, 75–82.

Enlight Software. (1995). *Capitalism*. North Carolina: Interactive Magic.

Ezzamel, M., & Hoskin, K. W. (2002). Retheorizing accounting, writing and money with evidence from Mesopotamia and ancient Egypt. *Critical Perspectives on Accounting, 13*(3), 333–367.

Hoskin, K. W., & Macve, R. H. (1994). Writing, examining, disciplining: the genesis of accounting's modern power. In A. G. Hopwood & P. Miller (eds), *Accounting as Social and Institutional Practice* (pp. 67–97). Cambridge: Cambridge University Press.

Huizinga, J. (1955). *Homo Ludens: A Study of the Play Element in Culture*. Boston, MA: Beacon Press.

Knechel, W. R. (1989). Using a business simulation game as a substitute for a practice set. *Issues in Accounting Education, 1989*(Fall), 411–424.

Koster, R. A. (2004). *Theory of Fun for Game Design*. Scottsdale, AZ: Paraglyph Press.

Lacan, J. (1977). *Ecrits*. Trans. A. Sheridan. London: Tavistock.

Lindon, A., & Butler, M. (2019). How to engage students. In K. Daniels, C. Elliott, S. Finley, & C. Chapman (eds), *Learning and Teaching in Higher Education: Perspectives from a Business School*. Cheltenham: Edward Elgar Publishing.

MacCallum-Stewart, E. (2011). Stealth learning in online games. In S. de Freitas & P. Maharg (eds), *Digital Games and Learning* (pp. 107–128). London: Continuum.

Moncada, S. M., & Moncada, T. P. (2014). Gamification of learning in accounting education. *Journal of Higher Education Theory and Practice, 14*(3), 9.

Nicholson, S. (2015). A recipe for meaningful gamification. In T. Reiners & L. Wood (eds), *Gamification in Education and Business* (pp. 1–20). New York: Springer.

Rucker, R. (2003). *Software Engineering and Computer Games.* Harlow: Addison-Wesley.

Shanklin, S. B., & Ehlen, C. R. (2007). Using the *Monopoly* board game as an in-class economic simulation in the Introductory Financial Accounting course. *Journal of College Teaching & Learning (TLC), 4*(11).

Sharp, L. A. (2012). Stealth learning: unexpected learning opportunities through games. *Journal of Instructional Research, 1,* 42–48.

SHORT THOUGHT: 'MATT, I TAKE IT ALL BACK!' – AN ATONEMENT REGARDING *COUNT FEFE*

David Yates

A few years ago, I was standing in a pub in Birmingham after being invited for drinks after work by Matt Davies, co-author and colleague. I was a PhD student at Aston University at the time, and Matt was one of the members of the Accounting Department who sought to include me in departmental activities and be part of the academic community within. We met with a couple of former colleagues.

At some point in the conversation, Matt pitched his bombshell idea (somewhat unexpectedly), containing words to the tune of: 'I'm developing a vampire-themed mobile game that helps students learn accounting.' This was met with some laughter from our contingent. I remember my comment at the time being something along the lines of: 'I get the app, it sounds great, but why vampires?' Thankfully, Matt wasn't deterred, despite the jibes from colleagues.

Knowing what I know now, I can put this down to a level of ignorance for what was being pitched, and the importance of 'the surreal' in gaming. What frustrates me is that even as a gamer from a young age, I failed to see the intelligence in the design of Matt's application until I began to use it.

Matt approached members of the department to assist in testing early versions of the application prior to release. I found myself playing the game most evenings, while relaxing after a day writing up my PhD thesis. Elements of the game began to strike me as poignant. The graphics were cartoonish, in the style of similar 'gothic comic' cartoons I had watched as a child. The music (annoyingly repetitive to some fellow testers) never became tiresome for me and reminded me of the soundtrack to *Theme Hospital* (Bulfrog Productions, 1997). Digital 'cards' flew across the screen and sound effects chimed when accounting entries were made. Surreal characters such as the 'Fat Cat Banker' (sadly removed from later versions) and competitor entrepreneur 'Business Racoon' made the game endearing to me, as a fan of the surreal business-strategy genre.

Stepping back, one can observe how this application transforms learning, taking the user to a different place by engaging with the realm of play. Trade-offs are made between depth of knowledge and playability, limiting the potential of the application, but also cementing its existence. I believe theory and philosophy to be the heart of university level education, and that there is no substitute. However, small applications like *Count FEFE* can supplement the educational experience, and can be useful for covering a variety of business concepts through experiential, stealth learning. The journey into the surreal audio-visual environment of the game facilitates and supplements this creation of a different, escapist 'real' for this to take place.

Matt, I take it all back.

REFERENCE

Bulfrog Productions. (1997). *Theme Hospital*. Redwood City, CA: Electronic Arts.

5. The use of in-class experiments to teach Behavioural Economics for Managers

Maria Kozlovskaya

CURRICULUM FIT FOR FUTURE BUSINESS LEADERS

The appropriateness of the mainstream Economics curriculum in the UK has been a subject of national debate at least since the Global Financial Crisis.[1] Most Economics degrees are still heavily influenced by the neoclassical approach, which other social scientists view as abstract, narrow and unable to explain out-of-equilibrium events such as financial crises. Students and employers are demanding a more diverse and more applied economic curriculum, relevant to real-life policy and corporate issues (Royal Economic Society, 2013). According to the progressive side of the debate, "Economics degrees are characterised by a lack of critical thinking, a lack of alternative perspectives, a lack of real world application and a lack of ethical and political context."[2]

A module on Behavioural Economics provides such an alternative perspective by challenging traditional neoclassical theory which, quite unrealistically, presumes full rationality of consumers, employees and managers. Behavioural Economics modules first started entering Economics curricula before the 2008 Financial Crisis; hence their arrival predates the Rethinking Economics movement. However, despite the heterodox subject matter of those modules (a behavioural economist is interested in how real people behave, not how perfectly rational economic agents should behave), they have until recently remained neoclassical in the methods they employed. A standard Behavioural Economics course teaches students to model irrational behaviour using formal mathematical models (game theory and decision theory). In these models irrationality is treated as just another assumption on agents' preferences. As a result, only students with a solid background in microeconomics and mathematics could succeed in such a 'first-generation' module on Behavioural Economics. Moreover, those modules did not broaden students' analytical toolbox, although they were useful in expanding their knowledge about economics research beyond rational choice model.

A recent movement advocating curriculum reform has been demanding diversity not just in the content of Economics degrees, but also in the range of analytical tools which students are taught (The Post-Crash Economics Society, 2014). In response, universities expanded the range of techniques with which they equip Economics students. The teaching of standard mathematical methods (econometrics and game theory) is now complemented with alternative approaches, including experimental economics.

Laboratory and field experiments are, in a sense, the perfect heterodox methodology to be taught in a Behavioural Economics module. The two areas of economic thought were developing in parallel in the second half of the twentieth century. Behavioural Economics research often relies on experimental methods. In its turn, much progress in Experimental Economics was driven by the need to study 'anomalies' in human behaviour. Those anomalies, or departures from rational choice model, were identified by the pioneers of Behavioural Economics such as Richard Thaler, Daniel Kahneman and Amos Tversky. Interestingly, Kahneman and Tversky's Nobel prize-winning research was inspired by classroom experiments they ran with their students.

There are multiple benefits of employing experiments in the classroom, apart from introducing students to cutting-edge research methodologies. Experimental methods facilitate more classroom discussion and let students experience Economics incentives first-hand (Guest et al., 2019). They also tend to be an effective way of teaching cohorts with varied backgrounds in mathematics. This opens up the module to all Business School students regardless of whether they have previously taken a Quantitative Methods course. Introducing classroom experiments in my Behavioural Economics module has increased the overall satisfaction score and has attracted very positive student feedback. Below I briefly outline the topics covered in the module and give examples of classroom experiments that I used to illustrate them.

BEHAVIOURAL BIASES IN THE MARKET AND IN THE WORKPLACE

Real-life consumers, employees and managers are not perfectly rational. Their preferences, beliefs and decision-making patterns differ from the assumptions of the Rational Choice Model (RCM) – the cornerstone of economic theory. According to RCM, the ultimate aim of an economic agent is to maximise long-term personal wealth. Moreover, if such an agent faces uncertainty, they base their decisions on objective probabilities of possible events (which they are presumed to know). Finally, they make all choices by carefully weighing up their options. Behavioural Economics challenges these assumptions. In particular, it argues that people have goals other than wealth, mis-estimate probabilities and often choose by impulse, inertia or rules of thumb (rather than careful deliberation). Those three features of real humans' behaviour are known as non-standard preferences, non-standard beliefs and non-standard decision-making (DellaVigna, 2009), and collectively they are referred to as 'biases'.

A course on Behavioural Economics for Managers prepares the students for selling to consumers and working with employees who are subject to behavioural biases. Perhaps more importantly, it teaches future business leaders to recognise those biases in themselves. The ability to identify and compensate for biased views is especially important for managers who evaluate their subordinates' work and choose positive or negative reinforcement measures. Below I give examples of non-standard preferences, beliefs and decision-making patterns taught in my 12-week undergraduate course, including their manifestations in consumers and employees. I then present classroom experiments which you can run with your students as subjects to help them appreciate the biases.

1.   Non-Standard Preferences

a.   Reference dependence resulting in anchoring, loss aversion and the endowment effect

Most people evaluate outcomes in relation to a reference point. Whether or not a final wealth of £100,000 is desirable depends on whether you have just won it in a lottery, or lost half of your £200,000 inheritance playing on a stock market. This seemingly obvious and widespread consideration, known as *reference dependence*, is ruled out by the Rational Choice Model, hence it is considered a 'non-standard' preference. As first described in Kahneman and Tversky (1979), not only do people evaluate all outcomes compared to the status quo, they also hate losing more than they like winning (a tendency referred to *loss aversion*). Loss aversion results in the *endowment effect*: people need more compensation to give something up (because it is perceived as a loss) than what they were happy to pay to originally acquire it. Reference dependence also gives rise to anchoring: people's choices depend on a recommended course of action they were exposed to, whether consciously or subconsciously. For example, recommended donation amounts have been shown to strongly influence the generosity of charity givers. A higher asking price for a house increases the winning offer, holding all objective characteristics of a fixed house.

b.   Time inconsistency, resulting in self-control problems

People often sacrifice long-term well-being for immediate gratification. Moreover, even when they make a plan to pursue long-term benefits (e.g. purchase gym membership), they then reverse their decision when the time of implementation arrives (e.g. fail to go to the gym, hence wasting the membership). Gyms are aware of the phenomenon and exploit it by marketing memberships more aggressively than pay-as-you-go rates.

c.   Social preferences, including altruism, fairness considerations and reciprocity

People can sometimes sacrifice material wealth in order to help or harm others. Consumers are happy to pay more for free-range eggs, compared to eggs from caged hens. Employees reciprocate generous salaries with higher workplace effort, even when their effort is not observable by their managers.

2.   Non-Standard Beliefs

Including misjudgement of own abilities (overconfidence) and misunderstanding of statistical laws (e.g. disregarding base rates and sample size).

3.   Non-Standard Decision-Making

Including decision fatigue and social pressure.

COOKIE TEST WITH A SWAP: AN EXPERIMENT ON THE ENDOWMENT EFFECT DISGUISED AS AN EXPERIMENT ON SELF-CONTROL

This experiment is presented to students as a test of their self-control abilities. However, it also implicitly tests their tendency to overvalue objects they already own (compared to objects they do not yet own), known as the endowment effect. The easiest way to run the experiment is in two separate groups (such as two seminar slots), although it can be run with just one group of participants as well. You will need two types of *consumable* prizes of approximately equal value.[3] I use two types of small chocolates, e.g. Roses and Heroes. The maximum number of treats you will need is one of each kind for every participant to allow for possible swaps; however, you are unlikely to use them all – see the explanation below.

The session starts with the instructor distributing treats to the class. If you are running it in two separate groups, every student within each group should receive the same type of treat (the groups should be of approximately equal size). If you only have one group of students, you can still run the experiment, but you need to distribute the treats randomly: do not allow students to choose their treat and do not allow them to swap treats between themselves. Importantly, the number of distributed treats of each type should be the same. The instructor then announces that this experiment aims to replicate the famous Oreo cookie test, where toddlers were left alone in an empty room with a cookie, and if they could abstain from eating it for fifteen minutes they received another cookie (Mischel and Ebbesen, 1970). Strikingly, toddlers who exhibited self-control in the experiment were significantly more successful as adults, being less likely to take drugs and scoring more highly on intelligence tests (Mischel et al., 1989). The instructor then invites the students to test their self-control ability by abstaining from eating the treat until the end of the class. I usually tell my students that, instead of the second treat, their prize for self-control will be their knowledge of their implied high intelligence (this helps keep the costs of the experiment low). Most students will not eat the treat (80–100% in my experience), so the instructor conducts the class as normal and congratulates students on their superior self-control skills at the end.

This is when the implicit part of the experiment begins. As a reward for their patience, participants who kept their prize intact are invited to swap it for an alternative treat if they wish (this opportunity should not be mentioned before the end of the class). Typically, across the two groups, significantly less than half of all participants choose to swap their treats. This is, however, irrational. To see why, let us assume that everyone in your total participant pool either prefers Treat A (e.g. a Roses chocolate) to Treat B (e.g. a Heroes chocolate), or prefers Treat B to Treat A. In other words, no one is indifferent to the two treats.[4] Consider a proportion of participants who prefer Treat A to Treat B. Recall that your division of the participant pool into the equal-sized 'Treat A group' and 'Treat B group' was random (because you distributed them randomly within one session, or because you used two seminar groups into which students are randomly timetabled). The random allocation means that approximately half of all people preferring Treat A will find themselves allocated to the 'Treat B Group' (since groups are of the same size). These people should want to swap their prize at the end of the class. For the same reason, half of all the people preferring Treat B will end up in the 'Treat A Group' and should also want to swap their prize. Given that everyone in your total participant pool either prefers Treat A to Treat B or vice versa, then half of Treat A fans plus half of Treat B fans equals half of the total participant pool. It follows that half of the participants (across the two groups) should take your offer of swapping the prize. In reality, the proportion will be much lower.

The reason behind this irrational behaviour is the *endowment* effect – our tendency to increase our valuation of an object once we have spent some time owning it. As a result, we need more compensation to part with something we own than what we were happy to give up to acquire it in the first place.

Once the implicit aim of the experiment and its results are revealed to the students, I discuss the endowment effect in the context of the course, including its role in consumer behaviour. Businesses exploit the endowment effect by offering free trials of their products, which boost sales. Even the widespread practice of using images of people consuming the good in promotion materials is designed to trigger the endowment effect. Viewers associate themselves with the people in the ad and feel like they already 'own' the good, which makes them more likely to purchase it to avoid 'losing' it. The endowment effect also contributes to real estate price rigidity during recessions. Home ownership creates a sense of attachment which makes house sellers overvalue their property. As a result, they are unwilling to reduce the asking price below what they themselves paid for the house in the past, even if the objective economic conditions have since worsened. This behaviour is irrational because it leads to houses spending longer time on the market, costing their owners in money and opportunity.

An important part of the exercise is critically evaluating the experiment. I encourage students to suggest what else, apart from the endowment effect, could have prevented them from taking up the offer of a treat swap. The alternative reasons they bring include indifference to the treats (which is unrealistically assumed away in the classic interpretation of the experiment), as well as the hassle of coming to the lectern and swapping the chocolates (the phenomenon known as transaction costs in economics).

THE ULTIMATUM GAME: AN EXPERIMENT ON SOCIAL PREFERENCES (FAIRNESS AND RECIPROCITY)

This experiment demonstrates that people are not motivated by their own material pay-off alone. In particular, they care about fairness – that is, they will sometimes sacrifice their own pay-off in order to achieve a more equal distribution of material goods in the group.

The Ultimatum Game is played between two players: a 'Proposer' (P) and a 'Respondent' (R). The Proposer is endowed with a sum of money (say £10) and decides how to split it between the Respondent and him-/herself. In particular, the Proposer offers £x to the Respondent, who can either accept, in which case R gets x and P gets 10–x, or reject, in which case both get 0. The only game-theoretic equilibrium in this game is the Respondent accepting any offer and the Proposer offering 0. This prediction is unambiguously refuted in laboratory tests of the game, where offers average about 30–40% of the total, 50–50 split is often the mode and offers of less than 20% are frequently rejected (Camerer and Thaler, 1995).

You can play this game with students using a stack of cards. Shuffle the deck and deal the cards to the students, instructing them to keep their card secret. The students who received red cards are assigned the role of Proposers and the ones with black cards are Respondents. Explain to the players that each of them is matched to someone else in the room with the same value, but opposing colour, of their card (i.e. queen of hearts with queen of spades, six of clubs with six of diamonds, etc). While keeping the pairings secret, announce the amount of each Proposer's endowment (say, two chocolates) and ask them to write down how much of it they would like to share with their Respondent. Then ask the black players to write down the minimum offer they would accept, meaning any smaller offer will be rejected, resulting in both players getting zero (in our example, no chocolates at all!). Afterwards you either call out each pair of players, or ask them to find their pair themselves, and implement successful offers (those where the Proposer's offer was within the Respondent's acceptable range). You will likely see a 50–50 split emerging as a salient (albeit theoretically irrational!) reference point. Rejected offers, and resulting burnt prizes, usually arouse a lot of emotion in the classroom, but serve as a powerful illustration of departures from textbook rationality.

This game has direct implications for workplace relations. If an employee thinks their colleague is being paid more for doing the same job, they may be less productive and even engage in acts of sabotage, resulting in everyone's prospects at the firm worsening. With reference to the stylised game above, they will be sacrificing their own pay-off in order to punish the unfair salary distribution.

Some behavioural biases can be demonstrated by simply running an opinion poll, rather than playing a classroom game. Below I describe two types of questions on which I polled my Behavioural Economics students. The first type involved asking the same question, albeit presented slightly differently, to two groups of students. The difference in students' answers highlights the effects of framing and anchoring on perception and decision-making. The second type can be described as 'trick' questions which reveal biases in judgement. Being subject to those biases can harm us in our role as consumers, employees and managers, so most students appreciate the exercise despite feeling tricked.

CLASSROOM TRIALS DEMONSTRATING THE EFFECTS OF FRAMES AND ANCHORS

Both experiments in this category were designed by Daniel Kahneman and Amos Tversky (Kahneman, 2011).

1.   How Old Was Gandhi?

This poll consists of two questions: the first requires a yes/no answer, whereas the second one prompts students to select a numerical value. The second question is the same for both seminar groups: 'How old was Mahatma Gandhi when he was assassinated?' The first question, however, differs. Group 1 is asked: 'Was Mahatma Gandhi older than nine when he was assassinated?' Group 2 is asked: 'Was Mahatma Gandhi younger than 140 when he died?' Although the first question is obviously a decoy, it influences the average answer given to the second question! When I ran the experiment last year, Group 1's average guess of Gandhi's age at assassination was 63, whereas in Group 2 it was 71. This experiment demonstrates the power of anchors. As discussed above, asking prices on housing markets and suggested donation amounts are examples of economically significant anchors.

2.   Flu Treatment Programme

This poll provided students with the following information: 'Flu is expected to kill 600 people in the UK this winter, unless the government takes action. Which programme should it adopt?' Group 1 was choosing between programme A (200 people will be saved) and B (there is a one-third probability that all 600 people will be saved and a two-thirds probability that no one will be saved). Group 2 was choosing between programmes C (400 people will die) and D (there is a one-third probability that no-one will die and a two-thirds probability that 600 people will die). Although both groups were presented with the same choice (programmes A and C have identical outcomes, and so do programmes B and D), student responses in the two groups differ. This experiment illustrates that choice depends on whether the outcome is framed as a gain or a loss. Framing plays an important role in business, especially advertising: consumers are more likely to by a '94% reliable' appliance than the one having a '6% failure rate'.

POLLS DEMONSTRATING BIASED BELIEFS

1.   *'Suppose you are testing for a rare disease (which only affects 1 in 10,000 people). The test is 99% accurate. You test positive. What is your probability of having the disease?'[5]*

The correct answer is 1%; however, it is given by the minority of students even when the question is asked in the MCQ form. The behavioural bias here is the *base-rate neglect*: students don't take the prior probability of the disease into account when evaluating their own probability of being ill, conditional on testing positive. In fact, if one million people get tested (100 of whom have the disease), there will be 99 true positives among the 100 genuinely ill people and 9,999 false positives among the 999,900 healthy people. This means that any given positive test result has only a 99/(99+9999) = 0.98% chance of being a *true* positive. Base-rate neglect has workplace consequences which we discuss in class. It contributes to stereotyping and subconscious bias against minority groups.

2.   *'Do you consider yourself more intelligent or less intelligent than an average person in the room today?'*

In my experience this question, when asked anonymously, reveals that over a third of students consider themselves more intelligent than the average student in the group. Contrary to how this seems, this statistic reveals how modest our students are compared to the general population. According to a YouGov poll, only 2% of Britons consider themselves less intelligent than average.[6] After the poll is concluded, I explain that the result is a mathematical impossibility (exactly half of group members are smarter than average) and we discuss the role of overconfidence in economic behaviour. Despite it being one of the factors behind financial crises, overconfidence has a bright side. Without overconfidence there would be no entrepreneurial activity – people who start a business must believe that the high failure rate of start-ups does not apply to them.

CONCLUDING REMARK

Classroom experiments increase student engagement, break up the monotony of a teacher-led session and help develop employability competences such as teamwork and peer learning (Guest et al., 2019). They enable students to directly observe market-relevant behaviour in themselves and their peers, hence they are a perfect pedagogical tool for a module on Behavioural Economics.

NOTES

1.   The examples of the national debate can be found at: The Post-Crash Economics Society (http://www.post-crasheconomics.com/); RethinkingEconomics (http://www.rethinkeconomics.org/); 'Do We Need a New Kind of Economics?' (https://www.ft.com/content/331ff894-f876-11e6-bd4e-68d53499ed71).
2.   'Why Reform the Curriculum?' available at http://www.rethinkeconomics.org/get-involved/why-reform-the-curriculum/.

3. The original experiment by Kahneman et al. (1990) used mugs; however, they only tested the endowment effect and not self-control, so their treats did not have to be edible.
4. Of course, the realism of this assumption can be subject to debate – quite literally, a post-experiment classroom discussion! I always invite students to question the assumptions of the methods we used in class, which helps them reach higher-order learning objectives, such as critical thinking skills (Bloom, 1956).
5. This question is based on Prof. Chris Wiggins' example posted in *Scientific American* (available at https://www.scientificamerican.com/article/what-is-bayess -theorem-an/).
6. Source: https://yougov.co.uk/topics/politics/articles-reports/2014/05/05/only-2 -say-they-are-below-average-intelligence.

REFERENCES

Bloom, B.S., 1956. *Taxonomy of educational objectives. Vol. 1: Cognitive domain.* New York: McKay.

Camerer, C. and Thaler, R.H., 1995. Anomalies: ultimatums, dictators and manners. *The Journal of Economic Perspectives*, 9(2), 209–219.

DellaVigna, S., 2009. Psychology and economics: evidence from the field. *Journal of Economic Literature*, 47(2), 315–372.

Guest, J., Kozlovskaya, M. and Olczak, M., 2019. The use of short in-class games. In K. Daniels, C. Elliott, S. Finley and C. Chapman (eds), *Learning and teaching in higher education*. Cheltenham: Edward Elgar Publishing.

Kahneman, D., 2011. *Thinking, fast and slow*. Macmillan.

Kahneman, D. and Tversky, A., 1979. Prospect theory: an analysis of decision under risk. *Econometrica*, 47(2), 263–292.

Kahneman, D., Knetsch, J.L. and Thaler, R.H., 1990. Experimental tests of the endowment effect and the Coase theorem. *Journal of Political Economy*, 98(6), 1325–1348.

Mischel, W. and Ebbesen, E.B., 1970. Attention in delay of gratification. *Journal of Personality and Social Psychology*, 16(2), 329.

Mischel, W., Shoda, Y. and Rodriguez, M.I., 1989. Delay of gratification in children. *Science*, 244(4907), 933–938.

The Post-Crash Economics Society, 2014. Economics, Education and Unlearning: Economics Education at the University of Manchester. *The PCES Report*. Available at http://www.post-crasheconomics.com/economics-education-and-unlearning/ (accessed on 2 October 2020).

Royal Economic Society, 2013. Teaching Economics After the Crisis. *April 2013 RES Newsletter*. Available at https://www.res.org.uk/resources-page/april-2013 -newsletter-teaching-economics-after-the-crisis.html (accessed on 2 October 2020).

6. A narrative-based game that can be used as an assessment tool in law teaching

Pieter Koornhof

1. INTRODUCTION

There is an adage that goes 'when the facts are against you, you argue the law, and when the law is against you, argue the facts'. Whereas some may find this a contentious statement, I have found that law, as both a profession and academic discipline, is characterised by narratives. There is the narrative that a client relays to their solicitor, which in turn must be abstracted into aspects capable of being addressed within the confines of the law. There is the narrative that a barrister (through the skilled use of evidence and testimony) provides to a court in order to sway a judge in favour of or against a particular matter. Sometimes, these narratives can be so compelling that they become the basis for popular television shows and movies even!

In order to both teach and assess the law, lecturers create narratives (in the form of problem questions) for their students to engage with. Often these problem questions are derived from popular or influential cases or matters that the lecturer may have experienced themselves. Problem questions can vary from short and simple (assessing only a very particular, discrete part of the law) to complex and interwoven. However, a problem question is still a one-shot game, and it cannot teach or assess the ability of a student to react to changing circumstances, something which is often crucial in practice. Whereas there are activities (such as debates, mooting and mock trials) which can both teach and assess this skill, considerations such as infrastructure, coordination and the size of a cohort may frustrate the ability to use such activities effectively, if at all.

A popular mechanic in both traditional tabletop games and video games is the use of dynamic narratives. They may branch depending on a player's choices (or contributions to the narrative), and past choices made may also impact on the options and opportunities available to the player in the future.

In written form, the most common example would be that of a 'choose your own adventure' book, something which heavily influenced the concept of the innovation discussed in this chapter. Because of the fact that a player effectively forms part of the narrative, they are more likely to be both engaged and mindful of their choices. Whether or not this is played out on a screen, or simply in the mind's eye of the player, the effect is essentially the same.

I believe that the above mechanic lends itself very well to application in the law in order to improve engagement and understanding. In this chapter, I provide the necessary background and context to reflect on why I chose to adopt such a mechanic in my teaching. I then propose how lecturers can adapt standard problem questions in a manner that transforms the narrative structure from one that is static to one that is both persistent and dynamic. I believe this allows lecturers to assess the ability of a student to react to changes without having to drastically alter their teaching activities. I will also reflect on how best to evaluate the success of the assessment, and how lecturers in other disciplines could also potentially benefit from it.

2.   BACKGROUND AND CONTEXT

In my first year at Aston I was tasked with teaching Intellectual Property Law, a subject that, as a result of the efforts of its previous lecturer, had gained a reputation for being particularly innovative. One of the key innovations in the subject was in how it was assessed. One of its two assessment artefacts was a piece of coursework which involved 'pairing up' law students with students from engineering or creative disciplines. A range of tasks would have to be completed by the law student, including entering into a confidentiality agreement and providing ongoing advice to their paired 'inventor'. Finally, an opportunity was provided to report on their steps and reflect on the experience. The underlying concept of the assessment was that a practical environment could be simulated for students, providing them with a safe space to develop their skills and, from time to time, learn from their mistakes.

One of the risks identified with the above assessment was its reliance on the assistance of third parties. If access could not be granted to 'inventors' – or if there was access, but the amount was insufficient – then the assessment would not be viable. Unfortunately, this risk manifested during my first year, which resulted in a new assessment having to be developed within the parameters of the module descriptor. This resulted in a diminished student experience (given that what they got was different from what they were expecting), and ultimately lower module feedback.

Reflecting on this incident led me to conclude that the assessment, while undoubtedly innovative, suffered from a potential fatal flaw. However, the positive feedback that it had garnered (not only from students but the broader university community) warranted that a means be found to still retain it. Additionally, the Law School had resolved to adopt a new overarching programme for all law students which placed a greater emphasis on developing employability and transferable skills. Teaching practices and assessments were expected to tie in to this programme to further develop and reinforce these aspects on an ongoing basis.

In the context of education, a game would be defined as a system in which students engage in an artificial conflict defined by rules and which results in a quantifiable outcome. While not exactly commonplace, the use of games in teaching the law is something that has been successfully implemented elsewhere. In a sense, many law degrees already incorporate such 'games' into value-added activities for students (such as through mooting and mock trials), with some schools also using them as assessments. Elements of gamification have been successfully introduced in legal studies on both an undergraduate and a postgraduate level in both the US and the UK. It has been shown to increase verbal skills, cooperation and confidence in students. Traditional game mechanics, apps and board games have been used in encouraging critical thinking and factual analysis in relation to subjects such as criminal law, legal skills and intellectual property. Often the feedback received from these innovations was overwhelmingly positive. This emboldened me to continue to develop my own innovation.

As a result of all of these factors, I accordingly resolved to develop an alternative assessment whereby students would still be able to advise a client, react to changes in circumstances and ultimately reflect on the choices they have made. The development of these skills is essential for law students, and so it was sensible to promote its acquisition. I decided to style my assessment as a type of coursework, given that it provides for a more flexible approach, generally leads to a more improved student experience and, at times, higher grades. It was also something that students knew and accordingly would feel less intimidated by. In addition, it also meant that many of the practical aspects focused on could be retained and directly assessed, ensuring constructive alignment within the various facets of the module.

3. USING A PERSISTENT NARRATIVE TO CREATE A SIMULATED PRACTICAL ENVIRONMENT

The idea to use persistent, branching narratives was born from the need to develop a functional equivalent for the student pairing combined with my own passion for narrative-based gameplay. In order to do this, I drew from my experience of dealing with clients during my time in legal practice. I recall that sometimes you would have proactive clients who have identified a potential risk and want advice to ensure that it doesn't manifest. At other times you would deal with angry individuals who had received bad advice (or no advice at all) and who would consult you after a problem had already arisen. In such instances, you would often find yourself painted into a corner by your own client, and it was your job to get them (and yourself) out of it. This was at times tricky, and, unfortunately, sometimes practically impossible. These are the moments, to my mind, where the skills, knowledge and lateral thinking often required in corporate and litigious legal practice are tested most.

At their core, the instructions a lawyer receives are a story told by a client, a story with various potential elements and problems, some of which the client may have identified, others which they likely have not. A lawyer must then take this story, abstract it, identify the problems that need to be solved, and attempt to solve them. In essence, if I could create a story which simulated aspects of this practical experience, it would allow me to set similar tasks and assess similar outcomes to what had been done in the past. This is not unlike what often needs to be done in other professional or business environments, something which is expanded upon later.

The proposed assessment followed a relatively simple structure in principle. First, students are introduced to a fictional client – someone who is either an inventor or in the creative industry. Initially I considered whether I would randomly assign the client's backgrounds to students, but ultimately opted to have them choose which one of the two they would ideally like to represent. The client's story would then develop at set points during the course, such as after certain content had been covered in class. Throughout the term there will then be coursework tasks that need to be completed. The initial task would be one where the student provides advice to their client on how to protect and strategically manage their intellectual property. Subsequent to this, an infringing event would occur (which naturally would differ depending on the client's background), and their client would approach them to institute action on their behalf. During this task the student would have to provide research and analysis on the potential outcome of their client's case. After the event, the student would have to finalise the paperwork related to the resolution of the problem. Finally, all students are given a chance to reflect on the advice they gave to their client, and what they would have done differently had they been given another chance.

In order to ensure that the above story is not just like every other problem question in law, the key lies in making the narrative persistent – and, in doing so, introducing novel elements to which the student has to react. This would have been done by stating that students should assume that their client implemented their advice during all the points prior to the infringing event. This simulates the situation where a lawyer is bound by the steps (or lack thereof) that a client took prior to coming to see them. This also means that a student who gave narrow or bad advice at the start needs to be creative when solving the problems that creep up as a result during the infringing event. In essence, this would mimic the experience where you would have to help both a proactive client and an angry one who only came to see you after the fact, the only difference being that you might be to blame for the things that have subsequently gone wrong!

When developing the assessment, it is important to ensure that a student's personal 'story' doesn't deviate too much or become overly complicated. The former concern is effectively dealt with automatically because of the fact that the story relates to a particular subject and its outcomes. For the latter issue, a foldback structure in the narrative is applied. This is a common method used in role-playing games and 'choose your own adventure'-style books to ensure that, no matter what the choices, there are always set points in the story. This is necessary in the assessment to ensure the application of similar skills and knowledge from all students. Whereas adopting such a structure means that the branching narrative is constrained, because of the persistent nature of each student's unique storyline it still allows for variation during the different phases of the assessment.

A simplified visual representation of the assessment would look something like Figure 6.1.

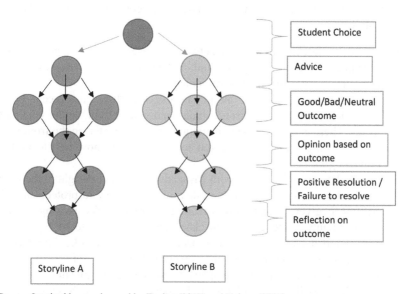

Source: Inspired by graphs used by Tucker (2017) and Nelson (2015).

Figure 6.1   Simple visual depiction of foldback branching narrative

One of the challenges in developing the assessment was in determining the distribution of marks for each set event. Initial bad advice shouldn't mean that a student would necessarily obtain a bad mark at the end, because the student may still be able to come up with a practical solution. Additionally, being placed in a situation where the client can't be helped at all shouldn't result in a fail, as the student may be able to learn just as much in the process when reflecting on their ultimate choices. Accordingly, I decided to weight both the initial advice and the final reflection at 25% of the final mark each, with the opinion in relation to the infringing event contributing 50% of it. It seemed sensible to provide the greatest weight to this component as it related not only to the skills and knowledge taught in the module, but also to skills being assessed on a programme-wide level. This also affords students the chance to essentially 'fix' the mistakes of earlier decisions, and not have one bad choice ultimately ruin the student experience. Finally, they are able to reflect on what they have done right and/or wrong (including what they learnt from the process) and due credit is afforded for this.

3.1   An Example of a Narrative-Based Game in Intellectual Property Law

Here is a brief overview of how the assessment could theoretically play out for a student:

- A student must initially choose between representing Steven, an engineer, or Janice, a children's storybook author. A brief background is provided for both clients. The student chooses Janice.
- Janice has found quite a bit of success with her most recent book, *Babagoogoo*, the protagonist of which is a mythical flying lemur with pink wings. There is also a striking depiction of the character on the front page of the book. Janice has asked you for advice about how best to protect *Babagoogoo*.
- The student provides Janice with basic advice about copyright in the book and in the art found therein. No other advice on how to protect Janice's creation is given, despite topics relating to trade marks, passing off and confidentiality being covered in class. This advice could be typified as neutral to bad, as Janice takes no proactive steps to protect her brand, comfortable in the knowledge that she is protected by copyright.
- Janice is upset to find that a company has started selling plushies of a character that is strikingly similar to 'Babagoogoo'. Someone has also started producing a 'Babagoogoo' TV series, and although the fictional characters she has developed appear in it, the storylines are not based on any of the books she's written. She now asks you for advice on what can be done.

- Because the student did not comprehensively advise Janice, she didn't opt to register trade marks and/or designs in the various distinctive aspects and visual expressions of her creations. She also didn't think of entering into confidentiality agreements when talking to toy manufacturers or TV producers when showcasing characters and ideas. Accordingly, the extent of her intellectual property protection is severely limited.
- Because of the fact that fictional characters are not protected by copyright in the UK, Janice's chances of successfully relying purely on copyright law in relation to the above set of facts are relatively slim. A student may be able to institute action based on passing off, and also to challenge any attempts from the plushie producers and TV production company of registering any trade marks from their side. Subsequent to successful resolution of these aspects, you could still register some trade marks in order to protect Janice's brand moving forward. Accordingly, the student can possibly make the best of a bad situation, and fix their mistake – even though most of it could have been avoided with proper advice at the start!
- Subsequent to this, the student can reflect on how their options were limited because they likely rushed their initial advice. Fortunately, in this instance the student would be able to rectify most of the problems caused by their advice, and would be able to reflect on how greater research and broader advice during the initial stages would have assisted both themselves and their client in terms of wasted costs and effort in resolving the situation.
- Alternatively, in the event that the student gives broad, detailed advice to Janice, they would be able to expand on the various protections available and analyse which, given the scenario, would be most fit for purpose. Whereas they would therefore not necessarily have to 'fix' any mistakes, they would have more to discuss and would still need to engage with what the best strategy would be for addressing the infringements that did occur. Admittedly the student's final reflection would likely be less focused on the lessons they have learnt, but there is still the opportunity to reflect on the choices they have made and how that affected the final 'outcome' of the matter.

In the above example there is only one set point and the branches of the narrative aren't too complex. This was deliberately chosen so as to not overwhelm the student or the lecturer. Naturally, the story and the solutions necessary to solve any problems that arise would differ based on how many events occur, though I would caution against too many, particularly when implementing this for the first time, or if the module is an elective that only takes place over one term.

4.   EVALUATING THE SUCCESS OF YOUR NARRATIVE-BASED GAME IN ORDER TO FURTHER DEVELOP IT

When developing any new teaching practices or assessments there is a need for self-evaluation and critical reflection, and also for evaluation to happen on an ongoing basis. Whereas it is not the only metric by which one should evaluate new practices, I believe that a significant factor in evaluating success would be to see what the impact has been on student experience and class performance. I was after all mindful of the fact that the assessment, while developed based on real-world experience, was not necessarily a tried and tested method.

Insofar as is possible, input from other stakeholders would be beneficial in evaluation and further development of such assessments. At the Law School we commonly make use of practitioners who are experts in their field to serve as visiting fellows and advise in content and course design. For my development, I was privileged to be in touch with lawyers who not only represented clients in the entertainment industry but also understood the relevant game mechanics. Using such resources greatly assists in determining whether there is merit in the assessment, not only in terms of how it assesses students, but also in potentially providing feedback on later performance in the workplace. Practitioners may also be able to advise on other considerations, such as whether the outcomes (and/or professional requirements) might unduly constrain the assessment, and how best to overcome this.

It is common practice to collect informal module feedback during the mid-point of the term. This interim feedback may also assist in gauging the initial interest and experience of students, while also assisting in identifying any initial concerns and providing an opportunity to tweak the assessment prior to its completion (to the extent that this is allowed within the confines of the externally approved assessment brief, naturally).

Last but not least, success shouldn't be determined solely by how students or others experience the assessment (though it is an important aspect). I believe that an important consideration when adopting any new practice or assessment is that it should be fun (for lack of a better word) for the person designing and delivering it. After all, if it isn't worthwhile for the lecturer concerned, they would have no reason to carry on with it.

5.   USING NARRATIVE-BASED GAMES IN OTHER MODULES OR DISCIPLINES

Because a narrative-based game assesses both specific knowledge and a general skill, the game can easily be used as a template for similar forms of coursework in other subjects. A model whereby client events may be simulated would be beneficial in a variety of contexts. For the majority of subjects, the only part that effectively changes is the specific knowledge being assessed. However, there could be some tweaks relating to the skills component if there are procedural aspects that a student needs to understand and engage with. An example of this would be in company law where one could build a persistent narrative based on decisions taken by the board or shareholders of a company.

At its core, the assessment is not much different from a business simulation, something which is often used as part of teaching and assessment in various other courses within business schools. Subject benchmark statements in a variety of disciplines have a general outcome whereby a student should be able to apply their knowledge in a dynamic environment, and this is a way in which this outcome can be assessed. Accordingly, the use of narrative-based games could be sensibly applied in other disciplines, particularly those where the 'problem' is derived from client interaction.

6.   CONCLUDING REMARKS

Individual knowledge and experience can have a significant impact on the choices you make when developing new teaching practices and assessment. My own practical experience provided me with the insight as to what intellectual property law students should be assessed on, whereas my love of games provided the inspiration for how to potentially accomplish this. That being said, because I had not created branching narratives before this, I struggled in actually determining how best to implement my idea. I am mindful of the fact that individuals versed in the use of such methods may find the way I have set out my model in this chapter to be somewhat basic. That being said, insofar as there is a need to develop new assessments, there will always be some risk that things may go wrong. I find I tend to learn as I go along, and often more so from my mistakes than my successes – a principle which, coincidentally, is echoed in this very assessment model!

BIBLIOGRAPHY

Bouki, V., D. Economou & P. Kathrani (2014). '"Gamification" and legal education: A game-based application for teaching university law students'. *2014 International Conference on Interactive Mobile Communication Technologies and Learning* (November).

Ferguson, D.M. (2016). 'The gamification of legal education: Why games transcend the Langdellian Model and how they can revolutionize law school'. *Chapman Law Review* 19(2), 629–657.

Hinebaugh, J.P. (2009). *A board game education: Building skills and academic success*. Lanham, MD: Rowman & Littlefield Education.

Jacques, S. (2018). 'Experimenting gamification in legal higher education: A thousand intellectual property rights'. *Nottingham Law Journal* 27(1).

Kirkland, K. & D. Sutch (2009, August). *Overcoming the barriers to educational innovation: A literature review*. Futurelab. Available at https://www.nfer.ac.uk/ publications/FUTL61/FUTL61.pdf (last accessed 24 October 2018).

Lerner, A. & E. Talati (2006). 'Teaching law and educating lawyers: Closing the gap through multidisciplinary experiential learning'. *Journal of Clinical Legal Education* (December), 96–133.

Lopez Torres, A. (1998). 'MacCrate goes to law school: An annotated bibliography of methods for teaching lawyering skills in the classroom'. *Nebraska Law Review* 77(1), 132.

Nelson, P. (2015). 'Designing branching narrative'. *The Story Element* (11 February). Available at https://thestoryelement.wordpress.com/2015/02/11/designing -branching-narrative/ (last accessed 28 October 2018).

Tucker, C. (2017). 'Managing the complexity of branching scenarios'. *Experiencing E-Learning* (18 July). Available at https://christytucker.wordpress.com/2017/07/18/ managing-the-complexity-of-branching-scenarios/ (last accessed 28 October 2017).

Webber, J. & D. Griliopoulos (2018). *Ten things video games can teach us (about life, philosophy and everything)*. London: Robinson.

SHORT THOUGHT: THE USE OF VIDEO GAMES IN LAW EDUCATION

Pieter Koornhof

One of my fields of research (and naturally also a personal passion) is video gaming. Despite its prevalence in society and the fact that its annual turnover now dwarfs traditional forms of entertainment, it is not particularly well researched or understood from a legal point of view. Given how pervasive it has become and the potential it has for immersion and engagement, I have long held the opinion that more should be done to use video games as a teaching tool in law. There are also a couple of ways that this can be done without it being onerous or the cost implications being unnecessarily high.

Firstly, where many jurisprudence or ethics courses may have a film or book study component, this could easily be replaced with a video game that explores a pertinent theme. A major benefit of video games over films or books is that the player is given agency (albeit usually constrained by the plot or game mechanics) rather than it being a passive experience. For instance, instead of watching a film detailing the horrors of war, a first-person shooter where the student potentially commits those very horrors may result in a much more engaging and meaningful thought experiment – a game that is particularly fit for purpose in this regard would be *Spec Ops: The Line*. Secondly, although there are not many games which have lawyers as protagonists, there are a select few that do. The *Ace Attorney* series is a fine example of games that use a compelling mix of fact-finding, linguistics and logical puzzles (coupled with rudimentary courtroom procedure). There are also other, less notable but equally fun, games of such a nature – including one where you are both a Parisian advocate and a falcon! Such games can be used to illustrate foundational concepts in modules such as introduction to law, criminal law or even the law of evidence. Lastly, those more adventurous and tech savvy could try their hand at creating simple games to be used for either of the above purposes. Narrative games allowing for player interaction, such as those explored in this book, can be built in engines such as Twine or Construct. In another chapter, my co-author and I explore the benefits of the use of fictional characters and world-building in legal education. This too, naturally, is something which can further be expanded on in a video game. In fact, basic versions of such games already exist and the impact on student experience has been published recently. Accordingly, while still in its relative infancy, it is not that ridiculous to suppose that video gaming will become an accepted (if not common) teaching tool in legal education.

7. Delivering games in a remote online teaching environment

Jon Guest and Matthew Olczak

1. INTRODUCTION

The playing of simple, short games in which students make decisions and find out the implications for their pay-offs (winnings) has become an increasingly common way to teach a range of key concepts and theories in economics. These are quite different from traditional business simulations (see the second section of this book) where a much more detailed scenario is played out. In such simulations, students typically have to make various decisions over a number of weeks and these choices are usually made outside of class time. In contrast, in short economics games, students typically have to make choices along just one dimension, e.g. what price to charge, how much to produce, or what quality to produce. These games typically take between 20 and 40 minutes in total to run and have traditionally taken place in face-to-face classes. During this time, students make decisions across a number of rounds and respond to the outcomes from their own and their classmates' previous behaviour.

In our experience teaching economics, using short in-class games in this way makes it easier to get across the underlying theory and bring out the implications of the resulting predictions. In Guest et al. (2019) we discuss a number of further benefits from using games in this way. In brief, we highlighted that games can help:

- break up the monotony of tutor-led teaching sessions and increase student engagement;
- support students with heterogeneous prior subject knowledge and learning styles;
- students to develop a range of transferable skills that will assist them in their future careers.

There are a large number of games that can be played in the classroom and these can be used to teach a diverse range of theories and applications. Many of these games require interaction between participants with a player's pay-off depending upon decisions made by other participant(s). For example, in the famous prisoner's dilemma game, two players must simultaneously decide in secret whether to confess to or deny committing a crime. Jointly they are better off denying the crime, but they each have an individual incentive to confess. Likewise, in some games participants represent buyers and sellers interacting in a marketplace.[1]

Traditionally, these short in-class games were played in a paper-based format, i.e. with photocopied instructions and decision sheets provided to the participants. In particular, in the late 1990s Charles Holt co-authored a series of influential articles (e.g. Holt and Laury, 1997) demonstrating that ordinary playing cards can be used to facilitate participant decision making and reduce the preparation costs for the tutor. In the last ten years, many online versions of the games have been developed.[2] Initially their use was constrained by the availability of computer rooms for teaching. However, with the vast majority of students now having web-enabled devices it is possible to play online games in any classroom or lecture theatre that has good Wi-Fi.

Over time, we have experimented with using technology to facilitate the face-to-face delivery of in-class games. This has enabled us to develop an understanding of the benefits and costs that switching to a technological approach brings. We will summarise our views on this in section 2 (see Guest et al., 2019, for more detailed discussion). However, we write this chapter at a time when the teaching environment is, at least temporarily, changing drastically. In light of COVID-19, much teaching for the forthcoming academic year will be delivered remotely.

When we started thinking about how to develop our teaching for this new environment, it became apparent that arguably all the benefits of using games listed above are magnified. First, there is concern that students could easily become less engaged when delivery is remote, communication is more difficult and a proportion of the delivery may be via pre-recorded lectures. Second, remote delivery makes it harder to identify different students' subject knowledge and learning styles. Finally, transferable skills will become even more important given the work environment students will be going into. In light of this, the aim of this chapter is to build on our understanding of how to use technology to deliver games (section 2) and provide insights into how games can still be used in a remote online delivery environment. We distinguish between synchronous delivery (section 3), where delivery is live and interactive, and asynchronous delivery (section 4), where students undertake learning activities flexibly at their chosen time. Then, section 5 discusses how, regardless of the means of delivery, appropriate follow-up activities are important to maximise the potential learning advantages of using games. Finally, section 6 offers some overall concluding remarks.

2.   ADVANTAGES OF PAPER V. ONLINE DELIVERY OF IN-CLASS GAMES

Before considering the remote online teaching environment, we first summarise some of the key pros and cons of using technology to assist in the delivery of in-class face-to-face games.

2.1   Advantages of Paper-Based Games

- Greater face-to-face social interaction can help motivate students and so have a positive impact on their learning. It may also help to develop a community of learners and lead to greater student interaction outside of the classroom.
- They may suit the personality and teaching styles of particular academics. As the tutor is facilitating the game rather than the software, they are likely to have greater direct involvement with the activity. This helps some individuals to convey their interest/passion in the subject and this in turn may help motivate greater levels of learning amongst the students.
- There are no set-up costs of ensuring that all participants log into the software successfully. It is also easier to make sure the participants understand the game.
- There is less anonymity. This reduces the chances that some students will hold up the progress of the game by either delaying or failing to make a decision.
- The tutor is able to change the pay-offs on the spot rather than having to adjust them in the software.

2.2   Advantages of Using Technology

- It reduces many of the cognitive and physical demands on the tutor. For example, it removes the need to: (i) change the room set-up at the beginning of the session; (ii) photocopy and distribute instruction/record sheets; (iii) physically move around the class collecting student decisions; (iv) calculate pay-offs and record results (i.e. inputting data into a spreadsheet). For some games, effective manual administration is almost impossible for one individual to undertake without some assistance from colleagues or other students.
- It enables tutors to more easily to present results to the class both during and at the end of the game. It is also easy to save and disseminate results for follow-up work and further discussion.

- It makes it possible to 'scale-up' games for use in very large classes, i.e. over 200 students.
- It increases the number of rounds that can be played in a given time period and makes it possible to play games that are more complex. For example, it is possible to have some rounds with stranger matching (random matching with different participants) and some with partner matching (matching with the same participants) in the same game.

3.   REMOTE ONLINE SYNCHRONOUS GAMES

At first glance it would seem difficult to play games synchronously through remote delivery. However, we believe the barriers to this are not insurmountable. It may be possible to deliver games in live webinar sessions that take place in a virtual classroom. Furthermore, as we highlighted above, online games may be feasible even if a large number of students attend such webinars.

Clearly, in a remote online teaching environment set-up costs become greater. There is a need to ensure that all participants are logged in to the software and there is greater potential for technological issues to arise. However, many online games are relatively simple to log in to and as long as clear instructions are provided, participants should be able to do this fairly quickly at the start of a session. Furthermore, if the same online games provider is used to run a range of games throughout a module, students will rapidly become familiar with how the site works.

It is also clear that interaction between students will be lost once the game is played remotely and it is harder for the tutor to interact with the students. One issue this presents is making sure that the participants fully understand the instructions before the game begins. This is crucial since if the students fail to comprehend the rules and make decisions in a random manner it will add greater noise to the results. This can make the implications of the results more difficult to follow and reduce the learning benefits. Therefore, it is important that the tutor spends some time at the start of the game talking through the rules and pay-offs. Screenshots of examples can also be used to show both the decision input and feedback displays the participants will see. In addition, the chat facility in the virtual classroom could be used to enable responses and questions from students. Likewise, raised hands could be used to indicate that students are logged in and have understood the instructions provided. Many online games packages also provide short quiz questions embedded into the instructions to assist understanding. Some also provide professionally made instruction videos to use. However, experience shows that a number of students will not fully grasp the rules until they have played a round or two of the actual game. For this reason, it is important that games are played across a reasonable number of rounds.

Once participants understand the game and are logged in, there is still the issue of how the tutor can provide commentary and feedback as the game progresses. As well as the chatroom, this can be done through audio delivery, for example by counting down the time until a round will end. Similarly, at the end of the round the tutor can provide a summary of the outcomes in that round. Typically, the game sites will provide a graphical display that the tutor can share via their screen and then discuss. Given the number of tasks the tutor will have to cover to run the game in this way, it may be worth recruiting a colleague or student to help, at least when you are inexperienced in running a particular game.

Finally, once delivery is remote, it should be recognised that the potential for problems caused by individual participants holding up the progress of the game by delaying or failing to make a decision is exacerbated. With this in mind, it is important to note that some online games include an option for the tutor to set a time limit on the decision-making process. Once this limit is reached, the software can impose a particular decision on players who have failed to respond. Therefore, it is important that the tutor knows exactly how to end the round and impose a decision on such participants, and what that decision will be. More generally, with online delivery it is arguably even more important that the tutor has a detailed understanding of how a particular game works. A good way to see this from the perspective of both the tutor and the students is to run the game and also play as a participant on separate browser tabs or devices.

4.   REMOTE ONLINE ASYNCHRONOUS GAMES

The previous section has demonstrated that, whilst there may be some diffi-culties to overcome, it should be feasible to run synchronous games remotely online. However, in the new teaching environment asynchronous delivery will also typically be common. This potentially provides an additional avenue through which games can be delivered. One advantage of this form of delivery is that with students living in different time zones and having different work/home responsibilities it might be difficult to find a mutually convenient time to play the games synchronously.

4.1   Individual Choice Games

The obvious type of game that could be used in asynchronous delivery are indi-vidual choice tasks where the decision of one participant has no impact on the pay-off of others. For example, in pairwise lottery-choice games, participants must typically choose between lower-risk options with a lower expected return and higher-risk options with a higher expected return. Similarly, the game site Moblab includes the bomb risk game where the participant has to choose how many boxes to open. At the start of the game one box containing a bomb is randomly determined. The participant's pay-off increases with the number of boxes opened unless they choose the one that contains the bomb. In this case, their pay-off falls to zero. The tutor can use the results from such games to discuss factors such as students' risk preferences and possible misperception of probabilities. In contrast, in intertemporal choice games, participants have to choose between receiving a smaller prize today or a larger prize at some point in the future. The tutor can use these results to discuss varying levels of impatience and time inconsistent preferences.[3]

Alternatively, there are games where the participants act as the manager of a monopoly firm.[4] The instructions provide relevant cost information, and the participants have to make the firm's strategic decisions. The software then simulates the role of buyers. The participants can adjust their decisions in each round as they try to maximise profits. The software can also add random shocks into the market to add some sense of realism. At the end of the game, students can see how their decisions compare with those made by the rest of their cohort, participants in previous games and the predictions of economic theory. Whilst such games could also be delivered synchronously, there would seem to be limited benefit to doing so and it may in fact be detrimental to require all students to progress through them at the same pace. These games should work well under asynchronous delivery. In addition, providing individual choice games for students to play asynchronously may be a good way to familiarise students with a game site. Once students are used to logging in and playing such games, it may become easier to use the same site to play more complex interactive games.

4.2   Interactive Games

In contrast, to the games discussed in the previous subsection, many of the games that have traditionally been used in class involve some interdependence between participants. This includes, for example, the market trading and the prisoner's dilemma game referred to in the introduction. In such games, a given participant's pay-offs depend not only on their own decisions, but also on the decisions of other participant(s) that they are playing against. This interaction between participants would seem impossible with asynchronous delivery. However, some software has previously enabled this in a limited way for some games by allowing students to participate against decisions retrieved from a database of previous results. Recent developments in technology have opened up another alternative – playing against robotic players that make decisions according to some pre-programmed rules.[5]

The use of games with robotic players in teaching is thus far an underexplored area. It raises a number of interesting issues. First, how will students respond to playing against robotic players? This may change the way they play in a systematic manner. It could also reduce students' interest and engagement with the game. Second, when playing against robotic players, students may be less likely to believe that the results provide insight into decision making in the real world. This could significantly reduce the potential learning benefits. Third, how sophisticated is the robotic play? In particular, to what extent do the decisions respond to those made by the human players? The more this is the case, the richer the learning experience for the students potentially becomes. In the future, AI technology may enable robotic players to learn to predict how student players will behave. It might also become increasingly possible for the tutor to choose the strategy adopted by the robotic players in certain games. For example, in a repeated prisoner's dilemma game the tutor may be able to control how a robot player responds in subsequent rounds, having discovered that it wrongly trusted its human opponent to deny the crime. If so, the tutor may be able to manipulate games in order to bring out particular lessons and broaden the range of learning outcomes. Finally, it should be noted that robotic players could also be used in the remote online synchronous delivery of games discussed earlier. An interesting question is then whether or not to inform the students upfront that they will be playing against robotic players.

There are therefore a range of different ways in which robotic players can be introduced into games. For now, what is clear is that they allow for interactive games to be delivered asynchronously. Increased use of games in this way will hopefully provide further insights into the issues we have posed. The increased demand for games that can be used in this way may also increase the speed at which this technology develops.

4.3   General Issues

The previous two subsections have suggested that a range of games could be delivered asynchronously. However, there are also a number of further issues that need to be considered when delivering games in this way.

First, for how long do you make a game available to play? Here, there is a trade-off between flexibility and focus. Given the possibility of technological issues and the difficulties logging in discussed previously, it is probably advisable to allow for some flexibility and not make the game available for less than 24 hours. However, to keep the student's attention on the game and to allow for timely feedback, it is probably sensible to make it available for no more than 4–7 days.

Second, we previously discussed the importance of making sure that participants can easily understand the game. Asynchronous delivery makes it harder for the tutor to answer any questions before the game starts. Therefore, it becomes even more important to provide clear guidance. Leaving the students to read the instructions of the game on their own may lead to misconceptions. Recording a video or showing instruction videos provided by the games package are possible ways to provide guidance. Students can also be encouraged to post any queries on a module discussion board. Another drawback of asynchronous delivery is that it is harder for the tutor to provide commentary and feedback as the game progresses. A consequence of this is that it becomes even more important how the tutor follows up the playing of the game with the class. We discuss the importance of follow-up work more generally in the next section.

5.   FOLLOW-UP WORK

In sections 3 and 4 we have demonstrated that there is the potential for games to be used in synchronous and asynchronous online delivery. Next, we highlight how, regardless of delivery method, appropriate follow-up teaching activities and assessment are important to maximise the potential learning advantages of using games.

After running a game, it is important for the tutor to facilitate an active learning environment that helps the students to make links with the underlying theory and what that theory predicts for decision making. Having played the game, students will hopefully have gained important insight into how decisions can be modelled in a simple experimental setting, the key factors that determine the decision-making process and how realistic the setting is compared to real-world decision making. Wherever possible, a preliminary debrief and discussion of these areas should take place immediately afterwards so that the game is fresh in the students' minds. In subsequent classes reference can then be made to the points raised in the discussion and the results of the game. The tutor may also be able to refer to a large body of research that uses experiments based on the same games to test theories and develop alternatives. Of course, an immediate debrief and discussion will not be possible with asynchronous delivery. Therefore, here, in the follow-up discussion the tutor may need to give a brief recap of the setting in which the game took place and encourage students to recall their thoughts whilst making their in-game decisions. Despite this, the results of the game can still be referred back to and analysed.

One concern which has often been expressed about using games in teaching is that they will not produce the expected results. Our standard response to such concerns has been that games typically produce consistent and broadly predictable results. Furthermore, results that deviate from what the underlying theory predicts can generate interesting and useful follow-on discussion about the design of the game and limitations with the theory itself. However, despite these reassurances, a relevant question is whether the possibility of unpredictable results from a game becomes more of an issue with remote delivery. After all, asynchronous material may well have to be recorded and released before the playing of the relevant game has taken place. This makes it impossible to refer to the results from the game in the recording and the best the tutor can do is to refer to the game in broad terms. Synchronously delivered sessions may then be the most appropriate for follow-up discussion of games. It is also then inevitable that the full package of teaching activities will to some extent be less integrated than they would be under the traditional face-to-face lecture and tutorial delivery method.

There is also evidence to suggest that the use of games is most effective when the student learning from playing the games is directly tested in the module assessment. One way to do this is to require the students to write an assignment reflecting on their experience participating in an in-class game. Cartwright and Stepanova (2012) provide evidence that students who were required to do this perform better on test questions examining knowledge of the underlying theory the game was designed to illustrate. Fully aligning games with the assessment could also encourage students to participate and engage more with the games. Given that participation and engagement are likely to be bigger issues in a remote online teaching environment, here it may be even more important that games are closely linked to the assessment.

6.   CONCLUDING REMARKS

This chapter has demonstrated that the new teaching environment that is emerging in light of the COVID-19 pandemic need not result in less use of games. This is reassuring since, as we highlighted above, the benefits of using games only increase in the new teaching environment. It will be extremely interesting to see how games are adopted and how students react. In addition, this new environment could alter how games are designed going forward. Alas, there are also some games which it seems cannot be delivered in a remote online delivery environment. For example, in the past we have run the international trade game in which groups representing countries must trade in order to obtain resources to produce paper shapes.[6] It would not seem possible to recreate the nature of the interaction within and between teams online.

NOTES

1. See Guest et al. (2019) for a detailed description of these games.
2. Sites providing these games include Veconlab, Economics-games.com, Classex and Moblab (web links below), where all the games on the first three sites are provided for free.
3. For example, see Veconlab for a range of such lottery and intertemporal choice games.
4. For example, see the monopoly simulation at Economics-games.com.
5. Moblab is leading the way in developing such games.
6. See https://www.economicsnetwork.ac.uk/showcase/sloman_game (accessed 29 September 2020).

REFERENCES

Cartwright, E. and A. Stepanova (2012). 'What do students learn from a classroom experiment? Not much, unless they write a report on it', *Journal of Economic Education*, 43 (1), 48–57.

Guest, J., M. Kozlovskaya and M. Olczak (2019). 'The use of short in-class games'. In K. Daniels, C. Elliott, S. Finley and C. Chapman (eds), *Learning and Teaching in Higher Education: Perspectives from a Business School*. Cheltenham, UK: Edward Elgar.

Holt, C. and S. Laury (1997). 'Classroom games: Voluntary provision of a public good', *Journal of Economic Perspectives*, 11, 209–215.

Web Links

Classex: https://econclassexperiments.com
Economics-games.com: https://economics-games.com
Moblab: https://moblab.com
Veconlab: http://veconlab.econ.virginia.edu/admin.htm

8. How to develop assessments based around teaching simulations

Jason Evans and Clive Kerridge

INTRODUCTION

The use of simulations in learning and teaching has long been considered essential in the healthcare and aviation sectors to ensure that 'safe-to-practice' graduates are released into the world to undertake their important roles in society. Whilst business schools do not necessarily view simulation with such a consequential concern, its use is now well established, if not ubiquitous. From the paper-based numerical specimen, to the modern fully interactive, graphical simulations that can be streamed through one's browser, simulations have been espoused as a tool that can be used to elicit a range of highly beneficial outcomes that are desirable to institutions and employers alike. Increased learner engagement, 'safe spaces' to practise without fear, opportunities to engage closely with teams – and the huge range of hard and soft 'employability' skills that accompany teamworking dynamics – decision making and, perhaps not least among them, a bit of fun are all reasons that teachers choose to engage simulations and simulation-based learning in modules and programmes.

Yet, whilst the potential benefits of simulation activity and simulation-based learning cannot be denied, they ultimately work best when undertaken as a component of a larger package of learning and teaching interventions. This chapter looks more closely at one element of that larger package of interventions – assessment.

Assessment in higher education institutions (HEIs) is debated, critiqued, adapted, challenged, despised and enjoyed by teachers and learners alike. Getting assessment 'right' is recognised as a challenge throughout the HEI landscape and therefore rightly forms a large part of any postgraduate learning and teaching certification programme. However, when it comes to simulations, getting assessment 'right' is critical to not only incentivise learners to engage with a particular topic's material, but also to achieve what we want a simulation-based learning activity to actually *do*. We have therefore structured this chapter to provide the reader with some critical background discussion to reflect upon, as well as presenting practical advice and tips that will prove useful to the reader's own teaching and assessment activity.

After considering the role of simulation in HEI business schools, we will consider the role of assessment, before synthesising with a discussion on the role of assessment in the context of simulation-based learning in HEI business schools. We then move to the more practical elements, discussing various approaches to assessment and simulations, considering how assessment can be developed for positive outcomes, and sharing our experiences to highlight some common pitfalls to avoid.

THE ROLE OF SIMULATION IN BUSINESS SCHOOLS

In recent times, simulations have been identified as a blended learning dimension that can be utilised as an integrated tool to enhance learner engagement and understanding. Simulations can be undertaken as a physical activity or purely in digital format or a mixed approach. Broadly speaking, the main aims of any simulation are to 'imitate a system, entity or process' (Lean *et al.*, 2006, p. 228). Yet when it comes to business simulation in the HEI business school context, we argue that there are two further key elements that simulation aims to achieve: experience of, and learning how to respond to, situations of both crisis and normality. Given the current context of the COVID-19 pandemic, and related economic, leadership and managerial challenges facing organisations, this would seem timelier than ever. One can only imagine that those who had the opportunity to complete a crisis management simulation prior to 2019/2020 would find themselves better prepared to deal with the situation.

Modern business simulations can trace their roots to the 1960s when experiential learning as a pedagogical approach began to be accepted as a tool for addressing the limitations of more traditional teaching approaches. Certainly, the use of simulations throughout HEI business schools has grown as a result of increased access to technologies and as evidenced through various studies (Goi, 2019; Blazic & Novak, 2015). Interest in simulation activity and how best to exploit the educational benefits continues to grow.

Within the academic literature, there is a clear debate on the implementation and use of simulations for learning and teaching in the HEI business school context. Detractors of the use of simulations argue that the simplifications can be misleading and trivial factual errors may also negatively influence learning. Others argue that the significant resource requirements needed to successfully run simulations may be restrictive. The time required to successfully plan, implement and assess can be considerable. In some cases, there may be a need to buy in professional staff that can be expensive. Others argue that simulations have no inherent learning advantages over the case study approach.

However, whilst these arguments should not be lightly rejected, the current management education literature is positively aligned to the use of simulation in the HEI business school context. The espoused virtues of simulation for business learners outweigh the critiques when correctly managed: the benefit of experiential learning and practical experience combined with an academic education in a well-planned manner, the development of managerial skills gained from experience, the production of more effective managers, utilising complex and realistic learning environments, working in a risk-free, experimentation-friendly environment, increase in dynamic knowledge, inherent engagement of learners, deep-learning as an outcome of the process of undertaking simulation activity and the ability for learners to engage in study on their own terms are all commonly lauded benefits. In addition, research demonstrates that learners respond positively to simulations, considering them engaging, fun and stimulating (see for example Evans *et al.*, 2013; Campos *et al.*, 2020).

The outcomes are also positive more broadly for both teachers and universities. The growth in business school enrolments has created a range of issues. Larger class sizes often translate into a lower level of interaction, resulting in learning and assessment approaches that often favour knowledge acquisition over rich learning experiences and individual skills development. Well managed, simulations appear to offer an attractive solution to the business school that appears to find itself a victim of its own success. They provide opportunities for learners to work in manageable teams and can offer a deep and enriching experience that is memorable when delivered well. They are also comparatively cheap when compared to other experiences such as field trips to organisations or interaction with business leaders.

THE ROLE OF ASSESSMENT IN BUSINESS SCHOOLS

The academic and professional literature surrounding assessment in business schools is large, dense and contentious. Debates include questions on form, format, timing, alignment and purpose. Yet, whilst some may go as far as to argue that assessment is extraneous and should be eliminated entirely, most are in agreement that learners must be assessed in some form – how else can we teachers know if learning outcomes are being met, or if learners have actively engaged with the studies at hand? What is clear, though, is that assessment in HEI business schools has changed dramatically in recent times.

In Britain prior to the 1990s, the formal qualifications one gained through a good business school were seen as something of a passport to ensuring employment, large salaries, increased status and secure futures. The MBA-holding graduate was seen as something of a rare creature, empowered with knowledge and networks, confident and assured, ready and fully able to make the big business decisions an employer required. However, the changing face of work and society and the ambition for 50% of all young people to go to university (championed by then prime minister Tony Blair and achieved in 2018) have significantly impacted the role of the twenty-first-century business school, and turned a more scrutinous eye upon it. Teachers, business leaders, learners and parents now understand that business education should reach far beyond the scope of the traditional chalk, talk and exam approach, producing graduates with a range of transferable skills. In particular, employers have become more assured and prescriptive in the importance they place on the knowledge and skills of a graduate employee – and it is rarely the formal qualifications that learners have studied for. Instead, employers seek a broad range of aptitudes, personal qualities and attitudes, in addition to basic numeracy and literature skills.

This emphasis on qualities that supersede the traditional subject qualification is therefore beginning to be reflected in the way business schools assess learners' attainment. The shift of perspective has also resulted in a focus on the relationship between the activity of teaching and learning, and assessment. Instead of the traditional stand-alone assessments that can be narrow in scope (multiple choice questions, focused essay writing), the emphasis has moved to integrated assessment of the type that is embedded in the teaching and learning itself and leads to 'deep learning' which in turn can support success in the world of work.

Within HEI business schools, then, business simulations are recognised as a tool to allow learners the opportunity to experience both crisis and 'normality' in the business environment. When properly planned and delivered, simulations can also service high-quality integrated and embedded assessment that acts as a vehicle for supporting learners to develop the aptitudes, qualities and attitudes desired by employers through these experiences and responses to them. It stands to reason, therefore, that any well-designed assessment should consider what the simulation is attempting to achieve, what learners are expected to do and what the expected (measurable) outcomes will be from doing it.

The next section in this chapter therefore turns to the practicalities of designing simulation-based assessment.

DESIGNING SIMULATION-BASED ASSESSMENT – MAKING IT WORK

When planning assessment, simulation-based or otherwise, it is important to ensure the fundamental principles are adhered to. The Higher Education Academy (2017) argues that all learning and assessment should be integrated and fully aligned and that, rather than being used solely to ascertain what learning outcomes have been achieved, assessment should provide feedback on performance in a way that contributes to learners' learning.

Simulations offer an opportunity to adhere to those fundamental principles. If well designed, the simulation experience itself can become the main vehicle for the assessment, resulting in a rich experience that has optimal outcomes for learners. If poorly designed, the experience can be confusing, frustrating and ultimately counterproductive. It is imperative, therefore, that time is given over to clearly understanding what you want a simulation to do and what you want learners to gain from doing it. What follows is a discussion on key points for consideration when designing effective assessment based on simulation activity.

Clarifying Assessment Outcomes

It is critical, before procuring a simulation, that tutor thinks carefully not only about what they want the simulation to do but also what they want learners to do with the simulation and what the outcomes of that will be. These last two points are very important, as, with any integrated and embedded assessment, constructive alignment is key to positive experiences. In a constructively aligned assessment, the intended learning outcomes are clearly explained, transparent and well-defined performance standards are in place, and the assessment measures progress against learning outcomes using the performance standards. In doing so, the entire process is clearly aligned to the assessment in a transparent way and is fit for purpose.

Assessed learning outcomes for a simulation activity should clearly demonstrate what a learner is expected to know, understand and/or be able to demonstrate at the end of the activity. Learning outcomes statements should be precise and measurable. Getting this right is important – if we are not clear on what is being assessed and how it will be assessed, how can we expect learners to know what they need to do in order to achieve their desired learning goals?

A good example of a simulation-based assessment outcomes' statement that is specific and measurable would be: '*... will be able to clearly justify, with reference to academic literature, decisions taken during the simulation activity*'. Compare this with a statement such as: '*... will develop problem-solving skills*'. The first is clearly linked to the simulation activity itself and is clear and measurable. When paired with a good marking rubric, learners would be able to clearly understand what they are required to do.

Defining the Assessment Approach

Having considered what the assessed learning outcomes will be and how they will be assessed, the next step is to design the format of the simulation-based assessment. There are a number of considerations at play here. There is no 'one best way' of doing things, but there are a number of pitfalls. In order to avoid the latter, it is important to plan and consider the assessment carefully before releasing it to the students.

INDIVIDUAL OR GROUP ASSESSMENT?

Simulations can often be completed in working teams or as individuals. Likewise, assessment based on simulation can be completed as a group or individual task, or a weighted mixture of both. The decision on this should be considered as part of the process of clarifying the outcomes of the assessment. A clear understanding of what learners need to do with the assessment, and what the outcomes of doing it will be, will help with deciding how the assessment should be completed.

Group assessment will allow for simultaneous assessment, and related time savings. It may also allow for simplification of instruction and process. Group assessment can also allow learners to work with one another towards a shared objective and continually develop and critique together throughout the process, supporting the development of a range of the transferable soft skills discussed earlier in this chapter. Groups are also able to break tasks into more manageable pieces and steps, allowing for a more complex and in-depth assessment piece to be developed than would be possible or acceptable for an individual to undertake. When paired with incentives (for example a regular 'leader board' approach for the simulation, or prizes for better outcomes) learners can often bond and work together more effectively towards a common goal. We have run simulations where we asked someone with perceived gravitas to view our final sessions and present the prizes – usually wine or chocolates or something similar. This person could be a local business figure, or maybe a senior member of the university management. We have even had prize-giving by representatives of core text publishers or simulation creators. For students, though, we have found that the recognition of their achievements amongst their peers is the main drive towards 'winning'. We have found leader boards to be particularly useful where the KPIs are both financial and non-financial – for example, share price increase (as a %) versus management of risk or management confidence. These metrics are more often than not managed through the simulation algorithm, thus representing no particular challenge nor increased workload for the simulation instructor.

Individual assessment will allow for a much more individual outcome demonstrating what the individual has learnt and whether or not the individual has achieved an assessed learning outcome. Additionally individual assessment allows for a more personalised response to an assessment task. Reflective pieces can be a very powerful tool for learners to demonstrate self-awareness and understanding of other actors' actions, both of which are key components of emotional intelligence. Furthermore, reflective practice encourages an active engagement in the process, resulting in a more meaningful and personal assessment experience for the individual.

If assessment can be designed for *simulated group activity, with provision for an individual reflection* on the process, it stands to reason, then, that the mix will encompass all the benefits outlined here. However, getting the mix right is important. Within most HEIs there is guidance for teachers on what percentage of an assessment weighting can be undertaken as group assessment. In addition to these guidelines, the teacher should also consider the right mix in the context of the assessed learning outcomes and the limitations of the simulation to be used.

FORMATIVE VERSUS SUMMATIVE ASSESSMENT

Formative assessment is assessment that provides constructive feedback to learners as part of the learning process, with the aim of allowing learners to develop their understanding or improve their work. Summative assessment refers to the evaluation of intended learning outcomes at the conclusion of a study programme.

In the context of a simulation-based assessment, the decision on how to approach formative and summative assessment can be directly influenced by the simulation itself. For example, many modern simulations offer immediate, interim feedback. Indeed, this may be a necessary element of the simulation in order for learners to progress with engagement. The feedback may relate to decisions taken across a certain period of activity, or it may take the form of broader expectations for performance in the future based on what has already been done. In addition, many modern business simulations provide summative assessment ideas to simulation facilitators and others may provide assessment embedded in the simulation itself.

Whilst these tools are often very useful and can save time, it is important that careful consideration is given to ensuring the specific assessed learning outcomes are fully addressed in a transparent way. Shoehorning a pre-prepared assessment into a learning programme can result in some of the pitfalls discussed later in this chapter.

ASSESSMENT FORMAT

Designing the format of a simulation-based assessment can be a rewarding process. As it tends to sit outside of the traditional approaches to assessment, tutors can be more creative with the design. Examples include teams working in dedicated 'private' rooms to manage a simulated crisis scenario in a pressurised environment, decisions taken within strictly time limited decision-making periods, or assessing a learner's development of critical thinking and response to environmental change in a strategic management simulation.

In designing the format, the teacher is likely to assess – across either both or individually – the outcomes of the simulated activity or reflections on the process of undertaking the simulated activity.

An *outcomes-based* approach might relate to, for example, a final share price position, or an increase in profitability or similar. This can be problematic, however, as learners are likely to become more interested in manipulating the simulated environment for short-term gain (the simulation outcome) over the development of other desired skills outcomes. Whilst this would be acceptable if the assessed learning outcomes were related solely to the final outcome position, it is unlikely to be the case that this would be an outcome in isolation. Even so, it could also be the case that though the assessment is not based on the simulation outcomes, but on a reflective piece for example (see below), the reflective grade could be 'adjusted' by a certain percentage based on the outcomes of the simulation. For example, a very impressive final share price might see the team's final grades increased by 5% or vice versa for a very poor performance outcome. An important point here is that the 'rules' are clearly explained and justified to learners, and that any such adjustments are fully transparent.

It is also useful to include a *reflective element* to a simulation-based assessment; indeed, Kolb (1984) would argue that experiential learning of the type simulation is aligned to should necessarily incorporate reflection. As outlined earlier in this chapter, reflective practice can be a powerful tool for learners to demonstrate self-awareness and understanding of other actors' actions, both of which are key components of emotional intelligence. In this case, the simulation transitions from being an end in itself to becoming more of a vehicle through which deep learning can be realised and evidenced through assessment.

There is also the question of the *time period* over which the simulation and its related assessment will be delivered. For example, some simulations are managed 'live' – that is they are undertaken in a simulated live environment and require decisions to be taken quickly and in a time-limited way. Similarly, the assessment could be based on such time-limited activity. Alternatively the simulation could be undertaken over a longer period of time, for example an entire semester. The assessment may allow for longer periods of analysis and decision making, and an assessment may be submitted sometime after the conclusion of the simulation itself, allowing time for reflection and considered analysis.

Whichever approach is taken, it remains imperative to ensure the approach allows for the intended learning outcomes to be assessed, and that learners are clear on how the task will do so.

ENJOYABLE EXPERIENCES

Much of what makes simulation attractive to both teachers and learners is that it can be a lot of fun to complete. In turn, learners are far more likely to engage more fully with activities that they enjoy, with the resulting outcomes better for all concerned.

When designing assessment, it doesn't have to be the case that the fun stops with the simulation activity. A well-planned simulation-based assessment will be fully integrated and embedded in the activity itself so will benefit from the halo effect of the simulation. Teachers can further enhance the enjoyment of simulation assessment by adding a competitive element. If you are assessing on performance outcomes, a teacher might consider creating a challenge, or making the activity more competitive, providing further desire to engage more fully with the task and the assessment.

PITFALLS TO BE AVOIDED

When beginning to design simulation-based assessment the creative juices can start flowing and it is easy to become carried away with innovative, exciting and highly ambitious plans, only to find yourself running round in circles and becoming frustrated with colleagues who do not share your enthusiasm. Our long history of working with learners has given us an excellent experiential insight into these most trying of moments (many times!) and we have built not only resilience but also an understanding of how not to go about it. We would like to share some of our learning with you in the hope that you can avoid the pitfalls that we have encountered along the way.

Time

As outlined earlier, simulation-based assessment needs to be very carefully considered and aligned with the desired outcomes and task to ensure success. The time it takes to do this well should not be underestimated. A well-designed assessment can take a lot of planning and development and go through many iterations and rethinks. A lack of consideration for the time it will take can see you end up with an ineffective assessment. However, whilst the time involved in developing a simulation-based assessment can be higher than for a more traditional assessment, it is definitely worth the investment, so stick at it!

Complexity

Be cautious of an overly complex assessment task. It is likely that learners will find the simulation process itself quite exacting. When you add on top of this a complex assessment task, learners can become overwhelmed. This will likely result in either tutors becoming inundated with learner pleas for help during office hours, an overloaded inbox or, worst of all, disengaged learners. Whilst simulation-based assessments should be challenging they need not be overly complex.

In our first attempts at running simulations, we had difficulty in clearly communicating what we wanted – the assessment was perceived as too complicated, being something very different to what students were accustomed to. The solution, we found, was to break the information into manageable, time-bound chunks (e.g., do A by March and B by April). In this way the task seemed more manageable and less complex. After some experience, we learnt which elements were considered less intuitive (by the students) and so sought ways either to simplify what we were doing or to drop more superfluous elements entirely as we iterated the assessment for future cohorts.

Accessibility

Accessibility should be a primary concern when developing simulation-based assessment. Any assessment should strive to be as inclusive as possible. A design error can have severe consequences for any learner with access issues. Consequently we would advise against any form of assessment that evaluates based on speed, manual dexterity, vision, hearing, or the physical endurance of a learner. Additionally, assessment design should always ensure adjustments are feasible for those with accessibility issues.

Buy-in

Buy-in is essential for the positive outcome of a simulation-based assessment. As the assessment will likely be embedded in the simulation activity, any teacher with either colleagues or learners that haven't bought in to the activity will find the semester ahead hard going indeed! We recommend that as the lead for such an activity, the teacher is clear on the commitment required from a teaching team or learner. However, we would also recommend that the lead is also enthusiastic in clearly explaining the outcomes for everyone involved. For teaching colleagues this might include explaining how satisfying the activity will be, that it will be different and stimulating for learners, and that they will experience learners that are fully engaged in the assessment task – likely a draw for teachers who have found themselves bored by many evenings marking drab or uninspiring written essays. Likewise, for learners, clearly outline the benefits for them in completing the simulation and its related assessment. We find it beneficial to be clear about how the assessment will enhance those elements that employers look for most, and how the task will support discussions about experiences in interviews and discussions with potential employers.

Fun for the Sake of Fun

In this chapter we have been clear – simulation-based assessment, when done right, can be an incredibly satisfying and fun experience. However, there can be a tendency to make things fun for the sake of being fun. After all, learners will be more receptive, talk about how great a teacher you are and how much fun your classes are and perhaps give you higher scores for your assessed teaching activity! This would be a disservice. It is incumbent upon us as educators to ensure that what we do is as engaging as it can be, but also to ensure that what our learners are engaging with is beneficial to them and their future selves. Ensuring that our simulation and assessment is helping to prepare learners for the world of work is paramount; simulation-based learning and assessment is certainly a fantastic vehicle for making that happen.

FINAL THOUGHT

In this chapter, we have laid out the background to simulation-based assessment in HEI business schools, discussed how to make it work and given some tips on what to avoid in designing assessment. This is based on years of painful experience in doing our best to get it right.

That learners enjoy and are enthused by well-done simulation-based learning and assessment is undoubtable. Yet in this chapter we have only really scratched the surface of what is possible and what can be achieved in this exciting area of pedagogy. As staff, we are often limited by previous practice and conventions but, as we demonstrate in this chapter, tutors can similarly be enthused and engaged in the process of designing assessments that are creative and attractive to their learners. We would urge any tutor to take the opportunity to experiment with simulation-based assessment design. You never know – you might become a convert to the possibilities, as we have over the years.

BIBLIOGRAPHY

Avramenko, A. (2012). Enhancing Learners' Employability Through Business Simulation. *Education + Training*, 54(5), 355–367.

Biggs, J. (1996). Enhancing Teaching Through Constructive Alignment. *Higher Education*, 32(3), 347–364.

Biggs, J. and Tang, C. (2011). *Teaching for Quality Learning at University*. Maidenhead: Open University Press.

Blazic, A. and Novak, F. (2015). Challenges of Business Simulation Games – A New Approach of Teaching Business. Available from https://www.intechopen.com/books/e-learning-instructional-design-organizational-strategy-and-management/challenges-of-business-simulation-games-a-new-approach-of-teaching-business

Campos, N., Nohal, M., Caliz, C. and Juan, A. (2020). Simulation-based Education Involving Online and On-campus Models in Different European Universities. *International Journal of Educational Technology in Higher Education*, 17(8).

Evans, J., Kerridge, C. and Loon, M. (2013). Campus Based Learners' Perspectives on Strategic Management Simulation: A Contextual Study. *World Journal of Social Sciences*, 3(2), 12–24.

Goi, Chai-Lee (2019). The Use of Business Simulation Games in Teaching and Learning. *Journal of Education for Business*, 94(5), 342–349.

Higher Education Academy. (2017). Assessment and Feedback in Higher Education. Available from https://www.advance-he.ac.uk/knowledge-hub/assessment-and-feedback-higher-education-1

Kolb, D.A. (1984). *Experiential Learning: Experience as the Source of Learning and Development*. Englewood Cliffs, NJ: Prentice Hall.

Lean, J., Moizer, J., Towler, M. and Abbey, C. (2006). Simulations and Games: Use and Barriers in Higher Education. *Active Learning in Higher Education*, 7(3), 227–242.

Levant, Y., Coulmount, M. and Sandu, R. (2016). Business Simulation as an Active Learning Activity for Developing Soft Skills. *Journal of Accounting Education*, 25(4), 368–395.

Lohmann, G., Pratt, M., Benckendorff, P., Strickland, P., Reynolds, P. and Whitelae, P.A. (2019). Online Business Simulations: Authentic Teamwork, Learning Outcomes and Satisfaction. *The International Journal of Higher Education*, 77(3), 455–472.

Loon, M., Evans, J. and Kerridge, C. (2015). Learning with a Strategic Management Simulation Game: A Case Study. *International Journal of Management Education*, 13(3), 227–236.

Salas, E., Wildman, J.L. and Piccolo, R.F. (2009). Using Simulation-Based Training to Enhance Management Education. *Academy of Management Learning & Education*, 8(4), 559–573.

Saunders, F. (2018). Designing Assessments that are Meaningful, Equitable and Manageable in UK Higher Education. Higher Education Academy. Available from https://www.heacademy.ac.uk/blog/designing-assessments-are-meaningful-equitable-and-manageable-uk-higher-education

9. Reflections on the value of simulations in developing employability skills in postgraduate business students

Jude Preston and Frances Rosairo

INTRODUCTION

This week I taught my first session of the new academic year. I was teaching a group of students enrolled on a technical degree apprenticeship. My module is an optional module – Team Leading and Managing People – and it is a far cry from the computer coding, digital and other technical content they are usually immersed in. These enlightened students have realised that technical skills alone will not be enough in today's competitive and ever-changing world of work, and 'employability' will not in future depend solely on technical expertise, but also on demonstrating many other competences – the 'soft skills' we have heard so much about in recent years.

The difference between these and the majority of graduates are that apprentices are already in full-time employment and are studying alongside their 'day jobs'. They are already used to working in teams, often remotely, communicating at multiple levels within their organisations, managing their own and the time and work of others, solving problems using sophisticated data analysis techniques and tools, and making decisions which have far-reaching consequences for them, their team and their organisation. Not so, however, for the majority of students who pass through universities today!

This chapter explores staff and student perceptions of simulations in postgraduate business education. It delves into my own experiences and those of colleagues, and offers comments from students' own perspectives, gleaned from analysis of reflective assessments and feedback. After briefly discussing the need for, and subsequent development of, transferable skills teaching in universities, we offer our reflections on managing learning via simulations at postgraduate-level business education. We offer insights into the challenges of staff familiarisation, and encouraging engagement in students, as well as some of the more practical aspects of delivering learning using simulations.

GRADUATE EMPLOYABILITY AND THE USE OF SIMULATIONS

As Succi & Canovi (2020) point out, perennial debates within the literature, and between employers' groups and higher education institutes (HEIs) over the last three decades or so about who, precisely, is responsible for the development of graduate employability, serve to both highlight the lack of transferable skills in graduates and the fact that for many students, employability and transferrable skills may not be very clear or very high on their list of priorities. Despite efforts over the years on the part of HEIs to address this skills deficit, employers still blame HEIs for not adequately preparing students for the world of work (Hurrell, 2016), and students often do not realise the importance of these skills. Additionally, there is a mismatch between the skills students consider desirable by employers, and what the employers actually want (Majid, Eapen, Mon Aung & Oo, 2019; Succi & Canovi, 2020); the top four skills suggested by students as important are: positive attitude, oral communications, self-motivation and self-direction, and problem-solving. Employers, while also requiring a positive attitude and problem-solving skills, cite teamwork and good ethics as their priorities (Majid et al., 2019). Professionalism and ethical awareness are also far more important to employers than students (Succi & Canovi, 2020).

Recently this skills gap has been addressed by HEIs in several ways; most universities include team-working and collaborative elements in taught modules, case studies facilitate the application of theoretical knowledge, students engage in presentations and other business-type communications, and many degrees include work experience, often for a full year. This latter initiative is invaluable in developing real-life employability skills; my own experience of teaching final year undergraduate students who have just completed a year-long work placement is that their understanding of how business actually works is enhanced significantly and this newly acquired ability to appreciate the bigger organisational picture enables them to make sense of their university learning. But for postgraduate students who have had no opportunity for work experience, either as part of their undergraduate degree or as career-based work, the lack of demonstrable, transferable skills can be a serious challenge when trying to gain early career employment.

The educational environment can be a closed one in which some learners, whether they admit this to themselves or not, take refuge from the uncertainties of the real world. Using a simulation is a way to bridge academic learning to the real world and this is an important step. Business simulations allow students to gain experience and develop the problem-solving, analytical and decision-making skills employers value, and an ability to work collaboratively in self-managing teams. The ethicality of the decisions becomes apparent while participating, and consequences observed and understood. I have seen this ability develop in students while supervising their learning using a business simulation. However, not all students willingly engage in simulations. Some fail to appreciate the potential learning they can gain from participation, while for a number of students the gamification of learning appears to trivialise the process. Engagement is one of the biggest challenges in teaching business using simulations and is discussed in more detail later in this chapter.

SO, HOW WAS IT FOR US?

My first experience of managing the delivery of learning using simulations was as the academic lead for our postgraduate Professional Development Programme (PDP). The PDP is a year-long module that aims to develop students' transferable employability skills. During the year students experience a wide range of skills workshops and careers events, and they are required to work in groups to produce an assessed Business Challenge presentation which is usually sponsored by a local organisation.

Students are also required to engage with one of four experiential learning 'streams': study abroad with one of our many partner organisations worldwide; an internship which may be with any approved employer globally; the Product Intellectual Property and Entrepreneurship stream (PIPE) for those with ambitions of starting their own business; or a group exercise involving a business simulation. Streams last for a minimum of four weeks. The four-week business simulation stream involves compulsory sessions where the simulation leaders present new materials and challenges as the 'virtual time' moves on through the simulation, plus students work autonomously in self-managing groups.

There were eight rounds of decisions to make, each round representing one financial period. Teams make decisions about a range of business areas including economic, political, financial, accounting, human resources, procurement, logistics, production, research and innovation, and marketing. In the year I became involved with the PDP, it was the simulation's fourth year of running.

The game encourages participants to formulate a medium to long term business plan based on background information. Decisions on product innovations, pricing, etc. reflect the team's decision on how they wish to position themselves in the market. Parameters set make clear that cash levels should not fall below a certain limit and that large capital investments only become operational after two financial periods even though the cash flow effect takes effect within one period. There is a need for the teams to react to changes or events within the business environment or the business decisions of the other teams. So here, the simulation requires the participants to decide when and if their plans need to be flexed to these events. Thus, the game simulated the 'norms' for many operations within a dynamic business environment.

Tutors are assigned to support the groups, and 'drop-in' sessions scheduled so that groups can ask for guidance if they need help.

My initial impression?

1. The system was complex and heavily focused on the ability of teams to interpret financial data. Tutors require a lot of familiarisation to become proficient at providing the guidance the students need to make decisions.
2. Levels of engagement with the simulation would be variable – a perennial source of intra-team conflict that, despite our best efforts to get the teams to self-manage, would often end up being something staff would have to sort out.

ENGAGEMENT

The business simulation stream on the professional development programme includes students from a range of business disciplines such as Accounting, Finance, Marketing and Human Resources. The aim of the simulation is to widen the gaze of these students to consider other aspects of the business or commercial environment that are not their area of expertise. As much of the detailed information provided in the simulation was financial data, we found students with a finance background were more comfortable with the material and so engaged with the programme more than others. This was the opportunity to encourage and allow good team-working skills, where students with financial expertise evaluate the data and report this to other team members, so enabling collective decisions to be made. There were, however, examples where those who were more able to interpret the financial data made the decisions, which left other students without a financial background unclear as to why certain decisions were made. Importantly this also meant that their sometimes-vital insights in to organisational and market behaviours were disregarded.

To overcome this, in 2018 we introduced an alternate business simulation experience specifically for our Accounting and Finance students. This alternate simulation had a greater emphasis on the accounting and finance implications and decisions but also required a wider range of business decisions, thus putting the spotlight on the non-financial aspects. Taking the Accounting and Finance students out of the mainstream simulation allows students from other business fields such as Marketing and Human Resource Management to apply their knowledge from their own field of expertise when making business decisions but to also consider the financial impact of these decisions.

In the first year we included the simulation as part of the Professional Development Programme; some of the more candid feedback showed that students did not always see or agree with the objective of using the simulation to learn.

Despite the changes made to the messaging and assessment, analysis of the simulation's reports from the last running of the simulation in 2019 still show variable engagement levels; most teams show the majority of logged-in time is down to just one or two students with others spending just a fraction of the time engaging. Of course, this doesn't mean that students are actively working in the system while logged in – they could have logged in and then gone for a pizza!

But the pattern, which is repeated over and over across teams, supports this input variability although those who spend less time may be doing other tasks which do not require being logged in. But I would argue that to fully understand the challenges, and the decisions and their consequences, a certain amount of logged-in time is needed to familiarise oneself with the system and the decisions, and those who have invested just a couple of hours (or less!) over the whole month are unlikely to have developed sufficient understanding to be able to fully benefit from the learning afforded.

Putting aside the amount of time spent logged in, my initial impression was that in some teams all, or almost all, of the team members (usually five individuals) were working well together and had embraced the task. This reflects their view of the authenticity of the tasks and exercises, as they threw themselves into their assumed roles. While walking around 'professionally eavesdropping' on the discussions, I heard not just discussions but at times heated disagreements, as well as laughter. I rarely, though, heard a student being rude, and I was impressed by the professionalism of many of the students.

Then I noticed students on the perimeters of groups, apparently engrossed in their mobile phones but not even listening to the discussion, and looking up, startled, when somebody tried to bring them into the conversation. Also some were trying to engage, but were clearly struggling to follow discussions and asking colleagues to explain. As the weeks and the sessions went on, some groups became smaller. When I asked about this, I was often told that such-a-person had dropped out. Then I began to really understand the importance of the facilitator's role in keeping students engaged – what was missing were clear signals to signpost to the students the value and relevance of what they were doing, to develop legitimate engagement. In other words, rather than teaching them, my role is to coach and stimulate the students' own curiosity so they engage with the exercise, and also to ensure that those who struggle don't get left behind and then lose interest, feeling the whole thing to be a lost cause.

This experience led me to approach the delivery of these formal and informal sessions slightly differently, and I always present ideas and concepts relating to the simulation by bringing them down to the lowest level to explain the task in the simplest terms, before gradually building them back to the level of complexity inherent in the simulation; in this way, it supports those whose language skills, rather than their analytical skills, are weaker and helps those from different cultures.

Critically also, the students need to fully appreciate that what they are experiencing are real tasks in an academic setting (Herrington, Reeves & Oliver, 2010), and that they are as close to reality as they can achieve.

WHAT DO OUR STUDENTS THINK?

With such a diverse student body, it is impossible to generalise about the value the students attribute to the simulation, and how easy or otherwise they found the exercise and the quality of their learning. To provide insights, I analysed their assignments, which provide a reflection on their experience. My recommendations for the delivery and management of business simulations follow the feedback from our students.

Did the Students Enjoy the Simulation Experience?

The overall feeling about the business simulation experience was positive. However, only a few students expressed 'enjoyment' using that term:

The business simulation was a fun and enlightening experience.

This group project was extremely enjoyable as it helped me to learn a lot about business first-hand.

Some were openly enthusiastic about their experience, but used the idea of excitement rather than enjoyment:

Seeing how each decision had repercussions in every department excited me.

Overall the business simulation was an exciting project...

Others expressed conditional enjoyment; their enjoyment of the simulation was to an extent dependent on how well their team performed together:

Can be enjoyable if each member of the group participated and did their part equally and fairly.

Others were more specific about which aspects of the team-working experience had positively added to their enjoyment of the simulation, especially where they had needed and received support from the team to enable and empower them. This clearly demonstrates growing maturity within the groups:

> *Every member of the team was exceptional. They encouraged me to express my thoughts and opinions.*

There was some constructive feedback highlighting where students had felt the simulation did not accurately reflect in sufficient detail the current global economic situation. It would of course be extremely difficult and time-intensive for staff to constantly adapt the simulation software in this respect:

> *It was frustrating that the global scenarios were fictitious.*

Another student expressed their distress at the amount of information they were expected to absorb right from the beginning:

> *The business simulation requires students processing overloading information [information overload].*

However, I am satisfied that the students' experience was positive and rewarding.

Of course, enjoyment of the simulation, while important, is not the only factor – the value and learning gained from it are paramount in justifying the use of such simulations.

What Did the Students Perceive as the Value of the Simulation?

Most students in some way expressed their appreciation of the closeness of the simulation experience to a real-life, real-world situation. It was particularly interesting that this was a sentiment from some of those students who have work experience, and who are therefore in a position to make comparisons between their employment challenges and those woven into the simulation:

> *...a highly authentic experience, and it can reflect a realistic business situation.*

> *All these skills are highly valuable when working in a real-life environment and highly demanded by employers.*

Those who do not currently have work experience were usually able to perceive the value of the work they were being required to undertake on this stream:

> *I consider it myself as a real workplace experience that made me learn a lot and prepare myself to the future career.*

Others clearly expressed their enjoyment of being able to apply their theoretical learning in a practical way, which emulates what they will be doing when they do enter employment:

> *Use[d] my accounting and finance skills and knowledge in a practical way... I had the opportunity to put what I had learned to real use.*

This student clearly expressed the strategic nature of the decisions they were making as a group, and that the true value for them was in developing understanding of market conditions, how their own organisation operated within the wider competitive environment, and that the necessity to scan the external environment was one key skill:

> *Strategic decision making was necessary... we had to predict what our competitors would do.*

A final word from one of our students on this topic, and for me perhaps one of the most gratifying – this student started out doubting the value of the simulation, clearly thinking it a pointless exercise simply to be endured in order to complete their degree. Their candid admission that as time went on their views changed, and they realised the authenticity offered by the simulation allowed them to make the sort of decisions they might make in the real world, does underscore the value of this type of experiential learning:

> *At first I did not think it would teach me as much as real work. As time went on though, I started to understand what I was learning and how like real life it really was.*

What are the Key Learning Points which the Students Have Taken Away From It?

Finally, we look at the students' views of what they have learned from the simulation exercise. Almost all students stated they had learned communications skills, decision-making skills, problem-solving skills, etc. For example:

> *The most meaningful learning outcomes of the business simulation are problem-solving, decision-making and analytical skills.*

The quotations I have chosen for the remainder of this section are those that complement this list, where students have identified other skills, competences and knowledge gained while working on the simulation.

One student expressed their dawning realisation that organisations are systems, and that managers cannot operate with a silo mentality when making decisions about one business area:

> *Decision making was crucial throughout the course. There were so many moving parts...*

Some students talked about how their analytical skills were honed, but focused on the need for attention to detail if mistakes were to be avoided:

> *I developed...a meticulous approach to research and information appraisal.*

Another student commented that often data is spurious, and that it is a skill to be able to realise which information is crucial and should be prioritised – to spot the red herring!

> *I learned how to evaluate the information and distinguish between relevant and irrelevant data to make well-informed decisions.*

Another student had been taken by surprise by the need for agility and nimbleness:

> *I need to act faster than I thought.*

For some students, the real learning was interpersonal soft skills, and the need to work as a team to overcome earlier mistakes:

> *When team members are under pressure and confusion, they must trust and rely on each other and act together to overcome difficulties.*

> *Our team went back to revisit the simulation rules and make sure the same mistakes were not repeated in future rounds.*

MANAGING AND DELIVERING LEARNING USING SIMULATIONS, TO OPTIMISE EMPLOYABILITY SKILLS DEVELOPMENT

In this final section, we offer practical observations and suggestions to facilitate the learning of students using simulations. These are based on our own experiences and those of our colleagues whose insights are incorporated into the earlier parts of this chapter.

Increase Student Engagement and Make the Learning Relevant

Don't assume that the students will be as enthusiastic as you are about the exercise! It is necessary to deliver a session at the beginning of the exercise to spell out how the simulation will challenge them, push them beyond their comfort zone, and force them to review and reconsider long-held assumptions and beliefs. This session should also clearly explain how and why the tasks are relevant for them in their future career.

As part of this session, it is also a good idea to talk to the students about professionalism; in the real world they will be expected to meet and maintain professional standards, and for the duration of the simulation exercise they must also meet these. This covers such things as attendance and punctuality, sending apologies if unable to make a meeting, submitting work by agreed deadlines, and conduct during meetings.

Another key aspect of any educational programme is assessment. If there is no impact on their grades, students do not see the point in 'game playing', resenting the time away from their dissertations which carry a significant assessment mark. They have a point; it's fun to take part in a game when you feel free and able to, but being forced to play a game, say football or chess, is not fun if you have a pressing assignment deadline to meet. Playing might be beneficial from a physical and mental health perspective but this is not easy to see. You might, however, be more willing to play if you were given some credit for doing so. The easy solution might be to allocate a proportion of the assessment marks to the simulation; however, some thought must be given to effective assessment. Marks cannot simply be awarded for winning. The 'win' comes from taking part and benefiting from the experience. We therefore introduced an individual as well as a team-reflective commentary which could be effectively assessed, and therefore graded, as the quality of the reflections would or should mirror the benefits and learning from the experience.

In the second year of running the simulation a further requirement was introduced for teams to formulate a short presentation, to be delivered to the whole cohort based on different aspects of the simulation. Examples of presentation topics were to attract investment and a recruitment campaign. The presentation did not affect the overall grades; however, 'assessment' came from their peers and academics who as the audience were able to scrutinise the presenters' expertise through a Q&A section at the end.

To help students see the relevance and value of the learning to their future career, try to bring real life into the learning environment. This enables students to relate their learning to specific contexts. This can be done in several ways; if you have a small enough cohort, you could, for example, arrange a field trip to visit an organisation whose industry sector is close to that being worked on in the simulation. Thus students can see for themselves how the business operates and can possibly discuss with the managers things such as the industry challenges, and the strengths and weaknesses of certain strategies.

Another possibility, and perhaps easier to organise, is to invite industry experts to talk to the students at strategic points in the exercise, to help them to contextualise the analysis and decisions they are making.

It is also very helpful to timetable as many sessions as possible – this increases the students' perception of the formality and importance of attendance. It may not be possible to timetable the teams' own meetings, but to encourage attendance and engagement ask teams to keep a record of attendance and contributions and submit this as part of any group assessment at the end. This makes it harder for people to hide their non-engagement!

In summary, the benefits of learning via simulation must be made clear from the start and reinforced throughout the simulation. For this, educators must be clear in themselves on the aims of including a game/simulation. These aims can then be honestly communicated to the students. Increased engagement was witnessed when there was deliberate messaging reinforcing the purpose and benefits drawn from the simulation, pulling together technical knowledge and the competencies desired by future employers.

Managing the Complexity of the Simulation: Facilitator Training

One challenge of the simulation we use for our postgraduate students is the necessary complexity – if this were not the case, authenticity would be compromised. Business is complex, and the simulation has to reflect this, similarly the systems structure of organisations must be reflected in the structure of the simulation. This does mean that facilitators need to have a very good grasp of the simulation and how it works, as well as an understanding of how businesses operate. This requires time and effort to develop the expertise with the simulation, but also, importantly, selecting the right people with organisational experience to support the student learning – don't rely on PhD students!

One of the best ways to achieve the knowledge of the system is to organise a 'dummy run' with just the facilitators, but with access to experts from the various disciplines – e.g. Marketing, Accounting, Human Resources – who can support the learning of the facilitators. Don't underestimate how long this takes! I recommend that a full series of the simulation is run, preferably twice, so that the facilitators have experienced the simulation from end to end and have had the opportunity to reflect and then have another go!

Don't Lose Sight of the Need for Collaborative Team-working and Communication to be Supported

One final point which is sometimes overlooked in teaching with simulations is that the learning for students is not only about the technical knowledge gained, but also the interpersonal and intercultural skills practised while working on the exercise. These are as important as technical knowledge.

All our students also experience sessions to explain and encourage exemplary team-working skills, intercultural awareness and leadership. This is an important prerequisite if students are to gain maximum development of their employability skills. It is also helpful to ask them to reflect on these skills at intervals during the exercise, so that they recognise this development in parallel to their technical expertise; unless the value of the simulation is reinforced, this point may pass some students by, especially those on more technical degrees such as Finance and Accounting.

CONCLUSION

There is clearly great potential for simulations to provide business students with an experience that is as close as possible to the real world when it is not possible for them to gain work experience via an internship or other employment opportunity. Additionally, it allows them to operate and make decisions at a much more strategic level than they would be able to do in an early-career capacity.

The challenge for universities is to capture and hold the interest of the students – by demonstrating the relevance of the exercise and its ability to deliver both technical and employability skills, and by giving it value by incorporating it into the assessment regime. The level of tutor skill and the training required to achieve this should not be underestimated if students are to be fully supported through their learning.

REFERENCES

Herrington, J., Reeves, T. C., & Oliver, R. (2010). *A Practical Guide to Authentic E-learning.* Abingdon: Routledge.

Hurrell, S. A. (2016). Rethinking the Soft Skills Deficit Blame Game: Employers, Skills Withdrawal and the Reporting of Soft Skills Gaps. *Human Relations 69* (3), 605–628.

Majid, S., Eapen, C. M., Mon Aung, E., & Oo, K. T. (2019). The Importance of Soft Skills for Employability and Career Development: Students' and Employers' Perspectives. *The IUP Journal of Soft Skills 13* (4), 7–39.

Succi, C., & Canovi, M. (2020). Soft Skills to Enhance Graduate Employability: Comparing Students and Employers' Perceptions. *Studies in Higher Education 45* (9), 1834–1847.

10. Business simulations to develop employability skills in Strategic Management students

Jason Evans and Clive Kerridge

INTRODUCTION

What is the purpose of a business school? This might initially appear to be a simple question to answer. But if you stop and think for a short time, the question becomes more complex. Is it to educate to a 'higher' level? If so, what purpose an academic education, founded in somewhat esoteric theory and poorly contextualized frameworks, in the modern workplace? Is it to prepare students for the workplace in a very practical sense? Surely yes, but then why do we not deliver photocopying 101 classes, or hands-on sessions on feigning interest in meetings that could really have been an email? Academic colleagues would balk at this suggestion, but it will surely lead to a more employment-positive outcome for students than, say, a shaky understanding of Maslow's Hierarchy of Needs! And lest we forget – the employability outcomes of graduates continue to grow in influence as a lead indicator for how 'good' a business school is. University business schools, then, find themselves pulled in two competing directions – those of the academic needs of those that manage and service business school programmes, and those of the business community that will go on to employ business school graduates and make us seem 'good'.

Within the business school there is of course a diverse range of students. We categorize these students in a range of ways, but most commonly we identify them by the subjects or disciplines that they are studying. As long-in-the-tooth 'lifers' in the world of academe, we the authors have found ourselves aligned to that perhaps least well-defined student group – the 'strategic management' group. This group of students typically consists of those studying a marketing or strategy programme or some combination of the two – 'marketing and strategy' or similar. This isn't to say that this group of students isn't very similar to other students within any given cohort. They still enjoy the company visits and many aspire to be the next Cher Wang or Elon Musk. They will have strong career aspirations and, in the main, have a good reason for the studies they are undertaking. But this particular cohort of student tends to be less well defined than, say, an accounting student or a law student. This means, then, that the often dichotomous relationship between academic knowledge and employer-desired skills can be starker, and potentially more difficult to achieve.

And so what is the point of this chapter – simulation and employability skills? Whilst simulation is used across disciplines, this chapter considers the application to this specific group of students. We will explore how simulation can support them in the development of both their academic knowledge and the employability skills that are specific to this student group. We will also present a case study of a simulation used in a business school in a 'strategic management' context to illustrate the points made in this chapter. Throughout, we aim to provide tips and findings for the reader based on our experiences of working with simulations for 'strategic management' students at university level.

SUBJECT SPECIFIC SKILLS VERSUS EMPLOYABILITY SKILLS FOR EMPLOYMENT OUTCOMES

A key motivator for students to invest in their academic education is to ensure they have enhanced employment prospects, i.e. get a well-paid/interesting job or develop their own successful business. And whilst evidence suggests that a mismatch exists between what employers want and the skills university graduates possess (see J.P. Morgan, 2020), there is little disagreement in academia about what skills students require to achieve their employment goals – students need to develop both their subject-specific knowledge alongside the development of those other skills that employers desire.

Are subject-specific knowledge and skills important outcomes from an employment perspective? Certainly, the knowledge and skills developed during a programme of study for a student are invaluable – employers recognize the time and effort required to gain a degree in a specific subject, with the 'best' graduate employment schemes requiring a 2:1 or above as a minimum requirement. In many cases, the subject-specific knowledge is essential for a role in an organization and employers expect graduates to have discipline-specific competencies developed from their degree studies. Marketing and strategy roles might seem to fit nicely here – a knowledge and understanding is likely to support a graduate in seeking employment. There is little doubt that this is true, yet, as UCAS (2020) points out, with a large number of major graduate schemes, the degree you hold doesn't have to be in a specific area and a degree is less important to employers than the employability skills students develop in university (QS, 2020).

It is in this context that UK universities increasingly focus on the employ-ability agenda and are keen to promote employability support and outcomes on their programmes. In the environment of an intensely competitive labour market, it is felt that employability skills are so important that their develop-ment should form a part of the process of educating – that is, they should be embedded in the discipline-specific knowledge and skills development.

What of simulation-based learning as a tool to support the delivery of these skills? As pointed out in Chapter 9 of this book on 'Reflections on the value of simulations in developing employability skills in postgraduate business students', business simulation allows students to gain experience and develop the skills employers value, along with an ability to work collaboratively in a self-managing team. It would seem, then, that simulations represent some-thing of a panacea – students are able to put into practice the subject-specific skills and knowledge that are so important to the attainment of their degree, whilst at the same time developing the other skills that employers seek. Hence, simulations help to overcome the problem faced by universities being pulled in competing directions.

Whilst this may, indeed, be the case, it doesn't consider the particular needs of any given student group. As we have already discussed, the 'strategy' student is slightly less well-defined. As we know, simulations have been demonstrated to support the development of more generic employability skills, so can simulation-based learning also support the development of specific employability skills required by this particular group?

WHAT SPECIFIC SKILLS DO 'STRATEGIC' MANAGERS NEED?

Strategic leadership in any given managerial position requires that the individ-ual observe, analyse, evaluate, formulate and advise on the implementation of a strategy, or range of strategies, for the achievement of goals. In this sense, responding to and delivering on a strategy (the role of 'any given manager') is not the same as strategic management and leadership in the way we have outlined here. It is this distinction, we argue, that means those students under-taking 'strategic management' programmes have specific employability skills needs. This point was made by Schoemaker et al. (2013) who argue that the successful strategic leader needs to learn and apply the following six key skills simultaneously: anticipate, challenge, interpret, decide, align and learn. These 'essential skills' are illustrated in Box 10.1.

BOX 10.1 'ESSENTIAL SKILLS' FOR STRATEGIC LEADERS

- Anticipate: By developing the ability to anticipate leaders can better identify threats and opportunities for the business that aren't immediately obvious.
- Challenge: The best strategic leaders challenge the status quo and ask 'why?' or 'why not?' They challenge themselves and others, and encourage divergent points of view.
- Align: Strategic leaders must engage in outreach and effective communication to gain buy-in from stakeholders who may have opposing views and differing agendas.
- Interpret: The ability to synthesize and interpret complex and ambiguous information to recognize patterns and develop new insight.
- Decide: Strategic leaders make tough decisions based on rigorous data and an understanding of options and trade-offs, taking both short- and long-term outcomes into account.
- Learn: Strategic managers promote cultures of enquiry and study both success and failure (both their own and their teams') openly and constructively to gain insight and learn lessons.

Source: Adapted from Schoemaker et al. (2013).

As can be seen, these skills are an addition, or a clarification in context, to the generic skills ubiquitous in any discussion on employability in university education. It is also important to point out that we aren't claiming these to be applicable purely to the student cohort we are discussing, either wholly or in part. What we are saying is that these essential skills complement those generic employability skills discussed earlier in this book for students involved in 'strategic management' programmes who wish to become strategic leaders.

SIMULATIONS AND DEVELOPING THE 'ESSENTIAL SKILLS' FOR STRATEGIC LEADERS

Anticipating

When it comes to simulations that are aligned to 'strategy' the vast majority are structured to represent a role-play of some kind. This role-play can take many forms; it could be a growth strategy that needs planning and implementing or perhaps the simulation represents a situation of crisis in which decision making needs to be formulated on the fly. Nonetheless, in every simulated situation that we have encountered, there has been a requirement to scan the (simulated or real-world) environment to identify opportunities or threats. More often than not, clues in the environment point to potential simulated events in the near or mid-term. As facilitators, we always work to guide students to anticipate the future – '*oh, you recognized that did you? Well done! – but what might that mean for the next trading period?*' There may be signals that a recession is on the horizon, or perhaps pointers that competitors have missed this, which in turn offer leverage opportunities for a simulation team. The key point is that by asking students to engage in simulated environments that require them to anticipate based on evidence, and in nudging them to anticipate based on what they see, the real-world skills are being developed.

Challenging and Aligning

Whenever we have undertaken a simulation, we have nearly always asked students to work in teams. Working in teams to navigate a simulated environment will elicit opportunities for students to discuss, debate and engage with one another's perspectives.

We have found that the best way to elicit challenge and alignment, both within groups and as individuals, is to ask teams to formally justify their decision making (see case study below for an example of this), either as part of a weekly wrap-up or preferably as part of the assessment for the class, aligned to the simulation. It is true that there will always be those students who want an easy ride and simply profess, '*yeah, let's just do what Angela says ...*'. Yet our experience has shown that when we have formally tasked students to justify, and we reward based on sound justification and judgements, students engage more deeply with one another. This write-up can take the form of an academic justification for a final position, or it can also include a discussion around the process of reaching that final justified position. We prefer the latter – as while the former does give an insight into the decision-making process, it doesn't incentivize the students to challenge one another and recognize that challenging the status quo is beneficial when seeking optimal outcomes to a task, and being challenged can be a positive experience. This approach is also useful when asking individuals to reflect and challenge themselves – perhaps more so. Individuals who take the simulation task seriously will reflect on the decision-making process, either justifying the outcomes or explaining choices that they felt were sub-optimal.

Interpreting and Deciding

As outlined above, students will develop the ability to challenge themselves and one another to achieve optimal outcomes, particularly where an assessment is involved as a component of the simulation. However, in order to reach a decision at all, they will need to interpret data. This can come in many forms. The most obvious starting point for a student is the academic text – usually the 'core' text for a module. We have found that early on in a module where the simulation spans the entire term, students tend to rely heavily on this source of information – they will often use it to justify any decision making in the earlier stages of the activity. We find that it is beneficial to advise students that, though the texts are good sources of information, there is much more available to them to aid decision making, not least of which will be the information provided as part of a simulation role-play. We therefore find ourselves not only guiding students towards this information, but also to other sources such as case studies of organizations that have found themselves in similar situations to the one in the simulation.

For many students, particularly those early on in undergraduate courses, postgraduate students or others who may have been away from university for a while, this information can be a little overwhelming and the ability to interpret it becomes difficult. As a result, we have found it important to undertake a little 'hand holding' early on in the process, supporting students in identifying what information may be more or less important to the task at hand. It has been our experience that, in turn, students very quickly develop the ability to interpret the data sources available to them and use it to inform decision making.

At this point, we are keen to ask students to consider the time horizons of their decisions – short, medium or long term. An example might be an opportunity to enter a market but with pay-offs that might not show positively on a (simulated) balance sheet for a long period of time, yet will still need funds to service the development of the business in that market. This consideration will, in turn, feed into their ability to justify the decision taking.

Whilst decisions made may not always be optimal, or even right (it is after all a learning experience), the development of the interpreting and data-based decision-making skills has begun, and will continue to develop through the current simulation, and any subsequent tasks.

Learning

The reasons why we have become so enthusiastic about the use of simulations for 'strategic management' students are manifold; simulated activity allows for an environment of application and experimentation that is free from fear of failure in the traditional sense. When properly aligned with an assessment that assesses the process and justifications for decisions made they are a powerful tool for learning.

Students will take the opportunity to study routes to decision making based in their discipline, as well as seek real-world examples of solutions to their dilemmas. When they are allowed the opportunity to reflect on the tasks they have completed, they are able to begin to identify their knowledge gaps and knowledge strengths, and learn from the experience in a positive manner – what information do I lack, and where can I find what is required to fill the gap?

The experience should offer the opportunity for students to learn about themselves too. We have had many cases where students have taken the opportunity to reflect as an individual and/or as a member of a team working towards a common goal. Many times, we have found this self-reflection to be very insightful. For example, students identifying how they contributed strongly to a decision, how they developed strategies to challenge, how they worked with a group of like-minded individuals to anticipate in a way that other teams had not and, based on the decision made, succeeded in achieving optimal outcomes, either for themselves or for their teams. Likewise, students identifying flaws in their logic, or identifying where they recognized their approach to a debate needed reorienting and learning from that experience.

BUILDING NARRATIVES

When we begin any simulation activity, we are keen to discuss with students the potential outcomes, i.e. why should they invest effort in this task? Of course, we outline all of the positive benefits as we have outlined in this chapter – and more! The fun, the experience, the depth of learning … However, one further thing that we discuss with students is the concept of 'building narratives'.

For students that wish to go on and work in the field of strategy post-degree we firmly believe that simulations offer students not only one of the very best educational and experiential experiences they can have, but also the opportunity to build a strong narrative for discussion with employers. The job market is competitive, even more so for students leaving university into economies likely to be severely hit by a global pandemic and less stable than at any point in recent times.

It can only be seen as a benefit to the employability prospects of any student to be able to build a strong narrative around what they have learnt during their university time. Students who complete a quality 'strategy simulation' experience should be able to confidently discuss what opportunities they have had to apply learning, to reflect in a meaningful way on the outcomes of these experiences, and to identify personal and professional development of skills. When students begin to understand the benefits of building strong narratives around learning, experience and development, engagement is inevitably increased, leading to better outcomes.

A CASE STUDY OF A STRATEGIC MANAGEMENT SIMULATION

Tutors, students and their prospective employers live in an era of imperfect information: What really matters? How do I evaluate competing or even contradictory sources? How do we balance the urgent (today) against the important (tomorrow)? These conundrums aren't unique to strategic management but they are almost always key ingredients in strategic decision-making processes. The case study chosen here looks at a business simulation with some of those characteristics.

BOX 10.2   THE CASE STUDY SIMULATION: WHICH? WHY? HOW?

This case study relates to a double-semester strategic management module for final year undergraduates that used a blended learning pedagogical approach. That included whole-cohort face-to-face lectures, a series of smaller tutorial seminars, a prescribed module textbook, and online content (including videos, self-assessment and further reading) via a dedicated in-house VLE site. In the second semester, studies and assessment tasks were based around an eight-week-long online simulation, in which students worked in 'management' teams of four to six members. This same simulation has also been run successfully over considerably shorter timescales for MBA and MSc student cohorts.

A proprietary strategy simulation was chosen that met an established rubric:[1] to be based on sound pedagogic principles; have an engaging story; involve mystery and opportunity for learner discovery; and be supported and integrated with instructional design. It required students to analyse strategic position and priorities for a virtual transnational advertising and marketing services company. Each group had to develop an outline strategic business plan, including three-year financial and non-financial KPI targets, prior to engaging in a final phase that involved a series of six 'board' meetings. The simulation provided occasional reports from 'business analysts' on changing environmental conditions and industry competition, etc. The simulation software presented a series of qualitative agenda item and action options, requiring critical evaluation and strategic decision making. After each meeting, choices were uploaded and the simulation generated resultant KPI data and feedback. Students were required to reflect on both their group-working experiences and the efficacy of their strategic choices.

The Six Essential Skills of Box 10.1 are not going to be equally represented and addressed in any study activity, business simulation or otherwise, but they do offer valuable guidelines for evaluating whether a chosen simulation will contribute to, or provide, an appropriate learning journey. Testing and developing some of these skills can be deliberately incorporated into simulation design; some other skills may be addressed more explicitly through the associated learning and assessment regimes in the course or module. How do these look in relation to our case study 'sim'?

- **Anticipate:** anticipation is a necessary element in devising the strategic business plan, with desired targets and metrics. But, as the sim progresses, there is also the need to recognize changing macro-environment, industry and other conditions, as opportunities or as threats, and how these may impact on options and choices.
- **Challenge:** here we are not just concerned with the discipline-specific challenges presented in the simulation (though there are plenty of those!) but more about whether the working groups – as 'management team' members – can challenge themselves to understand and take on board different perspectives and views on issues and priorities.
- **Interpret:** reflecting real-world dilemmas, the information provided to the strategy simulation participants is a deliberate mix of the insufficient, the excessive, the irrelevant and the ambiguous, i.e. it is necessary to synthesize different sources and define relative value and importance. In setting the simulation over an extended yet defined time period, there is the need to interpret how accumulated experience (e.g. results so far) and changing conditions (e.g. regulatory environment, competitive conditions) could or should impact on determining a framework – maybe an evolving one – for making informed choices.
- **Decide:** as for many strategy and marketing case studies and projects, we are often in a land of no 'correct' answers (which certainly does not mean any lack of scope for bad decisions!). If students fast-track their data analysis – which may be tempting, to 'get it done' and move on to see the next KPI outcomes – it is likely to distort understanding of their relative impact and the advisability/reliability of decisions. Coupled with a need to consider and balance different strategy horizons (short vs. medium term), there is plenty of scope for decision making of varying quality and efficacy.

BOX 10.3　EXAMPLE FROM OUR SIMULATION

At one board meeting, the students are presented with an opportunity to form a joint venture or alliance in an exciting Asian growth market. Interesting, yes. Attractive, yes, BUT … closer analysis would reveal it to be in a very different market segment, requiring very different capabilities (and a lot more people!) and unlikely to have synergies with their other established businesses. So, if students examine all the given data, they will decline the invitation. Too many, however, do just first-level analysis and take poor decisions. *The good news is that it provides an excellent subsequent opportunity, e.g. in a seminar, to reflect on and discuss the applicable strategic rationale for choices.*

- **Align:** considering buy-in for stakeholders is in two contexts. Firstly, for the simulation company an understanding and analysis of its stakeholders: issues such as investor pressures, community environmental factors, customer preferences, or business partner motivations and sensibilities are to be considered. Secondly (and often more memorably for the student), in communicating to and working with other viewpoints – not least accepting challenge and learning to negotiate, and sometimes to compromise.
- **Learn:** again, there are two layers of learning implicit here: evaluating and reflecting on the nature and efficacy of the simulation company decisions taken, not least their KPI outcomes in relation to intention and expectation; also insights deriving from the process of making collective strategic decisions within a team. The latter can be encouraged by having assessment regimes that require reflection and the identification of key lessons – strategy-related and for personal development. Both contribute to equipping students with the skill to continuously learn – a skill applicable long after the simulation is completed and one that is highly valued by employers.

What about the student perspective on all this? That was evaluated through a (rather detailed!) questionnaire survey, plus in-depth semi-structured 'exit' interviews and written student reflections. The questionnaire addressed knowledge (K), skills (S) and attitudes (A) acquired by the students. Overall findings have been reported elsewhere[2] but we can focus on just the skills which students (and we) considered most relevant to employability. These are summarized in Table 10.1, based on data from three consecutive annual cohorts (487 responses, 93% response rate).

Table 10.1   Employability skills acquired

Survey category (K-S-A)	Parameter (student responses on skills development, in relation to the simulation)	Agree or strongly agree	Disagree or strongly disagree	Mean (0–5 scale)	Std. Dev
B (S)	Helped to improve my team-working skills	81%	6%	4.02	0.83
C (S)	More confident in decision-making skills	71%	9%	3.75	0.92
D (S)	Helped to improve my interpersonal skills	58%	12%	3.47	1.06
E (S)	Helped to improve my communication skills	69%	10%	3.74	0.89
F (S)	Helped to improve my negotiation skills	68%	9%	3.72	0.86
G (S)	Helped to improve my problem-solving skills	69%	9%	3.74	0.87
H (S)	Helped to improve my conflict resolution skills	61%	10%	3.60	0.84
J (S)	Helped to improve my critical thinking skills	75%	8%	3.85	0.85
K (S)	Helped me appreciate the complexity of business strategies	78%	7%	3.90	0.88

As Table 10.1 indicates, responses on skills acquisition and development were very positive. In the questionnaires and in the exit interview comments, there was a series of interesting and pertinent responses. In terms of transferrable skills, most students felt they had improved team-working, communication, negotiation and conflict resolution skills, recognizing those as particularly relevant to developing employability skills and prospects. Feedback indicated team-working and project management skills were built up gradually, as group members became more confident in cooperating with each other to complete the tasks. Notwithstanding different levels of motivation and capabilities within the groups, students (mostly!) managed to negotiate team goals and 'recalibrate' personal expectations, to find a 'rhythm' that worked well for them collectively. Students stated they had learned to compromise, as they recognized the different personalities, characters and cultures within a team, and that they had to be flexible to 'make it work'.

Many of the students also reported enhanced communications skills, as the debates in the board meeting required clarity, tact and persuasiveness to get team members to buy in to their suggestions. A by-product of this was an improvement in listening skills, as students learnt to demonstrate that they had listened to and considered the views of others, establishing credibility with their team members. Several students felt they had acquired some leadership skills along the way, e.g. by taking the lead in board discussions.

This was not always a smooth process! There were comments that some debates within groups became very 'lively' and they had to learn to resolve conflict through tactics such as rational discussions (!), demonstrating empathy and learning to compromise. Some students believed that the cumulative experience, particularly within the board meetings, helped them become more confident and effective, enabling them to develop their portfolio of employability-related management and project skills.

> *The simulation is exciting (S9) and completely different from other modules (S3) and 'makes us feel what it is like working in a real company' (S2).*[3]

> *I think companies like people that have experience and this is as close to experience as you can get (S24).*

SUMMARY

As this chapter has demonstrated, simulations can be extremely useful tools to develop and elicit both generic employability skills and those skills that are essential for a successful career in strategic management. We have found, as shown in the case example presented, that, when done well, students enjoy simulations and perceive great benefit for them in terms of skills development.

NOTES

1. Proserpio and Gioia (2007).
2. Evans and Kerridge (2015).
3. Student quotes are from Kerridge and Simpson (2020).

REFERENCES

Evans, J. and Kerridge, C. (2015) 'Campus Based Students' Perspectives on a Strategic Management Simulation: A Contextual Study', Conference Proceedings of ACTC 2015 (Kobe, Japan), pp. 307–320, ISSN 2186–4705.
Kerridge, C. and Simpson, C. (2020) 'Tutor and International Student Perspectives on an Action Research Project: Use of a Business Strategy Simulation with Mixed Nationality Cohorts', *Journal of International Education in Business*. Published 4 December at https://doi.org/10.1108/JIEB-07–2019–0034
Proserpio, L. and Gioia, D. (2007) 'Teaching the Virtual Generation', *Academy of Management Learning & Education*, 6 (1) 69–80.

FURTHER READING

J.P. Morgan. (2020) Bridging the Skills Gap: Higher Educations Opportunity. https://www.jpmorgan.com/global/cb/bridging-the-skills-gap

QS (2020) Why is Employability Important in Higher Education? https://www.qs.com/employability-important-higher-education/#:~:text=Producing%20employable%20graduates%20forms%20part%20of%20the%20process%20of%20educating.&text=Generic%20employability%20skills%20are%20important,of%20tasks%20in%20different%20environments.

Schoemaker, P., Krupp, S. and Howland, S. (2013) Strategic Leadership: The Essential Skills. https://hbr.org/2013/01/strategic-leadership-the-esssential-skills

UCAS (2020) What Do Employers Look for in Graduates? https://www.ucas.com/careers/getting-job/what-do-employers-look-graduates

11. Bringing accounting courses to life using simulation-based learning (SBL): the case of Accounting Bissim

Matt Davies, David Yates and Martin Potts

1. INTRODUCTION

In this chapter, we share our experiences of co-developing and using 'Accounting Bissim'[1] (a business simulation software program) as part of a simulation-based learning (SBL) approach for introductory accounting courses for non-specialists. We observe a number of benefits to using this approach, while recognising some of its limitations. These benefits include an improvement in student engagement, confidence, performance and satisfaction. Anecdotal evidence suggests the approach has helped encourage active learning (Bonwell & Eison, 1991) and changed student perceptions of the subject.

2. BACKGROUND

Many students struggle with accounting courses. Preconceived notions that the subject will be difficult, dull and devoid of practical relevance contribute towards this perception (Mastilak, 2012). The challenge of learning what is essentially a new form of symbolic representation (language), with different rules, practices and forms, contributes towards this difficulty. Students therefore may view accounting as a subject to be endured rather than enjoyed resulting in a more surface rather than deep learning approach. The focus often becomes memorising enough to pass the final assessment.

Teaching accounting to non-specialists can therefore be a challenge. One recommendation has been for greater use of active learning and case studies (Libby, 1991). Whilst there is evidence to support the use of the case study approach (Boyce, Williams, Kelly, & Yee, 2001; Cullen, Richardson, & O'Brien, 2004; Hassall & Milne, 2004; Lee, Collier, & Cullen, 2007), there is an argument that it is less effective for introductory classes, since the use of cases requires students to have already acquired sufficient knowledge to be able to engage effectively.

We initially deployed Bissim in 2015 as a pilot for an accounting module of 120 MSc Business and Management students. Following the success of this initial pilot, we have used Bissim on more than 40 introductory accounting courses with approximately 1,500 learners across our undergraduate, postgraduate and 'post-experience'[2] programmes, covering all modes of delivery: 'face-to-face', 'fully online' and 'blended learning' programmes.

In order to maximise the benefit from utilising the SBL approach, a fundamental redesign of the modules was required. Unlike other simulation-based modules, we utilise the simulation to provide the business context for practical activities and module assessment. The learning process is based around applying accounting tools in the context of the management of a simulated business. In this way, accounting comes to life: students practise the application of accounting tools and the interpretation of accounting information, with parallels that can be drawn to 'real-life' organisations.

3.   PEDAGOGICAL CONSIDERATIONS

The driving force behind how we deploy SBL is to offer an alternative to the 'rote learning' approach that we have observed some students adopt. We wanted to approach the teaching of accounting in a way in which the student can connect on a deeper level with the subject. Therefore, the pedagogical concepts of 'experiential learning' and 'deep learning' form the heart of the student experience.

Deep learning involves the development of student understanding utilising higher-level cognitive skills and employing more critical thought (Biggs, 1987; Entwistle, 2000; Ramsden, 2003). Experiential learning is often referred to as 'learning by doing'. Kerridge (2019) discusses this aspect to simulation use, referring to Kolb (1984). The act of continuous reflection, conceptualisation, application and action on the part of the learner allows for this 'learning by doing' to take place.

SBL can bridge between these two related pedagogical concepts. The simulation software provides the 'field' for learning to take place: a simulated context, but one that the learner can connect with, provided that they engage with the simulation (assigning students to teams responsible for a single 'virtual company' promotes this). The context therefore allows for experiences with using and managing an (albeit fictional) enterprise, and allows for the deployment of more theoretical tools and calculative techniques from accounting. This apparent 'realism' provided by the simulation carries the potential to enhance learning (Adobor & Daneshfar, 2006), and facilitate student engagement. Deeper learning then comes from the problem-solving elements that the simulation provides. A team is more likely to be successful if they effectively apply their accounting knowledge and tools when making decisions.

4.   THE ACCOUNTING BISSIM SIMULATION

Accounting Bissim is a specially adapted version of Bissim, a piece of business simulation software developed by Simulation Training Associates Ltd. Students act as the management team of a domestic robot manufacturer operating in the year 2031. Bissim runs with up to six teams, each of which makes a range of decisions over a maximum of six 'decision years'. Bissim is an integrated business simulation in which students make a wide range of decisions related to:

- Research and Development
- Production and Operations
- Marketing
- Human Resources
- Finance
- Sustainability
- Information Technology
- Product Development
- After Sales Service
- Exporting

Unlike many other simulations, Bissim is a facilitated simulation that requires the tutor to input each team's decisions into the program and generate and distribute results to students. Students do not interact directly with the Bissim software, and whilst this does increase the input required of the tutor in comparison with 'online simulations', we would argue that there are several advantages to this approach (see also: Guest, Kozlovskaya, & Olczak, 2019). Students are not required to be trained in the use of the simulation software, and as students are not distracted by the data input requirement they instead focus on activities such as discussion, analysis of information and decision making. All that students require is a copy of the Bissim Participant Manual, which contains the preliminary information they need to get started.

4.1.   The Development of Accounting Bissim

There have been four key elements to the development of the simulation so far:

1.   Changes to the simulation decision choices
2.   Changes to the Bissim program and results reports
3.   The creation of Bissim-related exercises and assessments
4.   The introduction of role plays, videos and an annual news report

4.1.1   Changes to the simulation decision choices

We recognised from the outset that the introduction of a business simulation would inevitably mean sacrificing some time that would normally be spent on accounting-specific learning activities in order to give students adequate time to make decisions. This presented an issue: how to maintain learning surrounding the more technical aspects of accounting combined with utilising the simulation. Therefore, we reduced the nature and number of decisions to what we considered appropriate (see Appendix 11.1).[3] The retained decisions were:

1. Research and Development:
    a. A choice of product development projects each with a different cost to implement
2. Production:
    a. Production quantity
    b. Number of production staff
    c. Capital expenditure to increase production capacity
3. Marketing:
    a. Sales price
    b. Advertising spend
    c. Trade discount percentage
4. Human Resources:
    a. Wage rate
    b. Training spend
5. Financing:
    a. Share issues
    b. Overdraft facility
    c. Change of credit terms with supplier
    d. Change of credit terms with customer
6. Sustainability:
    a. A range of options for reducing the business's environmental impact and to ensure compliance with in-game environmental legislation

Although limiting the scope of decision making, this range of decisions has allowed us to design activities around the simulation and balance the time students spend making decisions regarding their company with that spent completing supplementary classroom activities designed to assist with learning the more technical aspects of accounting.

4.1.2   Changes to the Bissim program and results reports

We also made changes to the program and the results reports to help ensure the simulation was more suitable for our requirements. Working with the developer, we amended the way in which accounting is applied in Bissim to ensure consistency either with current practices or with the way in which we teach the subject.[4] In addition, we introduced new accounting and finance features that were not present, to help promote the achievement of the learning outcomes relevant for our accounting courses.

Making changes to existing features was relatively straightforward. Introducing new features proved more of a challenge. Some important accounting and finance concepts were absent from Bissim, and we therefore introduced the following features:

- Capitalisation and amortisation of research and development expenditure.
- The introduction of new accounting adjustments for accruals, prepayments and provisions.

These changes facilitated the creation of new supplementary exercises requiring students to identify appropriate accounting adjustments for their business based on a given scenario, which we discuss in the following subsection.

4.1.3   The creation of Bissim-related exercises and assessments

We felt from the outset that it was important for Bissim to be fully integrated within a module to ensure effective learning and constructive alignment (Barnett, 2009; Caulfield, Maj, Xia, & Veal, 2012). For each module where Bissim is used, each topic is supported by exercises that provide an opportunity for students to practise and explore application in the context of their own simulation businesses. Examples of these exercises include:

- calculation of relevant accounting numbers for their business such as depreciation, accruals and pre-payments based on given scenarios;
- calculation and interpretation of financial ratios for their business;
- calculation of the break-even quantity of production;
- evaluation of accepting an order from a potential new customer at a special price; and
- evaluation of a long-term investment decision.

These exercises were designed for students to not only practise the application of fundamental concepts and techniques, but also develop a more critical appreciation of their practical merits and limitations. For example, some of these exercises reveal that some accounting numbers require judgement and are therefore open to manipulation, thus introducing qualitative considerations outside of the 'black and white' answers often misattributed to the discipline of accounting.

4.1.4   The introduction of role-plays, videos and an annual news report

We introduced role-plays, videos and an annual news report as supplements to the experience of using the simulation. Our rationale behind the introduction of these supplementary elements was as follows:

1. We wanted to add another 'layer' of 'realism' to the simulation activity. This creation of the associated reports, videos and role-plays allows us to take elements from wider everyday life and add them to the simulated experience provided by the Accounting Bissim software. Via the addition of these artefacts,[5] we are therefore able to take the simulation closer to a 'real-world' environment.
2. The additions act as a communication tool that limits the amount of instructor-intensive guidance required. This also helps foster basic research skills within the student cohort, encouraging them to look up key information from the sources provided.

Role-plays involve the tutor taking one of the key stakeholder roles such as the bank manager, customer or supplier to meet with any team that, for example, is seeking additional debt finance or a change in terms. The tutor then has the ability to reflect the results of these negotiations via the data input process.

In 2019 we created a series of short videos (3–5 minutes duration) which cover some key aspects of the simulation including a summary of the perspectives of key stakeholders. There are eight such videos:

1. The Retiring Managing Director who in handing over the control of the business to the new management team provides an overview of the business and the industry in which it operates.
2. The Market Research Analyst who provides a forecast of likely future customer demand and an explanation of the price elasticity of demand for the industry.
3. The Bank Manager who provides a summary of the prevailing interest rates as well as the bank's lending criteria.
4. The Auditor who explains key accounting treatment in the simulation for Research and Development, Depreciation and Provisions.
5. The Investment Bank Representative who explains the process and funding available via a share issue.
6. The Customer who explains their negotiating position regarding payment terms.
7. The Supplier who also explains their negotiating position regarding payment terms.
8. The Lawyer who is acting for an injured customer. This video is relevant to any team that fails to invest in making their product safe by the end

of the fourth decision year. These teams receive a message that one of their robots has malfunctioned and the injured customer is suing for compensation.

These videos introduce a new type of resource, which suits some learning styles and contributes to the sense of 'realism' associated with utilising the simulation. Videos are released to students at the point in the exercise at which they are most relevant, providing a reference for decision making.

In addition to these videos, we introduced a four-page annual news report that summarises the state of each 'Simulation World' and provides key information relevant to the forthcoming decision year. The news report includes a summary of additional debt funding available to each team based on their current financial position and the lending criteria of the bank. This reduces the contact time required to brief students on the forthcoming decision year and has proved particularly helpful for new colleagues who are less familiar with how the simulation works.

5.   DEPLOYMENT/IMPLEMENTATION

We believe that for an SBL approach to be effective the simulation needs to be carefully integrated within the delivery and assessment of the module. In this section, we explore the different ways in which we have sought to achieve this and how these methods have evolved over time.

5.1   Organising Students into Teams

The first practical issue we face when using Accounting Bissim is how to organise students into teams. Each Bissim World has a maximum of six teams and works best with 5/6 students per team. Where possible we prefer to have a smaller number of larger teams as this reduces the data input requirement and reduces the risk that low student attendance for a particular session might adversely impact the learning process.

5.2   How We Use Accounting Bissim to Support Course Delivery

A feature of our approach has been to integrate the use of Bissim within the delivery of a module, and to dedicate time during synchronous sessions (both in-person workshops/seminars and online webinars) for students to work on two different types of Bissim-related activities:

• First, to make their business decisions.
• Second, to complete one or more Bissim-related exercises that address the relevant accounting topic of that particular week of the module.

From the outset we recognised that achieving an appropriate balance between these two simulation-related activities was important. As has been acknowledged already, the approach involves making a trade-off between the time spent in class to ensure: (a) the simulation is an enjoyable and engaging experience for students, and (b) the learning objectives are met. Wherever possible we run two-hour sessions, and allow at least 45 minutes for teams to work on their business decisions. We have found in the past that where lengthy sessions had been dedicated to the simulation alone, it had the potential to create a disconnect between wider learning and the running of the simulated business. The two-hour integrated session helps to reinforce the notion that the simulation is an aid to learning, facilitating the wider, educational objectives, and not simply an 'end' in itself. The remainder of the time is devoted to the completion of Bissim-related exercises, typically in teams, which provide a direct link between the module learning and its application within the context of the business simulation activity. Some of these exercises are based on the initial Bissim 2030 financial statements and therefore the solutions are identical for all teams. Others are based on the specific situation of their own business, and some of these link to the decisions required in that particular decision year.

Why don't we alleviate some of the time pressure by requiring students to complete their business decisions 'outside of class time'? There are many reasons why we prefer to make time for this activity during synchronous sessions. First, this approach gives greater incentives for students to engage in the synchronous sessions, as those who are absent will not have the opportunity to participate in the decision-making process. Second, this makes it easier for us to monitor 'team dynamics' and intervene where necessary. Third, this reduces the amount of student queries as the briefing is given 'in class'. Fourth, the role-play negotiations between tutor and simulation team are more effective if they occur during these sessions.[6] Finally, running the decision rounds in class allows the tutor to inject their energy and enthusiasm into the activity for example by providing a brief review of the state of the industry, highlighting any notable events and successes and providing support to teams who are finding the activity difficult. This helps maintain an environment in which students feel encouraged to apply knowledge and skills.

5.3   How Many Decision Rounds to Run?

Whilst running the simulation over too few rounds can lead to frustration, there are also problems with running the simulation over too many. After four decision years, some teams believe that they are too far behind the industry leaders, adversely affecting their motivation. As students become more familiar with the simulation there is a risk they will become less motivated as novelty wears off. To counteract this, the simulation has built-in events in the later years, and we also introduce our own activities and exercises to help maintain student interest. For example, we typically introduce the role-play negotiations with the customer and supplier in year three, and the ability to sell to a new overseas customer in year four. This means that there is always something new to consider even if the underlying dynamics of the activity become familiar.

While we are keen to ensure students do not find the activity too straightforward, we should emphasise that initially (at least) the simulation can be daunting, even with the reduced number of decisions. We believe therefore that it is vital that sufficient time is spent at the start of the activity to both build students' confidence in the simulation and help with team building. So, before students work on the full set of decisions in 2032, they first complete three separate activities designed to build confidence. First, students work in teams to complete a quiz that tests whether they have understood the key features of the simulation from their prior reading of the Bissim manual. Second, before we move to the first decision year (2031), students work in their teams to decide who will take on each of the key management roles for their business and choose their business strategy. The choice of business strategy itself is not input into the simulation program but can help students with the subsequent decisions they need to make, for example choosing between research and development projects that support either a differentiation or a cost leadership focus. Third, for the first decision year (2031) students are only required to make three decisions: production quantity, sales price and wage rate. This allows students to build confidence in the challenge before the full range of decisions are required.

5.4   Using Accounting Bissim to Support Course Assessment

Consistent with the principles of constructive alignment, we link the module assessment to the simulation activity.

Examples of assessed portfolio tasks include the following:

* Writing a report that provides a financial analysis of their business at the end of the 2033 decision year, including the calculation of relevant financial ratios.
* Writing a report that provides an analysis of the financial merits of a proposed investment decision.
* Drawing on specific examples, events and experiences from the simulation activity, critically reflecting on what has been learnt about accounting, including its merits and limitations.

Student performance centres on the ability to apply analysis to the specific context of their own business. By having a clear connection between the simulation and assessment, student engagement is enhanced. There are two specific aspects of our approach that facilitate this. First, most of the marks for the module are awarded on an individual basis, and, second, no marks are awarded for the performance of each business in the activity.

We accept that the use of individual assessment may seem counter-intuitive given the simulation is itself a 'team-based' activity. However, we seek to exploit the advantages of a collaborative learning experience without the potential disadvantages of group-based assessment; specifically the risk of 'free riders' achieving a mark with little personal contribution. We find that this approach also provides an incentive for engagement. We are also aware of colleagues (when using an SBL approach) who attach a small proportion of module marks (5–10%) for the performance of each team based on predetermined ranking criteria such as shareholder returns, profits, market share, etc. (see also: Dickie, 2006). We do not subscribe to this logic, as we believe that the SBL approach should create a realistic yet safe environment for students to try out the application of new knowledge and skills. We instead attempt to promote the idea of 'long-term value creation', based on a future business potential, rather than placing an emphasis on rewarding relatively short-term performance. Therefore, whilst at the end of each module we do declare a 'winner' for each 'World', we concede that this is somewhat subjective. We would be uncomfortable awarding marks based on such judgements.

6.   REFLECTIONS

The use of Accounting Bissim as part of an SBL approach has had a positive impact. Whilst there are costs and other drawbacks associated with the approach, overall we believe that an SBL module has the potential to enhance the overall curriculum in business-related disciplines. We discuss our observations in relation to this in the following subsections.

6.1   Student Engagement

As tutors on SBL modules, we have witnessed significant improvements in student attendance and engagement. For example, attendance on a second-year undergraduate module for non-specialists was more that 50% above that of other second-year accounting modules. This result is even more remarkable given the benchmark modules are for specialist students who we might expect to have greater levels of engagement.

We appreciate that attendance does not necessarily equate to active engagement, but we also find that activity levels in Bissim workshops tend to be greater than in other seminars. We are not suggesting an SBL approach is the only way to achieve this, but in our experience, the approach certainly has the potential to bring seminar workshops 'to life'.

6.2   Student Confidence

The SBL approach has helped students develop confidence in a subject that many approach with a sense of trepidation. By engaging on a deeper level, they inevitably spend more time learning and applying accounting knowledge and skills, which builds confidence. Second, the simulation provides a 'low-stakes' environment in which to explore the application of accounting concepts offering students the opportunity to learn from previous mistakes. Finally, through working in small teams students gain the benefits of collaborative learning. Students are able to share their concerns and misconceptions with team-mates and are able to help each other find solutions.

6.3   Student Feedback

Student feedback has been extremely positive. Overall module satisfaction scores are typically in excess of 90%, and sometimes in excess of 95%. End-of-module feedback surveys often include positive comments.

> *I loved this module, I never thought I would say that about accounting!* (Executive MBA student, January–March 2020)

We have found that the simulation activity helps students relate to a subject that can otherwise seem abstract and difficult. They seem more able to make connections between accounting and the underlying factors and decisions that influence it:

> *The business simulation helped to provide a real context for the theory.* (Online MBA student, March–April 2020)

> *The business simulation provided a practical way to learn the concepts.* (Online MBA student, March–April 2020)

7.   COSTS AND DRAWBACKS

We acknowledge that there are costs and drawbacks associated with the use of an SBL approach. Financial costs are involved when utilising a piece of simulation software under licence. In addition, there is the set-up time required. The use of SBL is not a 'quick fix' for improving student engagement. Instructors need to invest sufficient preparation time in becoming familiar with the simulation, and developing learning activities. In addition, the time inputting decisions into the software, along with ensuring logistical issues (such as appropriate physical space for collaborative learning, etc.) are managed appropriately should not be underestimated.

We also recognise that there are potential drawbacks of the SBL approach for learning. There exists the risk that students can become so engrossed in the simulation activity that it has a detrimental effect on the achievement of the intended learning outcomes.[7] We find that allowing time for in-class discussion and decision submissions helps to alleviate this issue. There is also the risk that whilst students gain an in-depth knowledge of the way in which accounting operates in the context of the business simulation, they may not gain a broader understanding of how accounting can operate in other contexts. It is important therefore that in the design of the module, references are made to other 'real-world' applications of accounting.

8.   CONCLUSION

In this chapter, we have shown ways in which SBL can be supplemented, enhanced and deployed. We have reflected on our experiences with 'Accounting Bissim' to illustrate how a simulation can be used to provide the organisational context for a number of exercises that promote the technical aspects of accounting, as well as offering a simulation of the management of an organisation.

We believe that SBL is an effective approach for teaching accounting to non-specialist students. While not offering a panacea for accounting education, the unique features of a simulation provide students with a different perspective on learning accounting, which we believe enhances the appeal of the subject and the learning experience, and allows access to aspects of learning that more traditional methods do not. We believe that the time commitment in designing and executing related content alongside the simulation carries with it a pay-off in terms of achieving learning outcomes and constructive alignment.

NOTES

1. Accounting Bissim has been developed in coordination with staff from Aston Business School, De Montfort University and Warwick Business School. For more information visit: https://www.accountingbissim.com
2. Programme tailored for corporate clients.
3. Appendix 11.1 shows the decision criteria in full, what was retained for the initial running of Bissim in 2015, and the current decisions that are enabled in the present form of Accounting Bissim.
4. For example, the initial accounting terminology that was used in Bissim was changed to comply with IFRS. Ratios were also changed in order to correspond with the calculation methods that we used in our courses.

5. Aspects such as the news report, videos and role-plays (in the form that we utilised them) could be considered elements and representations of the wider 'business environment'. These aspects enable a sense of realism to be established, presenting symbolic representations of the environment that exists outside of the simulation exercise (Žižek, 1989).
6. The interaction with another individual 'face to face' and the prospect of this form of negotiation is a key skill that we try to promote throughout the module, both in group discussions and through wider role-playing activity (see: Levant, Coulmont, & Sandu, 2016).
7. We have on occasion had to remind some students that the objective is to develop accounting skills and knowledge and not to become experts in the running of a domestic robot manufacturing business!

REFERENCES

Adobor, H., & Daneshfar, A. (2006). Management simulations: determining their effectiveness. *Journal of Management Development, 25*(2), 151–168.

Barnett, L. (2009). Key Aspects of Learning and Teaching in Economics. In H. Fry, S. Ketteridge, & S. Marshall (eds), *A Handbook for Teaching and Learning in Higher Education: Enhancing Academic Practice* (3rd edn, pp. 404–423). New York: Routledge.

Biggs, J. (1987). *Student Approaches to Learning and Studying*. Hawthorn, Victoria: Australian Council for Education Research.

Bonwell, C. C., & Eison, J. A. (1991). *Active Learning: Creating Excitement in the Classroom. ASHE-ERIC Higher Education Report No. 1.* Retrieved from Washington, DC: https://files.eric.ed.gov/fulltext/ED336049.pdf

Boyce, G., Williams, S., Kelly, A., & Yee, H. (2001). Fostering deep and elaborative learning and generic (soft) skill development: the strategic use of case studies in accounting education. *Accounting Education, 10*(1), 37–60.

Caulfield, C., Maj, S. P., Xia, J., & Veal, D. (2012). Shall we play a game? *Applied Science, 6*(1), 2–16.

Cullen, J., Richardson, S., & O'Brien, R. (2004). Exploring the teaching potential of empirically-based case studies. *Accounting Education, 13*(2), 251–266.

Dickie, M. (2006). Do classroom experiments increase learning in introductory microeconomics? *The Journal of Economic Education, 37*(3), 267–288.

Entwistle, N. (2000). *Promoting Deep Learning Through Teaching and Assessment: Conceptual Frameworks and Educational Contexts.* Paper presented at the ESRC Teaching and Learning Research Programme Conference, Leicester. http://www.leeds.ac.uk/educol/documents/00003220.htm

Guest, J., Kozlovskaya, M., & Olczak, M. (2019). The Use of Short In-class Games. In K. Daniels, C. Elliott, S. Finley, & C. Chapman (eds), *Learning and Teaching in Higher Education: Perspectives from a Business School* (pp. 231–240). Cheltenham: Edward Elgar.

Hassall, T., & Milne, M. J. (2004). *Using Case Studies in Accounting Education.* Abingdon: Taylor & Francis.

Kerridge, C. (2019). Experiential Learning: Use of Business Simulations. In K. Daniels, C. Elliott, S. Finley, & C. Chapman (eds), *Learning and Teaching in Higher Education: Perspectives from a Business School* (pp. 109–119). Cheltenham: Edward Elgar.

Kolb, D. (1984). *Experiential Learning.* New Jersey: Prentice Hall.

Lee, B., Collier, P. M., & Cullen, J. (2007). Reflections on the use of case studies in the accounting, management and organizational disciplines. *Qualitative Research in Organizations and Management: An International Journal, 2*(3), 169–178.

Levant, Y., Coulmont, M., & Sandu, R. (2016). Business simulation as an active learning activity for developing soft skills. *Accounting Education, 25*(4), 368–395.

Libby, P. A. (1991). Barriers to using cases in accounting education. *Issues in Accounting Education, 6*(2), 193–213.

Mastilak, C. (2012). First-day strategies for millennial students in introductory accounting courses: it's all fun and games until something gets learned. *Journal of Education for Business, 87,* 48–51.

Ramsden, P. (2003). *Learning to Teach in Higher Education.* London: Routledge Falmer.

Žižek, S. (1989). *The Sublime Object of Ideology.* London: Verso.

APPENDIX 11.1: DECISION EVOLUTION OVER TIME

Decisions	Full Bissim	Accounting Bissim 2015	Accounting Bissim Now 2020
Research and Development Projects	Yes	Yes	Yes
Production:			
Production quantity	Yes	Yes	Yes
Number of production staff	Yes	Yes	Yes
Capital expenditure	Yes	Yes	Yes
Production improvement projects	Yes	No	No
Marketing:			
Key customer segment	Yes	No	No
Key product benefit	Yes	No	No
Retail selling price	Yes	Yes	Yes
Advertising	Yes	Yes	Yes
Media choice	Yes	No	No
Number of sales staff	Yes	No	No
Trade discount %	Yes	Yes	Yes
Key outlet	Yes	No	No
Human Resources:			
Number of administration staff	Yes	No	Yes
Wage rate	Yes	Yes	Yes
Training	Yes	Yes	Yes
Finance:			
Credit period with suppliers	Yes	Yes	Yes
Credit period with customers	Yes	Yes	Yes
Bank overdraft limit	Yes	Yes	Yes
Dividend rate	Yes	No	No
Share issue	Yes	Yes	Yes
Bank loan	No	No	Yes
Sustainability Decisions:			
Product recyclability	Yes	Yes	Yes
Other sustainability projects	Yes	No	No
Compliance with environmental and pollution legislation	Yes	No	Yes
Information Technology:			
IT equipment	Yes	No	No
Website choices	Yes	No	No
Second Product	Yes	No	No
After Sales Service	Yes	No	No
Exporting	Yes	No	No

12. The value of simulations for mixed nationality/culture student cohorts

Clive Kerridge and Jason Evans

WHY READ THIS CHAPTER?

In recent years, recruitment at many university and college business schools has become more international, for undergraduate and particularly for post-graduate programmes. This has brought fresh challenges for both educators and students – not least in getting (and maintaining) student engagement and in selecting pedagogic methods that will best ensure programme learning objectives are met.

There is accumulating evidence that business simulations, which incorporate a considerable experiential learning element, can be particularly effective for mixed nationality, mixed culture cohorts, reducing the academic performance gaps (notably between domestic and international students) that are often features of more traditional, didactic course deliveries.

INTRODUCTION

Elsewhere in this book, the opportunities for, and benefits of, incorporating business simulations into undergraduate and postgraduate curricula and assessment regimes are discussed. Here we look specifically at issues and advantages of simulations for mixed nationality teaching. The term 'mixed nationality' in this context covers a variety of cohort types, in which students are drawn from different nations or regions, often different language groups and/or cultural backgrounds, and may have been taught previously in different pedagogic styles and traditions.

In the course of this chapter, we will focus on the particular challenges associated with teaching and learning in cohorts that comprise a mix of domestic students and international students, i.e. classes in which many of the learners have previously been educated in countries and cultures different from that of the host HE institution where they now study.

BACKGROUND: WHAT IS SPECIFIC TO INTERNATIONAL STUDENTS AND MIXED COHORTS?

International students are a significant proportion of recruitment at university level in many countries, most notably in North America, NW Europe, Australasia and Russia. In Australia, Canada and the UK, international students now constitute more than 20% of tertiary education cohorts (Statista, 2020). For Business Management subjects in the UK, international students make up about 27% of the total at undergraduate level but 63% on postgraduate taught courses (HESA, 2019). This recent increase has inevitably created challenges for both international and domestic students, also for faculty in the host country HEIs. Difficulties specific to the international students have often been seen to result in lower levels of engagement and academic achievement, relative to their domestic (host country) counterparts. Nevertheless, the principal learning issues for international students are similar to those for domestic students: engagement; integration; communication and employment skills.

Those very same issues apply beyond the classroom too. There has been extensive discussion in the business literature about their significance and importance, notably in the developing and managing of cross-cultural project teams. Examples in the academic literature include Hofstede's seminal work, *Culture's Consequences*; Pankaj Ghemawat's CAGE framework, with identification of cultural 'distance' as a key factor; and Erin Meyer's engaging recent book, *The Culture Map*.

So, this is not just about language differences (significant though they may be) but also about mixing students from different cultures and pedagogic traditions. With the recent increase in numbers of Chinese students attending overseas universities and colleges, there has been considerable research attention on the needs and challenges of East Asian ('Confucian heritage culture – CHC') learners in 'Western' HEIs. Earlier views of academic culture tended to focus on differences, contrasting Western/Socratic and Eastern/Confucian traditions, but those are being superseded by more positive views of the capacity of international students to adapt to new pedagogic approaches. To bridge a perceived 'gap' between learners from differing educational traditions, several educators have advocated the use of constructivist or active learning pedagogic approaches that require students to perform collaborative tasks, leading to more extensive interaction between domestic and international students, and higher levels of engagement with the academic content of their courses (Devlin & Peacock, 2009; Volet & Ang, 2012).

In the next sections, we focus on Experiential Learning (EL) which provides just such an approach. Business simulations that include group-working tasks can also provide an experience of working in mixed nationality, mixed culture workplaces – and this is recognised by students as a valuable tool for their future, with management roles and project teams involving cooperation with colleagues, clients and suppliers or partners across a range of countries and cultures.

AIMS: WHAT ARE WE SEEKING TO ACHIEVE WITH THE BUSINESS SIMULATIONS?

Improve Student Experience and Engagement

In this chapter, we consider the EL approach and the use and benefits of business simulations that incorporate collaborative working. Feedback from our own students, consistent with published research, confirms that such simulations are liked by many students – engagement levels are often high. They are applicable for different levels and varied class sizes; they work well with mixed cohorts (subject disciplines and/or cultural and language mixes); and they can be conveniently embedded into assessment regimes. Through the 'sims', students gain valuable insights into the multidisciplinary nature of business decision-making and entrepreneurship. Good business simulations can be fun and memorable too – for instructors as well as students.

Notwithstanding language adaptation issues, most international students will already have some experience of gaming – though not necessarily within a taught curriculum. There is a significant benefit in that simulation and gaming concepts are almost universal, so not language (or pedagogic tradition) dependent. This familiarity also renders the use of simulations a particularly effective way to facilitate collaborative learning.

Achieve Course/Module Learning Objectives (Through Appropriate Pedagogic Methods)

Simulations will rarely be of value if they are not linked with the associated learning disciplines and desired outcomes. Although much learning derives from the experience of *doing* the simulation activities, it is the associated reflection (as in Kolb's experiential learning cycle – see below) that reinforces cognitive and affective (feelings-related) learning in particular. Tutors and instructors – and assessment regimes – can play key roles in encouraging and directing students to reflect on their experiences, both during and after playing simulation game(s).

Facilitate [Better] Student Performance – Reduce or Eliminate Gaps between International and Domestic Students

There have been several recent investigations into the experience of international students taught in more constructivist or active learning environments, e.g. Bache & Hayton (2012), Loon et al. (2015), Spencer-Oatey & Dauber (2016), Chavan & Carter (2018), Bell (2020). Those studies generally report that it contributes to improved performance by both domestic and international students. Moreover, by exposing students to less prescriptive tasks, these approaches can partially replicate the complexity of authentic working environments, requiring a more active engagement with problems than is the case in less flexibly structured learning environments.

In line with active learning principles, a business simulation may provide a more loosely structured learning environment, within which students take on more proactive roles than in traditional, structured didactic contexts.

Accommodate and Encourage Effective Group-Working

Simulations played in groups offer various benefits to the participants, including all three types of learning specified in Bloom's taxonomy (Biggs & Tang, 2011), notably the behavioural (psychomotor) and affective learning which is more difficult to engender with traditional teaching and learning techniques. The higher levels of engagement (and more time spent involved with the subject matter) also influence cognitive learning.

There is evidence (for example, Simpson & Kerridge, 2019) that simulations are particularly effective for mixed nationality, cross-cultural student teams – minimising the linguistic obstacles to learning for international students and contributing to reduced attainment differentials versus domestic/home students. With the move to more off-campus, blended learning deliveries of university courses from 2020, student cohorts are increasingly dispersed across locations and between countries or regions. Business simulation designs and support features are often well suited to such conditions, providing a vehicle that aids and encourages cross-cultural group-working for both online and on-campus learners.

Develop Soft Skills that are Important (or Vital) for Business Careers[1]

Employers frequently comment on difficulties in recruiting graduates that have developed skills in effective group-working and can contribute well to project teams – all the more so for finding those who already adapt and function well in cross-cultural environments and teams. Shortcomings are particularly evident when it comes to collective decision-making; balancing differing opinions and views, data vs. intuition, evaluating short-term vs. medium-/longer-term benefits, etc. In many university programmes, there are few opportunities to engage deeply in such collaborative activities, even though these may be fundamental elements of subsequent employment roles. Students experienced in simulations can often put that learning (and associated confidence) to good effect in job interviews and employer assessment workshops.

LINKS TO THEORY AND RESEARCH

There have been many studies on the use and benefits of business simulations in management education, e.g. Faria (2001), Zantow et al. (2005), Lean et al. (2006, 2014), Kerridge (2019). A recent meta-review of the literature that focuses on studies in higher education (Vlachopoulos & Makri, 2017) reports that the use of simulations promotes affective, cognitive and behavioural types of learning. Positive impacts are also found on both students' attainment of learning outcomes and the attitude of tutors. The reported benefits are not just curriculum based: business simulations have often been considered effective tools in developing students' teamworking, collaboration, leadership and other soft skills likely to be valued by employers, e.g. Tiwari et al. (2014).

Several studies have sought to compare the effectiveness of online simulation-based learning with traditional didactic lecture-based teaching, e.g. Warren et al. (2016) reported an increase in student knowledge and confidence, based on reviewing the effectiveness of simulation games on satisfaction, knowledge, attitudes, skills and learning outcomes.

There have also been several studies on evaluating learning models for simulation-based training, including one by the authors of this chapter which endorsed the use of a prescriptive model developed by Salas et al. (2009) for effective application of experiential learning methods within a blended learning pedagogic approach (Evans & Kerridge, 2015).

In terms of optimising the use of simulations, Sitzmann (2011) highlighted the importance of integrating simulation games within teaching programmes but recognised that all too often they may just be supplemental teaching activities because "full integration requires high-quality mechanisms, students' engagement, and instructors' support". By ensuring that a business simulation runs over an extended period (days or even weeks), has instructor support and is fully integrated into a module/course teaching programme, we can meet Sitzmann's conditions for effective simulation-based learning, not least in relation to student engagement.

International students' comments quoted in a recent action research study (Kerridge & Simpson, 2020) supported the view that experiential learning, learning-through-doing within a reflective cycle (e.g. Kolb, 1984), and specifically through business simulations, contributed to reducing performance differentials versus their domestic peers. Notably, it enhances their ability to grasp and apply the theoretical content of their course. The study also presented comparative performance data on international and domestic students' grades over several cohort years of the same final-year undergraduate module on which the students commented. The module was delivered 'traditionally' via lectures and seminars in a first semester (A) but oriented around a multi-week business simulation, involving extensive group-working plus a final reflective assessment, in the second semester (B). Across the cohort, there was a significant improvement in engagement and performance in semester B but this was markedly more so for the international students. Figure 12.1 shows the grade differential between international students from the PRC[2] (approximately 40% of the cohort) and the non-PRC students. There is a convergence of grade attainment over the period that experiential learning pedagogies were embedded but this is most evident in the 'simulation' semester (B), where the difference is reduced to single figure percentage points. This is consistent with those comments made by the international students.

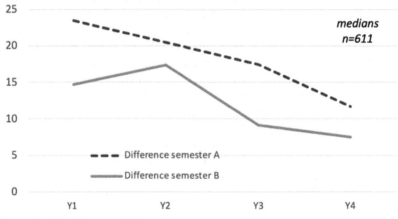

Source: Kerridge & Simpson (2020).

Figure 12.1   *Grade performance differentials between Chinese international and non-Chinese students: comparison of 'traditional' (semester A) and simulation-based (semester B) deliveries over four consecutive cohort years*

PRINCIPLES FOR CHOOSING AND USING SIMULATIONS WITH MIXED COHORTS

The established benefits of using business simulations make choice and incorporation of them a relevant issue for curriculum design considerations in most/ many HEI courses. In particular, this responds to a key challenge for business schools: to attract and retain international students, especially on taught postgraduate programmes, in an increasingly competitive recruitment market.

A recent article (Ogwude, 2019) elaborated some universal issues in mixed nationality teaching and learning, notably the need to actively recognise international students – but in ways that do not alienate or disadvantage domestic students – and to design assessments that do not substantially favour particular groups of students. Simulations can help on both counts, with attention to these key metrics: enhancing student engagement; improving student performance (including those reduced differentials between domestic and international students); and improving graduate employability prospects, as discussed elsewhere in this book. Of course, effecting a satisfactory and satisfying learning journey is vital for both domestic and international students.

Table 12.1   A categorisation of the main simulation choice criteria

Choice criterion	Options	Associated factors
Duration	Short/medium/long (multi-component)	May vary from just a single class session through to a sim conducted over several days or even weeks.
Participation	Individual or group/ collaborative	Self-teaching conducted individually, e.g. driving tests or flight simulators; teamworking, enabling development of soft skills, e.g. for employability.
Measurement	Qualitative and/or quantitative; 'numbers driven'	Metrics may vary, depending upon complexity; multi-component sims may involve several, e.g. be composites of financials and non-financials.
Competition	'Marketplace' or parallel competition; non-competitive	In 'marketplace' sims, choices and decisions taken directly affect the other 'players', e.g. pricing of products or investment. Even if independent of other players, a leader board system is often used.
Online/offline	Online, offline, or hybrid	Vary from an online video game style, to mainly offline, to hybrids, e.g. meetings but data input.
Feedback	Interactive or via instructors/peers	Automated and/or available online; interim or formative feedback with peers/instructors.

Source: Kerridge (2019).

So, are there some general principles to apply in selecting and incorporating simulations into teaching modules and courses? First, we need to recognise the wide variety of available 'sims'. As in Table 12.1, there is a range of options for scale, time, complexity, etc., and a judgement should be made on 'horses for courses'.

Practical constraints may limit or significantly influence the range of choices available for a particular study module or course. In the case of mixed nationality classes, *Participation* will often be the key criterion, with sim selection being made with a view to optimising cooperative and peer learning opportunities across a student cohort. Good simulations offer structured frameworks that are not overly prescriptive – encouraging a desirable mix of affective and behavioural, as well as cognitive, learning. The benefits of a *Competition* element should also not be underestimated – a leader board often contributes to enhanced levels of student engagement and commitment, especially if the sim is being run over extended periods of days or weeks. Above all, a simulation should be chosen which ensures good learning experiences – enjoyable but challenging – for both international and domestic students in group-working situations.

Also ... what not to choose?! Be aware of the dangers of 'bad' simulations – sometimes a simulation is chosen for teaching convenience, e.g. limited time and/or low cost rather than for its congruence with the learning objectives. The outcomes (or lack thereof) may be all the worse if the purpose and process of the sim are not well understood, i.e. not explained well by the instructors.

This brings us appropriately to the role of the instructor. Most business simulations benefit from – perhaps even need – significant instructor input, for example: outlining key principles (of how the simulation works) and specifying intended learning outcomes; identifying useful tools or sources of help and guidance; assisting with in-game guidance (which may be about team working or useful sources of reference), maybe offering some challenge. This does not have to be onerous – indeed, feedback from teachers is that it is often enjoyable and rewarding for the instructors too – but it is important, perhaps all the more so with the mixed nationality cohorts.

A Framework for Deciding on Appropriate Business Simulation(s)

Figure 12.2 represents a simple conceptual framework that considers the interrelation of four factors:

- issues/difficulties anticipated (for international and/or domestic students);
- appropriate pedagogic approaches, e.g. EL in examples discussed in this chapter;
- choice and design of the simulation, e.g. which of the categories in Table 12.1; and
- benefits sought from incorporating the simulation into the HE course(s).

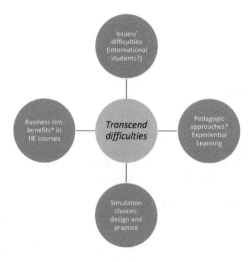

Note:
* Key benefits:
Engagement, Performance
Soft skill development
Decision-making
Cooperation and negotiation
Employability

*Figure 12.2   Conceptual framework for defining and selecting an
               appropriate simulation*

CONCLUDING POINTS

Well-prepared, well-explained business simulations are pedagogic tools for all learners – regardless of cultural background and prior educational experience.

Synthesising 'real management' processes and challenges, including negotiation, leadership and collective decision-making, is valuable to – and appreciated by – most business students.

There is ample evidence that the experiential learning involved with business simulations helps transcend language and other difficulties (for those from different cultures and pedagogic traditions) that often pertain to more traditional didactic learning processes.

The Dos and Don'ts on selection and application of business simulations apply as much to mixed nationality cohorts as to any other (see Appendix 12.1).

Finally, do remember: working through a simulation can be – and often is – FUN!

NOTES

1. There is a more comprehensive discussion on developing employment skills through business simulations in Chapters 9 and 10 of this book.
2. People's Republic of China.

REFERENCES

Bache, I. and Hayton, R. (2012) Inquiry-based learning and the international student, *Teaching in Higher Education*, 17(4), 411–423.

Bell, R. (2020) Adapting to constructivist approaches to entrepreneurship education in the Chinese classroom, *Studies in Higher Education*, 45(8), 1694–1710.

Biggs, J. and Tang, C. (2011) *Teaching for Quality Learning at University*. Maidenhead: Open University Press.

Chavan, M. and Carter, L. (2018) The value of experiential and active learning in business ethics education, *Journal of Teaching in International Business*, 22(2), 126–143.

Daniels, K., Elliott, C., Finley, S. and Chapman, C. (eds) (2019) *Learning and Teaching in Higher Education: Perspectives From a Business School*. Cheltenham: Edward Elgar Publishing.

Devlin, S. and Peacock, N. (2009) 'Overcoming Linguistic and Cultural Barriers to Integration: An Investigation of Two Models', in Coverdale-Jones, T. and Rastall, P. (eds), *Internationalizing the University: The Chinese Context*. London: Palgrave Macmillan, pp. 165–184.

Evans, J. and Kerridge, C. (2015) 'Campus Based Students' Perspectives on a Strategic Management Simulation: A Contextual Study', Conference Proceedings of ACTC 2015 (Kobe, Japan), pp. 307–320, ISSN 2186–4705.

Faria, A. (2001) The changing nature of business simulation/gaming research: a brief history, *Simulation & Gaming*, 32, 97–110.

HESA (2019) Higher Education Student Statistics UK 2017/18: where students come from and go to study. HESA Statistical Bulletin SB252.

Kerridge, C. (2019) 'Experiential Learning: Use of Business Simulations', in Daniels, K. et al. (eds), *Learning and Teaching in Higher Education: Perspectives From a Business School*. Cheltenham: Edward Elgar Publishing, pp. 109–119.

Kerridge, C. and Simpson, C. (2020) 'Tutor and international student perspectives on an action research project: use of a business strategy simulation with mixed nationality cohorts', *Journal of International Education in Business*. Published 4 December at https://doi.org/10.1108/JIEB-07–2019–0034

Kolb, D. (1984) *Experiential Learning: Experience as the Source of Learning and Development*. Englewood Cliffs, NJ: Prentice Hall.

Lean, J., Moizer, J. and Newberry, R. (2014) Enhancing the impact of online simulations through blended learning – a critical incident approach, *Education and Training*, 56(2–3), 208–218.

Lean, J., Moizer, J., Towler, M. and Abbey, C. (2006) Simulations and games: use and barriers in Higher Education, *Active Learning in Higher Education*, 7(3), 227–242.

Loon, M., Evans, J. and Kerridge, C. (2015) Learning with a strategic management simulation game: a case study, *International Journal of Management Education*, 13(3), 227–236.

Ogwude, U. (2019) 'How to Teach Students from a Range of Different Countries', in Daniels, K. et al. (eds), *Learning and Teaching in Higher Education: Perspectives From a Business School.* Cheltenham: Edward Elgar Publishing, pp.159–166.

Salas, E., Wildman, J. and Piccolo, R. (2009) Using simulation-based training to enhance management education, *Academy of Management Learning & Education*, 8(4), 559–573.

Simpson, C. and Kerridge, C. (2019) Narrowing the attainment gap between domestic and international students: use of a simulation and experiential learning in mixed cohort strategic management teaching, *Developments in Business Simulation and Experiential Learning*, 46, 108–110.

Sitzmann, T. (2011) A meta-analytic examination of the instructional effectiveness of computer-based simulation games, *Personnel Psychology*, 64(2), 489–528.

Spencer-Oatey, H. and Dauber, D. (2016) The gains and pains of mixed national group work at university, *Journal of Multilingual and Multicultural Development*, 38(3), 219–236.

Statista (2020) International student share of higher-ed population worldwide in 2019 by country. Published by Erin Duffin, 9 March 2020 at https://www.statista.com/statistics/788155/international-student-share-of-higher-education-worldwide/

Tiwari, S. R., Nafees, L. and Krishnan, O. (2014) Simulation as a pedagogical tool: measurement of impact on perceived effective learning, *The International Journal of Management Education*, 12(3), 260–270.

Vlachopoulos, D. and Makri, A. (2017) The effect of games and simulations on higher education: a systematic literature review, *International Journal of Educational Technology in Higher Education*, 14(22). DOI 10.1186/s41239–017–0062–1

Volet, S. E. and Ang, G. (2012) Culturally mixed groups on international campuses: an opportunity for inter-cultural learning, *Higher Education Research & Development*, 31(1), 21–37.

Warren, J. N., Luctkar-Flude, M., Godfrey, C. and Lukewich, J. (2016) A systematic review of the effectiveness of simulation-based education on satisfaction and learning outcomes in nurse practitioner programs, *Nurse Education Today*, 46, 99–108.

Zantow, K., Knowlton, D. and Sharp, D. (2005) More than fun and games: reconsidering the virtues of strategic management simulations, *Academy of Management Learning & Education*, 4(4) 451–458.

APPENDIX 12.1: TIPS ON WHAT NOT TO DO

- Don't overdo the use of simulations: like any good teaching techniques, they should be used sparingly – the greatest value is likely to be within the variety of a blended learning pedagogy. So, for a programme, by all means embed simulations in several modules BUT not in them all.
- Don't expect students to 'just do it', without a good explanation of aims and objectives or good guidance on the mechanics of how the simulation operates: do signal benefits but also set reasonable expectations.
- Don't forget that your instructors/facilitators need some instruction of their own before starting. If they have poor or superficial understanding of the simulation, this will inevitably impact on students' performance and enthusiasm too. Ideally do a 'dry run' of the simulation for new instructors.
- Don't choose generic simulations that are easy for staff to manage but offer little challenge or benefit to students – we should be providing an opportunity to build and develop business skills such as project management, scenario analysis and evaluation of priorities.
- Don't be intimidated by the 'inconvenience' of learning to use simulations as new teaching tools. Our own positive experiences indicate likelihood of a very good return on your investment of (really not so much) time and effort.

Source: Daniels et al. (2019), chapter 11, p. 118.

13. Ethical decision making in transnational business networks: making a case for the role-play teaching method

Bahar Ali Kazmi

ETHICAL DECISIONS AS TRANSNATIONAL BUSINESS PROBLEMS

Problem-solving as a design principle for business and management education is an uncritically accepted policy: Managers solve problems, and hence they should be trained in problem-solving. This approach transforms the business and management curriculum into a series of toolkits, guidelines, and procedural techniques. Important though these tools are for a particular sub-discipline of business and management education, their application in teaching ethical decision making in transnational business networks can be counter-productive.

Tools and techniques of business decisions are often inspired by the functionalist pattern of cognition and reasoning that is central to the value system that underpins the rationalisation of social relations. The transnational business networks involve the interface between multiple and often divergent value, cultural, and legal systems and therefore calls in question the moral intent that drives the rationalisation process.

In transnational business networks, the functionalist decision-making business tools and techniques can be seen as part of the 'ethical' problems rather than the source of their solutions: They stifle innovation which is essential to formulate and address an issue that for some stakeholders, involved in the decision-making process, is an ethical problem and for others it is neither an issue nor an ethical problem.

For example, the involvement of children in the manufacturing of apparel, sporting goods, toys, and carpets is a child rights issue. However, it cannot be resolved by merely removing children from the manufacturing process. Such an approach is likely to induce a range of ethical issues. Let me clarify this point by presenting a fictional dialogue among managers of international organisations on the issue of child labour in the manufacturing of hand-stitched footballs.

The dialogue is based on my own experience of managing the child labour project that inspired me to script and organise an ethical decision-making role-play scenario, presented in the chapter. The dialogue presents the debate among four characters – a modernist, a child rights activist, a regulator, and a behaviourist – who hold completely different standpoints on the nature of the child labour problem and how it should be addressed. The dialogue shows the opacity of ethical decision making in transnational business networks.

Four managers, representing international companies, trade unions, NGOs, and governments, in a formal boardroom, are trying to determine why local companies involve children in the manufacturing of hand-stitched footballs, why it should be seen as an ethical issue and how companies should address it.

BOX 13.1   SEEING THE 'WRONG' BUT AMBIGUOUS ABOUT WHAT IS 'RIGHT'

The Modernist: Children are involved in the manufacturing of hand-stitched footballs because the industry is home based and informal. We do not really know who is stitching our footballs. We provide stitching material to village-based contractors and they distribute it to home-based football-stitchers. We do not really know the exact locations of our workers. For us, it is impossible to monitor our subcontracting and workers chains. We need to, I strongly suggest, organise football-stitching factories. This system, as my factories already show, will eliminate the involvement of children in the manufacturing of footballs.

The Child Rights Activist: We fully understand that you are more focused on the channels that cause children to enter football-stitching jobs. We should not forget, however, that it is the children who should be the focus of analysis and actions. Our research shows that children stitch footballs because they and their families are poor, and if you do away with home-based football-stitching the economic lives of football-stitcher children and their families will definitely get worse rather than better. We suggest that a set of economic and social safety nets for football-stitcher children and their families must be in place before you stop providing football-stitching work at home.

The Regulator: We think that the idea of establishing football-stitching factories is really useful because it will make it possible for us to enforce labour laws. We all know it is actually the lack of relevant laws and the poor enforcement of existing laws that has caused the violation of labour rights in the manufacturing of hand-stitched footballs. However, we also think that football-stitcher children should be protected from further exploitation. So we recommend that we should also set up home-schools for football-stitcher children. This intervention, we are sure, will prevent the mistake which the garment industry in Bangladesh made. I suppose you all know that 30,000 children were removed from the garment industry in Bangladesh, none of them ended up in school!

The Child Rights Activist: Your intentions seem to be right but your approach is wrong. We believe that the western concept of childhood as a time of few responsibilities is shown to oversimplify the reality of the lives of Sialkot's children. Many football-stitcher children do have some education; it is not just a matter of stopping them from stitching footballs and sending them to school to grow into balanced and rounded adults. Their families' income must be protected and improved so that they will not suffer as a result of changes in the industry and so that children can afford to gain adequate schooling.

The Behaviourist: All the solutions, which you three have proposed, address the symptoms rather than the root cause of the problem that has led to the violation of child rights in the manufacturing of footballs. We believe that every child, whatever his country, race, or age, has the fundamental human right to education and our programmes take into account the individuals, their cultural and human dimensions, and give them basic schooling. Child labour can and must be ended before poverty is ended. We need to work on the values and beliefs of those communities whose children are involved in paid work. The involvement of children in the production of hand-stitched footballs is caused by the beliefs of their parents who do not see schooling as an inalienable right of children, and the only way, however slow it may be, is to educate parents and change their belief system and to send all children to school. This is a long-term solution rather than a quick fix.

The Regulator: We recognise the importance of a long-term solution but prevention is a much more cost-effective measure in the short and longer term. A much larger number of children are expected to benefit from the prevention of child labour through monitoring workplaces to keep them free of child labour. As we all know, one major problem area is the system of advances made against future work. In many countries, advances lead to bondage, as the labour contract is not clear. A second major challenge for the sporting goods industry is subcontracting, including home working which leaves home workers open to exploitation. The third problem area is recruiting agents, who tend to spring up hand-in-hand with the growth of the industry and operate in an almost completely unregulated and uncontrolled environment. All these issues suggest that we should pay more attention to the enforcement of FIFA's Code of Labour Practice and find an independent body to monitor implementation of the anti-child labour programme.

The Behaviourist: You do whatever you believe is right. We will continue our work in the region. We are working with community leaders, parents, and industry leaders to raise the level of awareness regarding children's rights. We have already witnessed a breakthrough in some villages of the region where many people in the community are beginning to see children much more as children and not as workers.

The Child Rights Activist: We would like to raise an important issue that has been ignored by all of you. Our research shows that the modernisation and the enforcement of FIFA's Code of Labour Practice will significantly reduce the income of football-stitcher families because many women will lose their jobs, particularly those who can only work at home. We strongly argue that if we plan to go ahead with modernisation and regulation then we need to find a solution for retaining the income of football-stitcher women. We are afraid that the current proposal will not only violate the rights of children, but also violate women's rights to employment. It is a recipe for social and economic disaster and we have already seen it in the case of the garment industry in Bangladesh.

It is obvious as the fictional dialogue shows that it is the interlocking of a range of moral issues that induces ethical dilemmas, stimulating emotionality, ambiguity, and radical disagreement. Crucially, these ethical dilemmas cannot be settled by using functionalist reasoning that is one of the building blocks that constitute ethical dilemmas in transnational business networks. Hence, we need a different learning approach to examine and address ethical issues that managers face, and for this reason I have begun experimenting with a role-play method.

A SKETCH OF A REFLEXIVE-NARRATIVE APPROACH

Broadly, role play, as a teaching and learning method, involves scripting and organising a transformative event that learners perform. In this sense, it is an enactment of a story or narrative. Initially I adopted this method with a view that it enables students to critically engage with their own managerial experience, i.e. question the beliefs, assumptions, and ideologies which structure their managerial truth and reality. It is, in this sense, an exploratory and developmental teaching method (Carter 1984). However, over the period I have noticed that teaching business ethics by using a role-play method is an emotional act: it places us – teachers and learners – in a learning situation where our personal sense of right and wrong comes under intense examination. This often triggers emotional response, induces ambiguity, and generates radical disagreement.

Crucially, it shows learners the emotional opacity of ethical decision making and helps them with generating novel perspectives to deal with it while analysing and solving ethical dilemmas that arise in transnational business networks. My experience of using role play as a method tells me that it can be used to set up a reflexive-narrative learning space. Using narratives for creating a reflexive learning space is easier to advocate than to do well. Below, I tell a story of scripting and organising a role-play scenario – 'Ethical decision making in transnational business networks' – which highlights the key features of a reflexive learning space, structured as a narrative.

I have developed this role-play scenario based on my own experience of managing a child labour programme and partnership between the global football manufacturing industry, NGOs, and the United Nations. It has taken me several years to fully develop a narrative structure, characters, and reflexive activities that constitute the role-play scenario. Initially, I conceptualised, developed, and organised it with the help of my academic mentor, Professor Alyson Warhurst. We have organised it several times for MBA students and mid-career managers. A brief sketch of the scenario and reflexive tasks are given below.

BOX 13.2 THE SCENARIO

Global Values and Actors: Throughout 2012, international trade unions, consumer groups in developed countries, and international non-governmental organisations accused international sporting goods brands of failing to prevent the use of unsatisfactory labour conditions in their supply chains, especially in Malia. As a consequence, several government ministers and consumer groups in developed countries have been demanding a complete boycott of the international sporting goods brands. The crisis has already started to impact negatively on the brand reputation, consumer loyalty, and corporate identity of the sporting goods companies. Some media reports in the last week have noted that three big sporting goods companies are now in real danger of losing a significant portion of their business in the European Union and the USA, if the problem is not addressed fully in the near future – hence the meeting.

Global Response: The international brands have mobilised their membership organisation, the International Sporting Goods Organisation (ISGO), based in Brussels, to evolve a rapid and appropriate response to the growing crisis. ISGO, in consultation with its members, has decided to hold a meeting in the UK, bringing together the sporting goods companies and their representative bodies, trade unions, local and international NGOs, and consumer groups. The purpose of the meeting, building on much preparatory work, is to draft a joint public statement outlining a socially responsible solution to the child labour problem.

You and Your Role: You are one of a group of ten people, acting as representatives of different organisations that are meeting on -/-/- during an international convention in the UK. You have been invited by the president of the ISGO. The group's mutually declared aim is to discuss and design a socially responsible response to the problem of child labour in the sporting goods industry in the South Asian country of Malia. The situation is critical, as consumer and trade union groups are threatening a boycott of branded sporting goods in the run-up to the lucrative football World Cup.

A public statement, which should include an outline proposed strategy for action, is scheduled at a planned press conference. As a group, guided by your chairperson, the president of the ISGO, you are to work through the ethical dilemmas of reaching a socially responsible solution through negotiation.

Tasks

A. Develop a socially responsible solution to the child labour problem in the sporting goods industry of Malia.
B. Draft a brief public statement for presentation (4–5 minutes), which should include: a statement outlining the solution and anticipated outcomes.

Note: While for the purpose of the scenario I ask you to contribute to decision making within your designated role, I do ask that you be creative in your approach. There are several possible responses to the scenario that participants may like to use in determining their personal and organisational positions. It is important to work through the ethical intent behind the position that you take.

MANAGEMENT EXPERIENCE

It seems to me that the epistemic assumptions which we make about the management experience of learners are central to designing a role-play scenario.

For example, I organised the role-play scenario for a second-year undergraduate class. The outcomes were at best unsatisfactory. Many students struggled to perform their characters and roles and had difficulty in grasping the scenario and the rules of the game. Also, they showed limited skills in using the language of management for articulating and presenting their individual and organisational positions on the ethical issues involved in managing the transnational business network of footballs. In particular, they seemed to find it hard to work in groups. This, I also noticed, was partly due to their reluctance to acknowledge the possibility of multiple valid answers to the same question and to recognise the merits of diverse definitions and explanations of the same concept.

Obviously, the role-play scenario seems to be a poor choice for introducing new and complex managerial experience. The conclusion is both reassuring and unsettling. It justifies the belief about the suitability of the constructivist approach to teaching and learning (Trowler and Trowler 2010; Biggs and Tang 2007) but it challenges us to be cognisant of the epistemic organisation of the learners' management experience.

The role play is designed, therefore, primarily for MBA and senior managers who have significant management experience, manifesting the tacit knowledge of management language, roles, situations, relations of power, and leadership games which are a precondition for performing the characters and reflexive activities. MBA and senior managers, I have observed, have understood the scenario, characters, and activities well and have completed the task successfully.

Scripting a role-play scenario, it can be concluded, involves taking into account the epistemic organisation of the learners' management experience. If a role-play scenario is designed in this way, it seems to transform, deepen, and reconstruct the knowledge of learners in ethical decision making.

NARRATIVE STRUCTURE

Knowing about the epistemic organisation of the learners' management experience alone, however, is not enough to design a productive role-play scenario. The narrative structure of the role-play scenario and the depth of characters play a vital role in performing reflexive learning activities. Narratives play several important functions in learning: they deliver knowledge, they produce communities by creating a shared sense of reality, and they transform or intend to transform behaviour (McEwan and Egan 1995). Crucially, I have observed that narratives enable learners to make personalised sense of the moral dimension of business practices.

A good narrative often introduces complex characters who struggle with a difficult problem that requires an urgent and innovative solution. This is often achieved by including a sequence of puzzles, riddles, and dramatic moments that the characters work through to solve the problem. In so doing the characters constantly change themselves, and influence each other, leading to the transformation of the characters. This can only happen if the characters are involved in social relationships. For example, I have scripted characters who know each other as friends and colleagues. They are also very well aware of the relations of power that facilitate or prevent them individually and organisationally to influence each other or shape the drama of solving the problem.

Furthermore, the narrative, it seems to me, can only produce a reflexive learning space if it is driven by a set of intersecting questions. For example, the role-play scenario asks, albeit implicitly, several questions: Will the international organisations find the solution? Will the children involved in the production of hand-stitched footballs get their rights protected? Will the boycott of the football industry be averted? Will the international brands move their production to another country? These questions are implicit in the narrative and emerge as the learners participate in the reflexive activities, which in this case means to constantly scrutinise and improve business practices by using the steady flow of information produced by the multiple value, cultural, and legal systems that drive and institute those practices (Giddens 1990). The process leads to modifying the ethical character of those practices.

In short, the design of role-play scenario requires overlapping social and organisational storylines or sub-plots and a set of reflexive questions (implicit) that together induce emotionality, ambiguity, and the likelihood of radical disagreement.

POINT OF REFERENCE

A simulation assumes reality. But, nonetheless, it is hypothetical, fictional, simplified, and therefore pretend. A role-play scenario as a simulation of what may happen and what actually happened can be seen as either scripting the future or reproducing the past. In this sense, a role-play scenario can have two distinct points of reference. It is the reproduction of a past which I have used as a point of reference. In my view, it is important to use a real-life event for scripting a narrative of the role-play scenario dealing with the ethical problems. For the purpose of the narrative, I have scripted an actual high-profile international event that happened in February 1997 which I witnessed and attended as a manager. A real-life high-profile event seems to offer a valuable learning advantage. The learners know that the event has happened and therefore they seem to be curious about what really happened, how did it happen, who played their individual character and what these characters did and how. At the end of the role play, I answer these questions and show them a short documentary on the child labour project that was made in 1998 for FIFA officials, and reveal the outcomes. This leads to a highly emotional debate about the ethical positions of the actual managers and their role(s) and motivation(s) in shaping the ethical or unethical decisions.

Furthermore, simulation of actual events demands more time. They cannot be simulated without grasping the contextual details and performance requirements. The role-play scenario presented in this chapter requires five full working days as it involves a large number of complex characters and a vast amount of contextual information and analysis. The students are required to go through their characters' briefs and learn the complexity of the characters and understand the social and power relationships that constitute the ethical decision-making setting. By using those relationships, they are expected to formulate their individual position on the child labour issue and the decision they wish to see at the concluding press conference.

I have observed that the extended duration of a role-play scenario contributes to the deepening of reflexive learning. The learners use five days not only to learn the contextual details but also to begin to get emotional, deal with the ambiguity, and enact radical disagreement – based on what they individually believe is right, what their social relations compel them to believe is right, and what their organisational agendas dictate. The process often leads to a highly emotional debate on the nature of the problem and its potential solution(s) in group tasks.

In short, it seems to me that the role-play scenario dealing with the ethical decision making in transnational business networks requires a real-life reference point and an extended learning duration for achieving reflexivity.

CONCLUDING REMARKS

I began this chapter with a view that the traditional problem-solving approach to designing the business and management curriculum can undermine the teaching and learning related to ethical decision making in transnational business networks. I have presented a case of a role-play scenario to show that a reflexive-narrative approach can be used productively to construct a learning environment that enables mature learners to engage in reflexive reasoning, structured as a narrative, and to apply it to examine the nature of the problems that result from the interface and intersection of the multiple, and often divergent, value, cultural, and legal systems. This approach, I have argued, makes it easier for the learners to enact emotionality, radical disagreement, and ambiguity. The point of teaching is not to eliminate these dimensions of the ethical decision making but to reveal them. I have argued that this can be accomplished by using a role-play method if it effectively utilises the deeper understanding of the learners' management experience, complex narrative structure, an actual reference point, and extended duration.

At a theoretical level, it seems, reflexive reasoning is a useful way to produce deeper knowledge of ethical issues, problems, and dilemmas but it is inherently tentative and impersonal. However, with the help of a simulated narrative of an actual event we can normalise uncertainty and augment personalised moral sense among the learners.

REFERENCES

Biggs, J. and Tang, C. (2007) (3rd edition) *Teaching for Quality Learning at University: What the Student Does*. Maidenhead: Open University Press.

Carter, Robert E. (1984) *Dimensions of Moral Education*. Toronto: University of Toronto Press.

Giddens, A. (1990) *The Consequences of Modernity*. Stanford, CA: Stanford University Press.

McEwan, Hunter and Egan, Kieran (eds) (1995) *Narrative in Teaching, Learning, and Research*. New York: Teachers College Press, Columbia University.

Trowler, V. and Trowler, P. (2010) *Student Engagement Evidence Summary*. York: Higher Education Academy. Available online: http://www.heacademy.ac.uk/assets/York/documents/ourwork/studentengagement/StudentEngagementEvidenceSummary.pdf

14. The positive impact of simulations and games in applied teaching and assessment in law

Chris Umfreville

1.   INTRODUCTION

Games and simulations are frequently viewed as a form of escapism, allowing us to get away from real life. They can, however, be used in quite the opposite way, providing us with an experiential insight into how detailed and technical academic concepts operate in the real world. In this chapter, I reflect on my use of simulations and games in the delivery of an undergraduate law module, with a particular focus on the integration of a simulated interview into the module assessment. The chapter will consider the design, delivery and ongoing development of the simulation together with analysis and reflection on its impact. This will include my experiences of the challenges and benefits of adopting a simulated assessment, which I hope will offer inspiration and reassurance to lecturers wanting to develop something similar in any discipline.

2.   DESIGN AND DEVELOPMENT

My teaching philosophy is underpinned by the application of experience, both my own and my students', and the concept of learning by doing. Accordingly my curriculum design is influenced by providing opportunities for students to engage with the subject content in a practical and meaningful manner. This can lead to deeper learning and understanding, with positive long-term benefits, rather than surface learning for assessment. This also has the advantage of engaging the class and developing key skills for both study and subsequent employment, which ultimately enhance the student learning experience. Whilst it is important to acknowledge the benefits of a liberal legal educa-tion, it is clear that aspirations of graduate employment opportunities drive university attendance. Simulation therefore has an important and innovative role to play in engaging students in learning but also, as Strevens and Welch

(2016) highlight, by breaking down barriers and preparing them for graduate employment.

Through regular consultation with graduate employers from a variety of disciplines, I have identified the importance of developing transferable skills and building student confidence to be able to demonstrate these. Oral communication skills are particularly important but can be challenging to develop in traditional undergraduate teaching and assessment. Whilst the tutorial or seminar has traditionally been a forum to develop such skills, a variety of factors including self-confidence, time constraints and financial pressures can prevent students engaging fully with such opportunities. An alternative way to ensure engagement is to embed such skills in module assessment.

It is with these objectives and challenges in mind that I developed a coursework portfolio assessment in a final year undergraduate Company Law module. The module is typically taken by around 80 law students with an interest in legal practice or commercial opportunities beyond law. The portfolio comprises two elements of linked assessment: a simulated client interview of up to 15 minutes, followed by a written memorandum of advice. These elements of assessment are completed in the context of advising a new client on matters arising in the operation of a company. Students adopt the role of a trainee solicitor in a law firm. They are initially provided with limited background information about the client and the issues at hand, with the instruction to prepare for and conduct an initial fact-finding interview with the client. The simulated interview allows students to gather the salient facts, as well as eliminating irrelevant facts. This factual matrix underpins a written memorandum of advice to a senior colleague, to support advice to the client. The written memorandum is targeted at another lawyer, rather than the client, to allow for full referencing to be included, thus retaining the academic rigour of the assessment by allowing students to demonstrate engagement with a range of resources as well as their practical problem-solving skills.

The central rationale for the client interview element of the portfolio was to introduce a form of authentic assessment to develop students' oral communication skills, professional etiquette and self-confidence. The marking criteria and guidance was designed with this in mind, with students awarded marks out of five across four key competencies: Professionalism; Relationship with the client; Structure of the interview; and Identification of client aims. Importantly, students are not directly assessed on their legal knowledge nor ability to provide advice in the interview. The students' subject knowledge, though implicit in the final two criteria as it will inform how they structure and close the interview, is instead assessed in the subsequent written submission for which they have more time to prepare. This is intended to remove an element of pressure and allow students to showcase their communication skills and professionalism, thus helping to build their self-confidence.

Following the interview, students are given the opportunity to raise further questions of the client by email (sent to me as module leader). This encourages students to reflect on their performance and seek clarification or further detail on any matters they consider to be relevant. Finally, the notes used by the client in the simulation are released so that all students approach the written element of the assessment with the same factual matrix. Students are not aware this will happen, so as not to undermine their preparation. The rationale for this is to ensure that students are not disadvantaged if they did not perform well in the interview assessment. This also provides further opportunity for student reflection, as all students can compare these notes with the notes they took during the interview and identify any information that may have been missed and why. Students also receive their interview marks and the opportunity for individual feedback prior to submission of the written element. The in-built opportunities for reflection and feedback allow for double-loop learning, enabling students to develop deeper knowledge and influence future behaviours.

This simulated assessment sits within a broader framework of games, playfulness and simulation throughout the module. One such example is the use of a modified version of the board game Snakes and Ladders to teach the topic of directors' duties. This sees students work collaboratively in teams (or boards of company directors) facing scenario-based questions on directors' duties whenever their team lands on a snake or ladder. If the question is answered correctly, the teams either avoid descending the snake or are allowed to climb the ladder, and vice versa if answered incorrectly. The students compete against rival teams (or companies) to see who can complete the game first by reaching the end of the board. In a slight deviation from the traditional game, teams have to stop at each snake or ladder, thus they could not complete the game without facing any questions. To improve their chances of winning, teams need to answer the questions correctly, so as not to breach their directors' duties in each scenario, and expedite their route to the end of the board.

Another example is the use of DUPLO® to demonstrate the various proprietary and contractual rights and obligations that make up a business and to illustrate the concepts of corporate insolvency and business rescue. Here I use a pizzeria playset, identifying assets owned by the operating company (the premises, pizza ovens, furnishings, stock and even the delivery motorcycle), the key contracts (such as telephone, payment processing and refuse collection), and I discuss the importance of the employees' skills and experience to the operation of the business, and the significance of goodwill and a loyal customer base to its trade. The tactile nature of the DUPLO® allows the demonstration of the dissipation of these assets, and the decline in overall value when the assets are (literally) broken up, compared to the benefits of keeping them together if there is a viable, yet financially distressed, business which can be rescued as a going concern. Having been thus introduced to the fundamental concepts that underpin the topic, students are better placed to engage with the technical specifications and their operation, as they can relate these to a visual and physical experience.

These playful interventions aim to engage the learner and make the content more relatable, and less intimidating. This holistic approach ensures familiarity for the student with participating in simulated situations, such that the simulated client interview assessment does not feel alien, but rather is a natural development of and is aligned to the learning and teaching experience within the module with which students have engaged.

3.   IMPLEMENTATION AND DELIVERY

Having identified the assessment rationale and design, there then follows the implementation of the new assessment process. This breaks down into two aspects: curriculum design and delivery on the one hand, and operation of the assessment process on the other. I address these practical aspects in this section.

Curriculum Design and Delivery

The simulated client interview assessed a skill which was new to many students. Whilst the fundamental underlying skill is that of oral communication, the conduct of a client interview in a professional context requires certain knowledge and understanding to facilitate its effective conduct. Some students would have developed, or at least had exposure to, this skill through participation in the University Law Clinic, a placement year or general work experience. The skill had not, however, been developed universally or uniformly as part of the programme at this point. It was therefore important to integrate the development of this skill to prepare students for the assessment. This was achieved by introducing a number of support mechanisms.

The first intervention was the delivery of an interviewing skills workshop. In the first year the assessment ran, this was delivered to all final-year students as part of an employability programme. The session included guidance on the importance of the client interview in legal practice and its effective conduct. Students were introduced to the marking criteria for the Company Law module assessment and given live examples of a good and bad interview to reflect on and mark. In a second workshop, students practised their interviewing skills in small groups and marked their performance using the marking criteria.

Whilst these sessions worked well, I felt that they suffered from two problems. First, the workshop was too far removed from the assessment, being at opposite ends of the semester. Second, whilst the skill is ubiquitous, engagement dropped as some students had not chosen the Company Law option module. These workshops were reformed for the second year of delivery, being incorporated in the module teaching schedule midway through the semester. The session addressed the same core content but was enhanced by involving a practising solicitor in its design and delivery. It also benefited from delivery closer to the assessment, allowing students to consider the assessment, and therefore appreciate the importance of the session.

In addition to the workshops, students were provided with a number of online resources through the virtual learning environment. These included further reading, formative exercises, and videos from practitioners offering interviewing tips. Students were encouraged to engage with these materials and given guidance on how to do this effectively. This included encouragement to work in groups on the practice exercises and the option to book mock interview sessions with me to practise and receive feedback.

Assessment Process

In addition to effectively preparing the students for the novel form of assessment, there were a number of practical considerations, and at times challenges, to address to facilitate the assessment process. These broadly fall into four categories: support; space; technology; and feedback, which are considered below.

Support

A fundamental requirement of the simulated interview is to have someone play the role of the client. Each interview also requires a marker to be present. For consistency and fairness I wanted to ensure all interviews took place in the same week. As this is a popular option module and the interviews had to be scheduled around both mine and the students' scheduled classes, it was not feasible for me to be present in all interviews. I was fortunate to have colleagues who were very supportive of the initiative and were willing to assist with the interviews.

I had initially hoped to involve PhD students to perform the client role, but for a number of reasons it was not possible to do this in the assessment window. As a result, my colleagues and I performed the role of both client and marker in each interview. Although not the initial plan, it proved a positive development, as the presence of familiar staff members can offer reassurance for students and the absence of a separate marker can relieve the pressure of being observed. To ensure consistency of delivery and marking I hosted a number of training sessions for colleagues, in which we covered the nature and purpose of the assessment, the marking criteria and the approaches to be adopted. This proved a valuable exercise, with moderation demonstrating consistent marking by all colleagues.

Space

Another key operational aspect was the identification and use of appropriate space for the simulated client interview. For effective running of the assessment we required a number of rooms to allow simultaneous assessment. I was also keen to provide a space for students to be able to reflect and consolidate their notes immediately after their assessment. These rooms needed to be in close proximity to one another in case of any problems, to ensure support could easily be offered to staff and students. Each interview was to last for up to 15 minutes. To allow students to settle, the interview to be conducted, marking to be completed and then changeover for the next student, each interview was allocated a 30-minute slot. This also made some allowance for potential technology issues, which are discussed in the next section.

This represented a potentially significant rooming demand. I therefore worked closely with timetabling colleagues to identify and secure suitable rooms at an early point in the planning process. I was fortunate that there was a suite of small tuition spaces, which were close to one another but also offered a realistic professional setting for the simulated client interview. This part of the process was quite time-consuming, but was an important and worthwhile investment. The process was smoother in the second year of operation as, with the desired rooms already identified, the rooming request was much more straightforward.

Technology

There were two key aspects of technology to assist with the operation of the assessment. First, I needed a facility for students to select and sign up for a suitable interview time. I identified a variety of time slots that would not clash with scheduled teaching for the students' core modules or the Company Law module. I then created an event booking page for the interviews, through which students were invited to sign up for their preferred assessment time. This proved a challenge to set up, as I was unfamiliar with the platform and was using it in a slightly unusual manner, setting up multiple and simultaneous sessions. This was another element which required an investment of time; however, once the site was set up it was easy to operate and allowed for reports to be generated to identify which students had signed up, and which students needed prompting. It was then straightforward to set up the platform the following year. Most students engaged with this process promptly, though it was necessary to follow up with a small number of students and, in a very small number of cases, allocate times. Although additional work, this was not particularly time-consuming and engagement with the booking process was generally better than I had expected in the first instance.

I also needed to record each student assessment to allow for internal and external moderation. I secured funding to purchase a number of tablets to record the assessments. These were recorded using Panopto™. There were again a number of challenges in terms of procuring and setting up the tablets and then setting up the recording, which were resolved by working closely with colleagues from our IT and Digital Services teams.

Feedback

A key aspect of the assessment design was to provide an opportunity for students to reflect on their performance in the interview assessment prior to submission of the written assessment, as discussed above. The overarching purpose was also to develop students' oral communication skills and self-confidence. It was therefore important to provide the opportunity for individual feedback and release of provisional grades. Tutors marking the simulated client interviews completed a marking sheet for each student, providing a score out of five in each of the four competencies detailed above as well as providing a written commentary. These marks, broken down by category, were compiled in a spreadsheet and then emailed to students' university email accounts using mail merge. Students were invited to make appointments with me as module leader to review their recorded interview and/or seek further feedback.

4.   ANALYSIS AND BENEFITS

The development and implementation of the simulated client interview as part of the coursework portfolio assessment required a significant investment of time and rigorous planning. Whilst this was challenging at times, it was, without doubt, worthwhile when I consider the impact on student performance in the assessment, the wider student benefits, and also the personal benefits for me as a module tutor. Furthermore, the initial investment paid dividends in subsequent running of the assessment as the infrastructure and understanding were established, resulting in much quicker processes second time around.

The first and most clearly quantifiable benefit was that of student performance. In previous years students had been required to complete a stand-alone piece of coursework. This was presented as a problem question addressing a range of issues. Performance for this assessment was satisfactory, with the majority of students achieving a grade in the upper or lower second class range. Around a fifth of students achieved lower grades than this, with a small number not achieving a pass mark. Following introduction of the coursework portfolio there was a marked improvement in performance, with an increase from 40.5% of submissions awarded an upper second class mark or higher to 61% in the first iteration. Students performed very well in the interview assessment, achieving very good scores. Improvement was also noticeable when excluding the interview grades. Performance in the written assessment saw an increase in first class grades (13% to 22.5%) and a decrease in third class marks (20.3% to 12.5%), whilst no one who completed the portfolio failed (compared to 2.8% previously).

My initial reaction was that this improvement in performance was primarily down to the splitting of the assessment into two staged components. Scheduling the interview assessment several weeks before submission of the written assessment required students to engage with the assessed content earlier than they might do otherwise. In preparing for the interview and planning their questions, students needed to engage deeply with the module content. In some cases this early work may have encouraged students to attempt the written component well in advance of the formal deadline, allowing them more time for development and reflection on their work. However, even for those students who may have started the written component closer to the submission deadline, they would have benefited from a longer incubation period to develop their thoughts following the deep engagement required for the interview assessment. Conversely, where students did not perform well in the interview assessment, release of their provisional mark acted as a prompt that they needed to do more to develop their understanding and achieve their desired grade. Feedback from students on the new form of assessment supported my reflection, that the longer incubation period was beneficial, even where students did not start the written work until much closer to the submission deadline. No students confirmed my second reflection directly, though the ability to reflect on performance in the interview and any gaps in knowledge was identified as a positive feature. Feedback revealed that some students would have preferred a shorter period between the two assessments, but this was necessitated by the university calendar, with the two assessment elements falling either side of the Christmas vacation and January assessment periods.

There were also wider benefits for the students completing the interview assessment in terms of self-confidence and preparation for future careers. I observed that a number of students were nervous in advance of the interview assessment, but that this apprehension was quickly assuaged following completion of the interview, even before results were released. By being forced to engage with the process rather than it being optional, students developed confidence and resilience that will help them in other scenarios, including employment interviews and work experience. The interview exercise also offered an important opportunity for students to develop their applied understanding of professional etiquette and standards. This included appreciating the importance of body language and personal presentation.

There were also personal benefits for me as a tutor in introducing this assessment. As discussed above, I developed a number of new skills that have proved useful in other areas. I also developed positive working relationships with colleagues across the university, which have proved mutually beneficial subsequently. The integration of employability skills into the assessment also offered an opportunity to bring practitioners into the design and delivery, ensuring an authentic experience for students and allowing them to build professional connections, whilst also showcasing our students' talents to employers. This then facilitated wider discussions on curriculum and skills development with the practitioners, which helps to ensure the currentness of the curriculum in light of a constantly evolving practice area. Finally, the assessment has allowed me to engage more meaningfully with a wider number of students, especially those who may not attend seminars for a variety of reasons. This has allowed me an additional means of building rapport with and supporting students on the module.

It is important to recognise that introducing a two-stage assessment with an in-person skills element does increase the overall time required for marking, in addition to the initial investment in setting up the assessment. Whilst the improvement in the written submissions did reduce the temporal demands in comparison to the previous coursework, the fixed-time nature of the simulated interview necessarily increases the overall marking demands. As a counterpoint, the nature of the interview assessment and the level of student engagement, together with the wider benefits identified, compensate for this. Additionally, the improved pass rate reduced the need for referral support and marking.

There were two broad aims behind the introduction of the simulated client interview assessment:

1. The development of student oral communication skills, self-confidence and professional etiquette which would provide transferable skills and improve graduate employability.
2. The promotion of deeper learning and understanding of the module content.

The positive student results in the interview assessment demonstrate that excellent levels of professionalism and oral communication were evident. As discussed above, these will have been developed through a number of student experiences, including prior work experience, but also through the support systems implemented within the module. Student feedback further revealed that students' confidence increased following completion of the interview assessment, though students did not necessarily appreciate the employability benefits.

A marked improvement of student performance in the written assessment compared to previous years highlights an increased level of understanding and practical problem-solving in the student body. The early engagement, and the opportunity for double-loop learning provided by the separation of the two elements of assessment together with the various feedback opportunities, appears to have aided this.

Adopting a simulated form of assessment has delivered clear benefits for student learning and attainment. The interview element of the assessment represents an evolution of the traditional legal problem question – where students are presented with a number of facts to mine – to one of acquisition, with students required to determine what information they need and obtain this through judicious questioning. As Yuratich (2020) observes in respect of gaming, simulation similarly necessitates an active and experiential form of learning, which immerses students in the practice rather than simply presenting them with the salient facts. The presentation of the facts following the simulated interview and prior to the need to provide formal advice does represent a slight deviation; however, it operates as a form of safety net which students were not expecting, as discussed above.

5.   REFLECTIONS AND TAKE-AWAYS

Introducing a simulated assessment presents its challenges. Not least it requires a lot of work to design and establish, and then a lot of organisation and coordination to deliver. These processes do become easier over time, and the student outcomes more than warrant this extra work. I have found this a much more satisfying assessment to deliver. Importantly, the students bought in to the assessment, with high levels of engagement (including 100% attendance at the interview two years running) and attainment.

The potential challenges are ongoing. The COVID-19 pandemic has prevented, and likely will continue to affect, on-campus assessment. With the move to remote working and online meetings, it is possible that the assessment could be developed to operate through platforms such as Zoom and MS Teams. This is not a straightforward development, however. Careful consideration will need to be given to factors including student access to technology, reliable internet connections and suitable working environments from which to conduct the simulated interview to ensure equality and fairness in assessment. Furthermore, the need to manage the technology could put students under a different kind of pressure to that experienced in the face-to-face assessment. In all, the technology-based solutions could potentially distract from the underlying purpose of the proposed assessment. Instead, it might be more appropriate to develop the assessment to operate asynchronously whilst still building the same competencies.

I set out seeking to share my experiences of developing a simulated assessment, including the challenges and benefits. I have done this with the hope of inspiring wider adoption of such assessments, and of offering encouragement to help address the types of challenge that may arise. As I hope I have made clear above, these are worth it for the positive outcomes, for both students and staff. I will therefore close with four brief take-aways that underpin my experience.

Be Bold. Be Ambitious. Be Innovative

I found that students, whilst perhaps lacking self-confidence initially, embraced the novel form of assessment and ultimately performed really well. They benefited from being pushed outside of their comfort zone, although they may not have appreciated it initially.

Plan Early

There are lots of elements to bring together. Many of these will take longer than you think. Some may take you by surprise. I learned the hard way at times but was fortunate to be helped by supportive colleagues across the university.

Be Flexible

Not everything will work exactly as you planned, and you may need to make adjustments throughout. Rather than dwell on potential failure, embrace it as a positive opportunity. The alternative will often ultimately be an improvement.

Build In Support Mechanisms

A novel form of assessment is a great way to engage students and develop important skills. But for this to happen, students have to arrive at the assessment confident and prepared. This can be achieved with a variety of support mechanisms to help students develop the necessary skills and generally enhance their confidence.

BIBLIOGRAPHY

Biggs, J. and C. Tang (2011). *Teaching for Quality Learning at University*. Maidenhead: McGraw-Hill Education.

Bone, A. (2009). 'The twenty-first century law student'. *Law Teacher* 43(3), 222–245.

Guth, J. and C. Ashford (2014). 'The Legal Education and Training Review: Regulating socio-legal and liberal legal education?' *Law Teacher* 48(1), 5–19.

QAA Subject Benchmark Statement: Law (2015, July). Available at http://www.qaa .ac.uk/docs/qaa/subject-benchmark-statements/sbs-law-15.pdf?sfvrsn=ff99f781_8 (last accessed September 2020).

Strevens, C. and R. Welch (2016). 'Simulation and the learning of the law: Constructing and using an online transactional assessment in employment law'. In C. Strevens, R. Grimes and E. Phillips (eds), *Legal Education: Simulation in Theory and Practice*. Abingdon: Routledge.

Webb, J., J. Ching, P. Maharg and A. Sherr (2013). *Legal Education and Training Review: Setting Standards: The Future of Legal Services Education and Training Regulation in England and Wales*. Available at http://letr.org.uk/ (last accessed September 2020).

Yuratich, D. (2020). '*Ratio! A Game of Judgment*: Using game-based learning to teach legal reasoning'. *The Law Teacher*. DOI: 10.1080/03069400.2020.1773677

15. B(l)ending the truth: using fictional characters and worlds in law teaching

Kris Lines and Pieter Koornhof

INTRODUCTION

In Chapter 6 a suggestion for how to use narrative-based games in law is explored. In this chapter, we focus on the intrinsic value of the narratives themselves, specifically in relation to world-building and the use of fictional characters. We believe that effective use of this may improve content for increased engagement and have value as both a teaching and an assessment tool. In a sense, lecturers already implement some of these tools when crafting problem questions for their modules. However, by being more mindful of how this is done and can be expanded upon, both newer and more experienced lecturers may use this knowledge as a point of departure for reflecting on and adapting some of these aspects into their own teaching practices.

The purpose of this chapter is to scratch the surface and expose the reader to as many of the pertinent concepts relating to this. In doing so, we will first provide a brief background and context on the use of narratives (and, in particular, transmedia storytelling) in law teaching, before expanding on the mechanics of world-building and the value of creating immersive worlds. Subsequently, the benefits of using fictional worlds are explored and reflected upon, followed by an analysis of and reflection on the use of existing fictional characters. We then discuss means of adapting (and even revising) real-world examples to form part of such worlds. Finally, we reflect on how such worlds can be used to transform assessment practices within law.

BACKGROUND

The use of stories and narratives to drive student engagement is nothing new. Indeed, most cultures have engaged in visual and oral storytelling to capture ideas from one generation to the next. We have all used hypothetical problems or thought experiments to challenge students to apply their learning. Storytelling has also been variously linked, particularly in law, to a range of teaching theories, most notably: the case method (or Langdellian approach), and the Harvard Case Study Method. In the former, students dissect previously decided exemplar authorities with a view to teasing out key principles. In the latter, the case study contains real-life examples of businesses struggling with an issue or dilemma. Yet, while each of these approaches can exist as a stand-alone problem or scenario, it is possible, with very little development, to enhance these problems through the use of transmedia to become even richer and more engaging content.

The leading definition of transmedia storytelling seems to have been adopted from Henry Jenkins' book, *Convergence Culture* (2006: 97):

> A transmedia story unfolds across *multiple media platforms*, with each new element making a distinct and valuable contribution to the whole. Ideally, each medium makes its own *unique contribution* to the unfolding of the *story*.

There are three straightforward ways to apply this to university teaching:

1. Making a series of interwoven, yet independent, stories or problems. For example, the Marvel Cinematic Universe does this very well. Each film may be tonally different from the others and may be understood without watching every movie. For fans though, each movie enhances the overall world and adds a different perspective or storyline.
2. Conveying different messages through different media. For example, introducing content via a Talking Head video or podcast, or via authentic looking documents, rather than a (more traditional) written statement. This will help to engage students who prefer using different approaches.
3. Developing 'bonus' content that is ancillary to the main resources. For example, gamified elements, encouraging student-generated social media, or revision material. The use of 'props' and physical artefacts, such as a replica of the painting that the parties were fighting over, or a shoe that the manufacturers were trying to source ethical labour to create, might add fun and creativity, but is ultimately unnecessary to solve the problem being discussed.

Teaching Tip: Be careful of making any transmedia too complicated or too dependent on students engaging with every resource, otherwise this will lead to failure. A good example of this comes from the Matrix franchise. While the Wachowski sisters created a complex and overarching transmedia story system to underpin the movies, ultimately the sheer number and range of resources excluded all but the most passionate fan. Students may not be used to having fragmented and multi-sensory information within their learning environments, so this may need to be implemented gradually, rather than in one go.

WORLD-BUILDING

While struggling to grasp certain concepts during their intermediate year of the LLB, one of the authors of this chapter was told by a close relative (who was also a lawyer) that "the law is everywhere, and the best way to understand it is to just go and look for examples of it in the world". At the time, the advice seemed esoteric, but the value of it became clearer over time. Employed as a thought experiment, one can start seeing the law of contract at work in every-day transactions, the law of tort in potential incidents, and how the various things taught to you as a student intersect. The ability to immerse himself in a 'world of law' effectively turned a student with (at that point) mediocre grades into a passionate law lecturer! We believe that this shows the value of consistent and effective world-building – whereas that student had crafted their own world, imagine what could have been if that very thought experiment had been employed on a programme-wide scale, or could be reused and extended for future cohorts?

An integral part of every fictional world is the decisions as to its extent and the medium in which it appears. At its simplest, a fictional world might exist only in the mind of its readers. For example, Terry Pratchett's Discworld exists primarily through its novels (and more recently its television adaptations). While each novel can be read independently, there are also a number of story arcs involving groups of key characters (The Wizards, The Watch, Death, The Witches, etc). The Harry Potter franchise also started out through a book series (and movie adaptations), through its tie-ins with Warner Bros. Studios, it now exists in both physical (theme parks) and virtual (Pottermore/ Wizarding World) locations.

For many academics, this paper-based environment will be the limit of their fictional world. However, what elevates it to the status of a world as opposed to a collection of disparate resources is the degree of integration within their course(s). For example, at Aston University, both the Law of Tort and Medical Law & Ethics modules take place on the fictional island of Nousanto. Every problem, seminar question, case study and examination from both modules are set within this world. Characters also reappear and move between modules. For example, a child might be injured in a road accident in Tort, and then treated (negligently) by a doctor in Medical Law. As a result, students get sucked into a willing suspension of disbelief, and can start to recognise and react to common characters. From a teaching perspective, the fictional nature of the location also means that it is easier to create new problems because key buildings, locations and characters are already in existence, or can be fabri-cated quickly.

Teaching Tip: If you wished to enhance the realism of the world that you have created, consider developing the motivations and interactions between the characters. Twitter is an easy way to do this as tweets can be scheduled to be sent in real time as the scenario is unfolding in tutorials. Just be careful that any accounts are clearly labelled as parody accounts though, otherwise they are liable to be deleted.

THE USE OF POPULAR WORLDS AND CHARACTERS – A COST/BENEFIT ANALYSIS

An easy way of starting off with creating a fictional world for one's teaching is to make use of fictional characters and settings that have been developed by others and which are accordingly well known and established within popular culture. There are even instances where entire academic critiques have been, and continue to be, written on the legalities of the actions of comic superheroes and villains (although, often with a uniquely American law perspective!). Whereas this may be an easy way for lecturers to dip their toes in the metaphorical waters of world-building, we believe that there are a variety of reasons why it is better to ultimately develop one's own world if choosing to implement a fictional world beyond the scope of a single subject (or even question, for that matter). We briefly set out these reasons in this section.

An obvious benefit of using established worlds is that a lecturer does not have to go through the time and effort of developing their own characters, settings and narratives. It is also nearly instantly recognisable for students. However, what one must be mindful of when using established worlds and characters is that there is a profit incentive to continually expand the universe. This means that there is a lack of control in the direction of a particular character or event. A lecturer making use of popular worlds would likely find themselves over time naturally diverging from them in order to make sure that their own particular narrative maintains an internal consistency. Given this, lecturers run the risk of simply using the names of popular characters and doing their own thing in any case, which detracts from the potential immersion by creating a dissonant narrative to the one in popular culture.

If implemented on a larger scale, the use of such established characters and settings may also create problems from an intellectual property point of view, particularly given the commercial value of these worlds. Whereas fictional characters are not given copyright protection in the UK, they do enjoy some level of protection in other countries. In addition to copyright, characters and names are also protected through the use of trade marks to ensure broad and more universally recognised protection. This means that the use of such characters poses a legal risk in any event. Whereas there are generally accept-able means of using copyrighted works in an academic context, the use of trade-marked characters (even in an academic context) is significantly less clear-cut. Accordingly, the nature and extent of what constitutes infringement and what is acceptable use may differ from place to place.

Whereas the odd use of a fictional character or world in a discrete problem question is unlikely to be problematic in practice, these issues become far more complex when implementation happens on a larger scale. For these reasons, we believe it is best practice to develop one's own world from the start. Naturally, there is nothing wrong, when initially doing this, to draw inspiration from your knowledge of existing characters, settings and events, as long as you don't constrain yourself in the process!

Teaching Tip: If lecturers develop their own unique worlds, the risk of inadvertently using a story or setting that has been used (and/or analysed) by another is infinitesimal. This means that, aside from the legal risks not cropping up, the risks of students being able to plagiarise from existing sources (such as those very critiques mentioned earlier) are also diminished.

IMMERSIVE WORLDS

At a more advanced level, there are options for lecturers who wish these fictional worlds to be fully immersive experiences, either through virtual expe-riences or physically through augmented realities and live-action games (see Chapter 19, 'Quality lecturing is like a walk in the park'). However, it is worth noting that the resources and complexities involved in creating, and supervis-ing, these experiences exponentially increase. It is therefore important from the outset to be clear as to what the expectations of the simulations should be.

The simplest option, used by many business schools, involves the purchase of programmable software to simulate specific business environments, for example the Business Game™. Often though, these resources are specific to individual modules, and lack continuity across the degree programmes or business school.

At the other extreme are experiences that are highly reliant on user-generated content. Perhaps, the most infamous example of this is Linden Lab's *Second Life* web platform. A decade ago, this software promised users a virtual experi-ence, with the ability to create their own avatars, objects and classrooms. While a number of universities created virtual campuses (see for example, Harvard's Berkman Center, or Stanford's virtual library), ultimately the platform was not successful in becoming an educational environment. Indeed, problems with the complexity of joining instructions, the high degree of autonomy given to users, and the increasing prevalence of adult-oriented content led to many universities withdrawing.

Between these two extremes lay the Jisc-funded 'SIMulated Professional Learning Environment (SIMPLE)' project – initially at Glasgow Graduate School of Law, and then at five other institutions. The simulation here revolved around the fictional Scottish town of Ardcalloch and intended to replicate a professional environment between student 'law firms' and their simulated clients. What made this world different from other offerings though, was its transactional document-based nature. Unfortunately, while the concept was well regarded, take-up across the Higher Education sector was low. In part, this was because of the complexity of the software requirements and the perceived cumbersome nature of the interface.

Teaching Tip: Consider whether a fully immersive world is really necessary? If it is, you may be able to replicate some of these functions through modern learning management systems. For example, the adaptive release tool in Blackboard allows the use of rules to manage when content is made available to specific users. This and other lo-tech solutions, such as automatic out-of-office email replies containing 'new information' may replicate some elements of these simulations.

REBOOTING REALITY

In an era of decolonised curricula and smashed glass ceilings, it is worth considering whether lessons can be taken from comic books' reimagining of history. At their core, Black Lives Matter and related social justice movements argue for removing the inherent barriers and structural or systemic inequalities that have (often, but not exclusively) been installed, by a Western, white, male, heterosexual patriarchy. However, a key problem with this approach is that historically much of the classic literature or case authorities are firmly rooted in these problematic contexts. These texts either have to be replaced with works from a more diverse authorship, or alternatively contextualised as products of their time.

Comics and popular transmedia offer three alternative approaches that could be used to alter source material: Retconning, Rebooting, or the use of Parallel Realities (the Multiverse). 'Retconning' (a portmanteau of 'Retroactive Continuity') is where multiple writers might take very different, and mutually incompatible, approaches to a topic. For example, the most recent film in the *Star Wars* franchise (*The Rise of Skywalker*) undid a number of the plots and sub-plots explored in the preceding film – in the process reviving a character that had previously been thought to have been killed off in an earlier episode. By contrast, rebooting is essentially the nuclear option, destroying everything that existed prior to the 'change' in favour of a new reality going forwards. In many of the popular science-fiction franchises, writers have periodically 'rebooted' their worlds; see for example, the Marvel Cinematic Universe (Thanos' click in *Avengers: Infinity War*), the DC Arrowverse (*The Crisis on Infinite Earths*) or Star Trek (*Nero's 'Red Matter'*). This narrative device allows writers the scope to alter previously 'sacred cows' or inconvenient historical plots, without affecting the integrity of the whole world. The final approach utilises parallel realities, often referred to as the 'multiverse', to suggest that an infinite number of alternative worlds exist, thereby allowing characters to be transposed into different contexts. For example, in *Red Son*, Superman fell to earth in Ukraine rather than Kansas. Similarly, in *Spider-Gwen*, Gwen Stacy rather than Peter Parker was bitten by a radioactive spider.

What all of these techniques demonstrate is that historical events, literature and case authorities can be effectively reimagined into different formats, whether through the introduction of new interpretations, or by transposing the events to an alternate setting. Indeed, there are already good examples of this approach starting to be published in the mainstream. For example, in *Feminist Judgments: From Theory to Practice*, a group of feminist legal scholars have written the 'missing judgment' in key cases, whether as additional concurring or dissenting judgments, or from a fictitious appeal.

For teachers wishing to engage students in challenging current societal norms or beliefs, reimagining concepts in light of institutional racism or social privilege could be an effective medium to accomplish this debate.

> **Teaching Tip:** Consider adding a transmedia element to this new interpretation by creating it in a new medium. For example, if the judgment should be revisited due to changing societal values, this may be more effective via a video?

ADAPTING ASSESSMENT PRACTICES

Whereas the use of a fictional, immersive world is a great way of creating narratives in teaching, such large worlds are relatively superficial even when implemented on a programme-wide level. Accordingly, use of the entirety of the world in order to assess particular knowledge or skills is not fit for purpose. For assessment, the focus shifts from the world in itself to the student within that world where they become the 'major player' in a discrete aspect of that world. As we have noted earlier, most lecturers already apply a rudimentary form of world-building when drafting problem questions. While they are usually based on the facts of existing cases or events, in this chapter we show that this does not necessarily have to be the case. There are also many assessments in law which naturally suit themselves to the use of fictional worlds in this manner. In this section we reflect on how the concepts and tools discussed above can be used to adapt (or, dare we say it, transform) assessment practices within law teaching.

A common example of a simulation within a fictionalised setting would be the use of Objective Structure Clinical Examinations (OSCEs) such as those applied in the assessment of medicine and related health sciences. Essentially, these OSCEs are skills stations employing fictional patients and scenarios to test a student's competency to engage with practical tasks. These types of assessment are also increasingly becoming used in other professions. In the context of law teaching, they will arguably become even more prominent with the eventual introduction of the Solicitor's Qualification Exam in the UK. Existing assessments at law schools which naturally lend themselves towards implementation in a fictional world (or already make use of it) include that of mooting, oral assessments and interviews (something explored in another chapter in this book). Furthermore, problem questions can be adapted with relative simplicity to incorporate elements of a fictional world (shared or otherwise), irrespective of whether they are standard problem questions or dynamic ones (such as the narrative-based games discussed elsewhere in this book).

There is already evidence of how the above assessment practices can be successfully adapted within law. One such example can be found at a South African law school in the form of their Integrated Assessment Project. This project, which runs across every year of the programme, chooses a particular skill (or set of skills) to develop within a year group. The lecturers teaching within that year group then coordinate to create assessments focused on the particular skill. Whereas students know what the skill being assessed will be, they don't know which subject (or subjects) they will be assessed on as these are randomly assigned. This then culminates in the creation of a shared narrative between clusters of subjects in the final year, where aspects of the skills taught and assessed in previous years need to be used in 'solving' a comprehensive problem drawing from separate yet related areas within the law.

Whereas the above example doesn't make use of a fully realised shared world, we believe it is a model which can easily be adapted to do this. Doing so would create an internal consistency and allow for greater immersion (very much like one of the co-author's own thought experiments did). Admittedly, effective implementation of such a programme-wide world is not a simple matter. It requires planning, coordination and sufficient buy-in from staff, and it is not advised to simply implement it in one fell swoop. A more sensible approach, like the one implemented with the Integrated Assessment Project, is to first coordinate among the years regarding particular skills to be focused on and to subtly introduce common characters and events. From this point of departure, as both staff and students become used to the practice and can see the value therein, one can over time coordinate and organically craft a shared world. Once this is well established, development of further narratives and assessments within the world should be relatively simple, and if 'tweaking' of the world is required as new laws or cases emerge, the tools discussed in previous sections can be used to do so.

Teaching Tip: The earlier that a broad framework can be mapped out, the easier it will be to integrate across years and modules. It will also be helpful to agree common branding for linked documents. However, where the resources reflect different characters, perhaps as the inclusion of their 'personal correspondence' on the client file, some idiosyncratic content can actually make the material seem more realistic and should be encouraged.

CONCLUSION

As we have noted, developing hypothetical problems to test student learning is a skill that many lecturers already have. This chapter does not advocate for the replacement of that skill, but rather the transformation thereof. Accordingly, it provides a range of tools that can develop, enhance and extend these practices. Indeed, there is a strong argument to be made that transmedia (like multi-modal learning before it) is simply a logical extension of the current approach to teaching and learning, and that over time some will naturally gravitate to such an approach. As we transition in this post-COVID-19 world to an increased online presence, transmedia techniques give us the opportunity to create authentic and diverse content that will more readily prepare students for the demands of the workplace. Naturally, it should come as no surprise that most if not all of the tools and suggestions discussed in this chapter could easily be applied to disciplines other than the law.

While the chapter has provided a short overview of examples of world-building and the advantages and disadvantages associated with each, this is necessarily just a snapshot of the resources out there. We would therefore encourage you to explore the area further and develop your existing resources incrementally. Building immersive and integrated learning environments can be daunting, particularly in the early stages of development. It will also necessitate an investment of time, planning and resources. However, once it is established, it will streamline your assessments and more importantly make learning more engaging and fun, for both you and your students!

BIBLIOGRAPHY

Daily, J. (ed.), *Law and the Multiverse: Superheroes, Supervillains, and the Law*. Available at http://lawandthemultiverse.com/ (last accessed 15 September 2020).

Daily, J. and Davidson, R. (2013), *The Law of Superheroes*. New York: Gotham Books.

Giddens, Thomas (ed.) (2015), *Graphic Justice: Intersections of Comics and Law*. Abingdon: Routledge.

Hughes, Michael, Gould, Helyn, McKellar, Patricia, Maharg, Paul and Nicol, Emma (2008), SIMulated Professional Learning Environment (SIMPLE): Programme Final Report. JISC, UKCLE, University of Strathclyde.

Hunter, Rosemary, McGlynn, Clare and Rackley, Erika (2010), *Feminist Judgments: From Theory to Practice*. Oxford: Hart Publishing.

Jenkins, Henry (2006), *Convergence Culture*. New York: New York University.

16. Pursuing play in crisis management education

Lauren Traczykowski

INTRODUCTION

Exercises and simulations have long been a tool for educating crisis and emergency managers. 'Wicked' problems require intellectual investigation and practical solutions (Loreto et al., 2012). As with doctors, soldiers and essential service providers, responders cannot get things wrong in the middle of an emergency; if they do, people die. 'Serious' games have been the traditional space for emergency exercise development as well as the go-to mechanism for crisis management pedagogy (Hoff & Hoff, 2011; Loreto et al., 2012; Oulhaci et al., 2013; Radianti et al., 2017). One of the benefits of a game is the limited time frame and reduced space for debate which mimics real-world, real-time emergency scenarios (Loreto et al., 2012).

That said, exercises are still just practice for the big event and implementation of lessons learned from previous disasters. We cannot be frivolous in our dealings with real people in real scenarios, of course. However, if leaders will resort to 'what they know' in an emergency, we need a mechanism that allows leaders to feel comfortable challenging accepted rules and operating procedures and hence un-/relearn their occupation. Exercises and classroom environments are a chance for practitioners to play, explore and challenge preconceived or entrenched ideas about how they should respond to a given emergency situation. I argue herein that learners would benefit from debate time and free space to not only 'get things wrong' but to find for themselves what is 'wrong', and learn how to build complex relationships with those working around them. Crisis management is very serious business, but I suggest that by removing the formality inherent to 'serious games' in crisis management pedagogy, we will allow learners the freedom to explore alternative response ideas and the space to challenge preconceived ideas (Bateman, 2005).[1] I therefore make the argument for play in crisis management education in this chapter.

I establish this argument by first defining terms related to crisis management education in section 1. In section 2, I provide a brief history and validation of the use of 'serious games' for crisis management education. In section 3, I suggest ways that play might fill the gaps of using 'serious' games exclusively. Finally, in section 4, I offer mechanisms for the integration of play into crisis management education.

1.   DEFINITIONS

The term 'disaster' is rather complicated. It is often described as an event which disrupts the normal way of things and will usually involve some harm to people (Quarantelli & Dynes, 1973; Zack, 2011). Meanwhile, a crisis can be defined as "an occurrence that is either natural or human-instigated that affects the normal operation of business and political systems" (Saleh, 2016). We plan for crisis to protect people, homes, businesses and, increasingly, ways of life. Crises occur globally and consistently by way of war, natural hazard, civil unrest, poor leadership, etc. I understand a disaster to be a specific event and a crisis to have an ongoing nature, but this distinction and the term used are irrelevant to the type of learning I discuss in this chapter. In fact, I mean this analysis to consider our approach to any real-world disruption that requires or triggers some sort of official humanitarian response.

Crisis management can be defined as "the management of exceptional or out-of-the-ordinary situations" (Roux-Dufort, 2007). So, crisis management is how we organise ourselves and the world around us when nothing is normal. Crisis management can, and often does, involve preparedness assessments, mitigation efforts and, depending on the type of crisis, the delivery of humanitarian aid and the development of new policy for humans affected (UN Environment Programme, 2020). Like disasters versus crises, for the purpose of this analysis we can use the terms crisis management, disaster management, crisis/disaster response, and emergency management interchangeably, though they are distinct response mechanisms outside of this text.

From a more philosophical perspective, Roux-Dufort explains a crisis as an "accumulation of ruined equilibriums + ignorance of management" (Saleh, 2016, p. xiv). The goal of crisis management education is therefore to educate the crisis managers such that they are not 'ignorant'. By educating crisis managers we improve human ability to respond to and recover from an emergency. Hence, it is appropriate to explore different pedagogical approaches to crisis management education so as to ensure the best possible outcomes for those affected by an emergency.

2. SERIOUS GAMES FOR CRISIS MANAGEMENT EDUCATION

A traditional approach to crisis management has long involved the use of exercises and simulations and hence 'serious games' are standard. I engage here with a brief explanation of this current norm in crisis management education before moving forward with my playful approach.

'Serious games' are 'things' of play, but are not specifically play (Sicart, 2014). Hollywood offers us examples of how serious games are/can be used by military and political organisations (Alvarez et al., 2011). Consider films like *Ender's Game* and *War Games* where we are taught the value of engaging with a game to test response mechanisms to some realistic and possible future in an attempt to ensure peace on Earth (*Ender's Game*, 2013; *War Games*, 1983). In *War Games* we find the futility of war through a game of Noughts and Crosses (Tic-Tac-Toe for my American readers) in which the computer plays itself. Noughts and Crosses is considered the first video game (Alvarez et al., 2011). It was developed purely for fun but, in *War Games*, it is used as a learning tool first, and entertainment second, and in that way, *War Games* has used Noughts and Crosses as a 'serious game'.

Simulations are versions of 'serious' games which give players an immersive experience and an opportunity to understand what the activity in question feels like as well as what 'winning' looks like (Frasca, 2003; Pelletier & Kneebone, 2016). Think of video games as simulations and something like *Call of Duty* as an example (Alvarez et al., 2011). People play *Call of Duty* (and similar simulations) for the experience, to work within certain rules of the game and, ultimately, to win (Frasca, 2003; Sicart, 2014).

Moving to the experience of real emergency managers, 'exercises' have long been a tool to test emergency plans and prepare crisis and disaster responders. Exercises can involve a handful of people talking through a scenario; a formalised step-by-step discussion of what to do and when; a 'table-top' exercise where participants take on their role, respond to timed/queued challenges and real-time scenario updates; a fully interactive test of equipment and personnel, and the drilling of plans, response facilities, and communications. Exercises are rule based and goal oriented and in this way adhere to the 'serious' game or simulation approaches. Emergency managers are incredibly familiar with exercises and their use for continuing professional development and as assurance that response plans are operational.

Teaching student emergency managers and crisis response teams can be very similar and both seek opportunities to test systems for proof of concept, exploit flaws in existing systems, judge individual and system capacity, etc. Modelling crisis response, for example, as a form of preparedness helps those engaged in the process to know contributing factors to and viable ways out of the crisis (Saleh, 2016). Medical and healthcare exercise training and simulation can likewise be discussed under the umbrella of crisis management education. The reoccurrence and normality of these simulations in crisis education provides participants with a mechanism for building relationships with others as part of a 'cultural practice' fully integrated into their profession (Pelletier & Kneebone, 2016).

For crisis management education, simulation is the bridge to play. Fictionalisation and removal of 'intended outcomes' as a goal – something so ingrained in 'games' – allows the players to go off-script and learn the realities of a scenario when 'nothing is normal'. Some working in psychosocial care who utilise the exercise 'serious game' or 'simulation' technique suggest that whilst the goal of learning knowledge, attitudes and skills exists, there is also need for "increased and complementary familiarity with one another's specialities as an aid to more holistic care and more efficient and effective use of consultation with specialists" (Hoff & Hoff, 2011). Simulations start to provide the freedom for players/learners to learn about possible ways of successfully working together, even if this does not bring them to the intended or pre-decided outcome, but, as I argue in the next section, there is space for adding play as a pedagogical approach (Loreto et al., 2012, p. 353).

In sum, 'serious games' are hugely beneficial training supports within emergency management. They are scenario based and can be carried out at a lower cost than full interaction with a disaster; this allows for safer training of more people (Radianti et al., 2017). Skills learned from serious game crisis management education include: anticipation, teamwork, responding with quick judgment, resilience, 'lateral thinking, and creative skills' (Loreto et al., 2012). Likewise, simulations often test our responsiveness and capability (Loreto et al., 2012). If the testing of a plan, the identification of chains of commands, or practice of certain activities or actions is the reason for engaging in the game, then 'serious games' like those normally used should continue to be used.

However, there are skills not taught in 'serious games' – enhanced relationship-building, for example. Play/playful learning is therefore in a unique position to offer communication and interaction skills. And so, whilst there is value in using simulation and serious games, these may not always be sufficient. Instead, I argue that we can move beyond serious games to playful approaches to crisis management exercise and learning.

3.   THE SPACE FOR PLAY

Play is something slightly different to games: it is free. The focus is more on the doing within the play, the 'practising' of skills, than the winning (Whitton & Moseley, 2019). Think about 'playing' catch. You are free of rules, you play not to win but to practise throwing and catching. The thing thrown can be anything – a ball, an egg, jelly beans, whatever; one can catch with anything as well – hands, a basket, a mouth.

With 'catch', that which is thrown and caught is irrelevant; skills of throwing and catching are had no matter the object, and fun is had. Likewise, the type of playful learning used will not inhibit the skills learned in crisis management education. I herein argue for play in crisis management education as an alternative pedagogical approach to enhance the variety and skills adopted by the learners.

Whilst related, there are known and distinct differences between play and games (Bateman, 2005). Where (serious) games have normally dominated, the pursuit of play is a valuable addition to crisis management pedagogy. Games do not provide us with the space or time to hone our ability to reason and develop practical wisdom. Play will provide its own, additional, set of skills: risk management, how to fail safely, and how to be resilient (Whitton & Moseley, 2019). Hence, from a pedagogical perspective, the desired learning achieved through serious games in crisis management is at least possible through the use of play, with some additional benefits.[2]

Adults, especially those with 'serious' jobs, are not always good at letting go. That said, hand-to-hand 'play' combat would not be advisable in a classroom environment either. Improvisation, though, is key in a crisis. So how do we make people feel comfortable with the idea of improvising and remove the rules around outcomes (Bateman, 2005)?

Play is that loose and safe space where rules do not dictate a goal. By allowing adult 'players' the space to feel safe to explore options and trial alternative mechanisms, they learn how to adapt and improvise without judgment or backlash. Additionally, rules within play guide behaviour not outcome, and there are no necessary winners or losers (Frasca, 2003). If 'rules' do not apply, then peers rely on relationships and 'out of the box thinking' within a crisis management exercise. Crisis responders have rules and corresponding expected rules of behaviour, but playing a role does not require that we adhere to expected roles or even play the game; hence, play can be helpful.

Further, on the topic of rules, there are specific aspects of crisis management education that would benefit from conversation and conceptual development as opposed to rules- and outcomes-based practice: equality and diversity, integration of local communities, ethical decision making, etc. There are of course laws and guidance that emergency managers use in their decision making around these topics. However, reliance on traditional relationships and/or interactions between roles may serve the unanticipated outcome of reinforcing gendered or racialised mechanisms of response by removing/discounting other voices. By using a playful approach we can spend time on decisions, unpack/debate concepts, challenge laws/accepted wisdom, get things 'wrong', and discuss the why (as opposed to simply the what) of our choices. We can even 'play' to the extremes of gendered and racialised operations. A reflection on how one feels at the end of this will be just as important as, if not more important than, learning the 'rules' against gender and racial discrimination. To allow learners to truly learn from their experience, they have to be able to create imaginary scenarios and suspend any kind of social etiquette or legality to see what results from their decisions.

I move now to the thought-provoking characteristic of play. 'Mind or subjective play' includes daydreams and ruminations (Sutton-Smith, 2006). Scenario-based/exercise activities to test something like ethical decision making in a crisis are, quite appropriately, a rumination. It is the space for deep thought and consideration where the dialectic is helpful and decisions must be justified. Hence, the play I suggest herein may not help learners understand logistical mechanisms or operational tactics. Instead, the play of this chapter is an opportunity to take on a role, test boundaries, consider relationships and see what happens; nip at the ear of an issue and see if/how, and maybe ask why, the issue bites back (Bateson, 1976). Citing Sutton-Smith (1997), play 'deconstructs' the world such that learners can put the pieces back together themselves (Pelletier & Kneebone, 2016). This is particularly valuable when we want to practise, test or challenge our mechanisms for response in more contentious areas like ethics, inclusion, etc.

Often, though, a very practical objective is hampered by sociological and political debate. For example, the provision of calories to affected humans in the aftermath of a bombing can be settled through somewhat practical discussion. A human needs x number of calories; the road to that person's village is blocked by landmines. The objective/goal is to ensure that the specific humans affected receive the right number of calories whilst, at the same time, the crisis responder is able to safely carry out this objective. Instead, though, conversations tend to focus on whether providing food to that human is in fact supporting the needs of the aggressor, whether the requirement of neutrality by those managing the village checkpoint being foisted on you is something you and your organisation are willing to agree to, etc. Hence, problems in an emergency are ethically and socially layered such that there is a need for the discussion and 'rumination' that play provides. Hence, the benefits of playful learning are valuable to responders and play should therefore have a place as one of the pedagogical approaches to crisis management education.

4.   INTEGRATING PLAY INTO CRISIS MANAGEMENT EDUCATION

Now, there are playful learning approaches to disaster management but they have focused on digital/online games (Fujima & Woelfert, 2012). Here, I offer some ways to make traditional, in-person exercises more playful. I begin with some basic assumptions about module content and structure. Then, I move to the objects, as well as the roles, 'tools' and activities of play in crisis management education. I explore the use and continued value of 'injects'. I finish by discussing the type of assessment that can be used in a playful crisis management exercise that will arguably encourage risk management, applaud 'failure' as well as understanding, and support resilience and deep thought inherent to serious games.

Module Content and Structure

As with any constructively aligned module, the assessment of a playfully designed module leads the module design (Biggs, n.d.). In this way, using a reflective assessment will allow for playful participation even if the learner does not engage with the actual play of the activity. Observation of decisions made and relationships developed, tools used and the expectation of reflection will enable learning outcomes to be met.

The content of a module which uses play/playful learning will likely have a stronger grounding in the humanities than in any sciences. This is because the humanities are an appropriate, but not exclusive, place for 'rumination' including philosophising and dialoguing. To that end, this playful approach will lend itself to a concept-heavy module as opposed to a module like maths (for logistics and operations) that requires the learning and application of rules.

Toolkit

Teaching forces us to consider what concepts and skills we want our emergency managers to have upon module completion. The intention is to build student understanding and their specific 'toolkits' over the course of a module. Think of student learning as similar to a child's playful experience playing catch, running after frogs and swatting at bugs. Just as we give children a ball and a bat and tell them to go play, I suggest that we give learners play tools. Baseball, with winners and losers, is a possible outcome of providing a ball and bat, but is not required. Likewise, having an operations manager, a medic, a journalist and a politician sitting around an earthquake scenario, having learned about equality, may not result in the type of exercise 'serious game' one might imagine. It would be helpful for the players and the module leader to see what happens without the restrictions of 'rules'. So the approach here: teach your students and provide tools for their toolkit. 'Play' by giving the class a scenario. See how those tools are used, which they struggle with and whether they try to interact with others or play in solitude.

The teacher or moderator is able to provide the learners/participants with extra knowledge or a change of circumstance as the learners work through the scenario. Adaptation could be described as the pedagogical term for an 'inject' (Oulhaci et al., 2013). Imagine the child playing baseball is sprayed with a hose. That has not changed any rules of the game – there were no rules. Instead, it encourages the learner to adapt to the new environment, utilise different skills, use the tools (bat) already being used better, or do away with the tools entirely.

Assessment

The objective of the given exercise scenario and allowing students to 'play' with it is not about 'survival' or building teamwork skills specifically (Loreto et al., 2012). The objective is to understand how the tools (knowledge) provided in the module may be useful, appropriate, or not. There is no 'outcome' of the play itself other than having played.

The assessment can/should exist separate to the actual play activity. As there are no rules and no expected outcomes, students should be expected to reflect on what they learned, what tools they used, what tools they couldn't or didn't want to use, etc. The most important aspect of this will be the student's own analysis of why they or others seemed to play as they did. Over the course of several 'play times', students may start to play and use their tools differently. But this will be an individual decision based on the play activity that each wants to participate in.

Indeed, reflective learning is difficult to achieve when only real-world achievements are used (Loreto et al., 2012). One possible achievement a student may decide to reflect on was a complete lack of understanding of a certain concept or how it could be used. Likewise, a student might realise that the laws that govern a certain emergency response are counter-productive. This would be similar in my baseball metaphor to an individual not being able to throw or catch a ball, but seeing the (non-) value of such ball-throwing/catching.

Reflection may instead involve observation of and analysis of someone else's actions through mutual agreement. Through this kind of reflective practice students learn to dialogue with peers and build relationships. Importantly for a sense of play, this also allows students the chance to take risks and build their resilience.

CONCLUSION

Within this chapter I made the case for a playful approach to crisis management education as an additional pedagogical approach. Play offers more flexibility as well as training in risk management, resilience and how to fail safely. Also, without the stress of the goal that serious games reinforce, we are able to see why certain actions 'fail' and if there is any benefit to unexplored nuances. In making the case for a playful approach to crisis management education I suggested conditions under which this approach might be most beneficial to students and learners. Simply put, a playful approach to crisis management education is an alternative to serious games, another tool in our tool belt.

NOTES

1. We may also encourage a wider uptake of crisis management as a profession because interested parties will feel less intimidated that they will get the 'wrong' answers or don't have enough training to 'get the job done'.
2. It can be argued that any required activity ceases to be 'play'. To overcome this paradox, Whitton and Moseley suggest that the term 'playful' learning is useful as it encourages the whimsy inherent to play, even if a person is being forced to engage in a play activity (Whitton & Moseley, 2019). Whilst I think this distinction is helpful and accurate, I don't think that the crisis management training I am suggesting in this chapter is derailed by the aggregation of these terms. Individuals participating in crisis management education are either present because they want to be, because they recognise the need for such training (again, a sense of willing), or are being forced ('Go or you aren't qualified to do your job'). Those in the latter grouping need not participate in the actual play I suggest to engage in the learning (and hence will not be forced). This will be explained more thoroughly in the discussion of constructive alignment and reflection as assessment.

BIBLIOGRAPHY

Alvarez, J., Jessel, J.-P., Rampnoux, O. & Djaouti, D., 2011. Origins of Serious Games. In M. Ma, A. Oikonomou & L. Jain, eds, *Serious Games and Edutainment Applications*. London: Springer, pp. 25–43.

Bateman, C., 2005. *The Anarchy of Paidia*. [Online] Available at: https://onlyagame .typepad.com/only_a_game/2005/12/the_anarchy_of__1.html (accessed 15 May 2020).

Bateson, G., 1976. A Theory of Play and Fantasy. In R. Schechner & M. Schuman, eds, *Ritual, Play and Performance: Readings in the Social Sciences/Theatre*. New York: Seabury Press, pp. 67–73.

Biggs, J., n.d. Aligning Teaching for Constructing Learning. *Higher Education Academy*.

Ender's Game. 2013. [Film] Directed by G. Hood. US: Summit Entertainment.

Frasca, G., 2003. Simulation versus Narrative. In M. Wolf & B. Perron, eds, *The Video Game Theory Reader*. Abingdon: Routledge, pp. 221–235.

Fujima, J. & Woelfert, C., 2012. Professional Training for Disaster Management Improved by Playful Home Edutainment. Conference paper presented at the 1st IEEE Global Conference on Consumer Electronics, GCCE 2012, Tokyo, Japan, 2–5 October 2012.

Hoff, M. & Hoff, L. A., 2011. *Crisis Education and Service Program Designs: A Guide for Administrators, Educators and Clinical Trainers*. Abingdon: Routledge.

Huizinga, J., 2016. *Homo Ludens: A Study of the Play-Element in Culture*. Kettering, OH: Angelico Press.

Loreto, I., Mora, S. & Divitini, M., 2012. Collaborative Serious Games for Crisis Management: An Overview. Conference paper presented at the IEEE 21st International WETICE.

Oulhaci, M., Tranvouez, E., Epsinasse, B. & Fournier, S., 2013. Intelligent Tutoring Systems for Serious Game for Crisis Management: A Multi-Agents Integration Architecture. Workshops on Enabling Technologies: Infrastructure for Collaborative Enterprises.

Pelletier, C. & Kneebone, R., 2016. Playful Simulations Rather than Serious Games: Medical Simulation as a Cultural Practice. *Games and Culture*, 11(4), pp. 365–389.

Quarantelli, E. & Dynes, R., 1973. When Disaster Strikes. *New Society*, 23.

Radianti, J. et al., 2017. A Crisis Management Serious Game for Responding Extreme Weather Event. Conference paper presented at the 4th International Conference ISCRAM-med 2017, Xanthi, Greece.

Roux-Dufort, C., 2007. Is Crisis Management (Only) a Management of Exceptions. *Journal of Contingencies and Crisis Management*, 15(2).

Saleh, Y., 2016. *Crisis Management: The Art of Success & Failure*. Maitland, FL: Mill City Press.

Schertz, M., n.d. Empathic Pedagogy: Community of Inquiry and the Development of Empathy. *Analytic Teaching*, 26(1).

Sicart, M., 2014. *Play Matters*. Cambridge, MA: The MIT Press.

Sutton-Smith, B. (1997). *The Ambiguity of Play*. Cambridge, MA: Harvard University Press.

Sutton-Smith, B., 2006. Play & Ambiguity. In K. Salen & E. Zimmerman, eds, *The Game Design Reader: A Rules of Play Anthology*. Cambridge, MA: The MIT Press, pp. 296–313.

UN Environment Programme, 2020. *Why Do Disasters and Conflict Matter?* [Online] Available at: https://www.unenvironment.org/explore-topics/disasters-conflicts/why-do-disasters-and-conflicts-matter (Accessed 15 May 2020).

War Games. 1983. [Film] Directed by J Badham. US: MGM.

Whitton, N. & Moseley, A., 2019. Play and Learning in Adulthood. In N. Whitton & A. Moseley, eds, *Playful Learning Events and Activities to Engage Adults*. New York: Routledge, pp. 11–24.

Zack, N., 2011. *Ethics for Disaster*. Plymouth: Rowman & Littlefield Publishers, Inc.

17. Playful learning in accounting education

Ozlem Arikan

INTRODUCTION

The recorded history of the world starts with the invention of writing and writing was invented to record specific amounts of livestock or commodities, which is accounting. In other words, it is the accountants who gave the world the ability to make sense of the past. This happened centuries ago, but accounting never lost its importance; if anything, it became much more important with the formation and globalisation of financial markets. Corporations fail as a result of accounting scandals (Toffler and Reingold 2004) with tens of thousands of people losing their jobs. For example, millions of households lost their savings only in the 2002 financial crisis due to accounting manipulations (Tooze 2018). On the other hand, we owe it to accounting for the creation of many jobs, industries, and the living standards we have acquired so far. Were it not for accounting, which is a process of measuring performance, we would not have the markets necessary to exchange stocks and commodities; thus, corporations would not be able to raise money efficiently and employ their employees. Moreover, the efficiency of any system, be it hospitals, schools, or corporations, could not be measured in order to make any improvements. Accounting is a vital part of our lives. Yet, to the world, accountancy is boring (Bougen 1994). Obviously, such an important, delicate practice embraces a diligent system of thinking distilled through centuries of experience, and thus is far from boring.

However, this stereotype of accounting being a boring profession extends to the new accounting students. Students in the accounting programmes rarely, if ever, choose the course because of some inherent love, or proven ability; rather they choose it for vocational purposes linked to future monetary rewards (Marriott 2004). This lack of intrinsic motivation, at least at the beginning, places a higher importance on the use of playful content as a teaching method in accounting, as such content increases students' interest in the course (Haywood et al. 2004). Indeed, the first official game used in higher education was a board game called the Landlord's Game; patented in 1904 it was designed for accounting courses to teach tax theory and later inspired the popular game of Monopoly (Moncada and Moncada 2014).

Perhaps most important of all, however, the accounting profession tries to solve ill-structured problems in a dynamic business environment where there is no right or wrong answer in many cases; therefore 'knowing' about concepts is not enough; students need opportunities to learn to solve problems by creating their own representations of the situations and developing their acceptable solutions (Springer and Borthick 2004), and some playful techniques such as role-playing are great tools to teach students such skills.

For all these reasons, I use playful learning in my teachings from the very first day to the last; to teach my students the importance of attendance, a seemingly complicated formula with exponentials, the meaning of efficient markets; how universal concepts such as being good or fair are related to accounting. I even merge playful techniques with assessments. The below gives some examples of the playful learning I employ in my modules.

THE POETIC BEAUTY OF ATTENDANCE

I cannot imagine any lecturer who claims that attendance is not important for his or her subject and I am no exception. With its many detailed rules which are intrinsically linked to each other and are inherently vague to allow discretion, in turn necessitating critical thinking skills, accounting is best learned in a dynamic environment such as a classroom, where all these factors can be successfully blended. Therefore, I urge students to attend all classes, and I underline the importance of attendance in my first interaction with students.

To ensure that students remember how important attendance is, I communicate it via a poem at the beginning of the term, written by a fellow academic, when he felt sufficiently frustrated by students who had been asking him what they had missed as a result of their absence (Wayman 1993). The poem consists of a dialogue between a lecturer and one of his students, the student asking him what s/he missed, and the lecturer answering the student. The lecturer's answers range from 'student did not miss anything, as in their absence nothing important could have possibly taken place, to student missed everything as the lecturer is just about to give a quiz worth many marks about the lecture's contents'. Needless, to say, the poem is funny and entertains the students which is one of the aims of playful learning tools: teaching whilst entertaining. Nevertheless, it gets more serious in the end. The lecture, it says, was one microcosm of experience specifically created for the student to examine, but s/he was not there. I love the poem because it is not only funny, it also carries a meaningful message. After reading the poem, I briefly go through an interview with the poet where he explains all the effort a lecturer puts into their preparations and why he thinks it is important for students to appreciate this and participate in classroom activities. This activity gives me the opportunity to convey important messages to students while having some fun and a laugh. It allows me to situate attendance as a pleasant subject, and the story embedded in the poem and the interview is aimed to help students retain the message in their memories (Bower and Clark 1969).

PLAYING WITH EXPONENTIALS

Accounting is all about valuation. After all, it is about summarising trans-actions and reporting them as a single value. Valuing a past transaction is relatively straightforward but accountants often have to deal with the valuation of future transactions. A company is defined to be a nexus of contracts (Jensen and Meckling 1976) and contracts typically include projects where some future cash flows are expected. The problem about valuing future cash flows is that they are less valuable than the same amount of cash flows received today. The main reason for this is that the future is risky. No matter how robust the contract is, there is some chance that the promised money will never be deliv-ered. The future also represents some foregone opportunity costs. After all, if you had £10,000 right now rather than a year from now, the least you could do is deposit the money in a bank account and earn some interest. The longer you wait to receive your money, the less valuable your money becomes; waiting for two years is riskier than waiting for just a year, and the amount that could have been in your bank account is larger if you waited for two years rather than one. All these issues are resolved by the accompanying formula:

$$Value = \sum_{t=0}^{n} \left(\frac{FutureCashFlow}{(1+i)^t} \right)$$

With its sigma sign and exponentials, the formula looks scary, at least to some students. However, once you know the logic above, it is straightforward. The value is equal to the sum (hence the sigma sign) of the future cash flows starting from the cash flows generated this year ($t=0$) until year n (when the contract ends), all discounted (hence the fraction) by a factor i, representing the cost embedded in the future for that particular setting (the level of risk and the foregone opportunity cost) and getting smaller as the years pass by (hence the exponential).

I can hardly imagine a single accounting core module at any level that does not use this formula or its variation. Hence, it is important that students under-stand its logic in an intuitive way. I accomplish this with a role-playing game. Two students play the game. One says to the other, 'I want to give this money (typically a £5 note supplied by me) to you. Do you want it now or a year from now?' Almost all the responses to the first question are correct: students intuitively know that money received now is more valuable than money received in the future, known as the time value of money. Then the second question comes: 'Why do you want the money now rather than a year from now?' Surprisingly, students struggle here. Their answers, if any, are typically technical, such as 'money has time value', rather than reflective. At this point I step in and ask, 'What does that mean; why does money have time value?' and almost always I have to further prompt them to help them to come up with an answer. 'You are reluctant to receive the money a year from now. Why? What could happen in a year?' This seems to be the magic question, after which students are much more able to reflect on the difference between now and the future. Now they can come up with answers such as that their fellow students can change their mind in a year, or they may not be able to find the student, all reflecting on the riskiness of the future; as well as with answers such as that they may start a small business, or invest the money in a bank account, reflecting the opportunities foregone in a year. In the third part of the game the students discuss whether they would prefer to take the money a year from now or two years from now. At this point, students grasp the idea that the longer the time it takes one to receive the money, the less is the value of the money. I then explain the relationship between the above formula and the game.

The game is fun and informative – not only for the players but also for the rest of the audience. There is always a lot of laughter in the class whilst the game is being played, and when their poor fellow student struggles to answer the questions, many students enthusiastically raise hands to answer on their behalf! All the evidence, whether assessments or class discussions, reveal that students thoroughly grasp the logic of the above formula after this game. What is surprising though is that no matter what the level of the students is, be it first, second, final or postgraduate, all students at first struggle to rationalise why they would prefer to take the money now rather than in the future. Most of them have already seen the above formula many times when we play the game, but they do not seem to have grasped the rationale behind the concept of the time value of money, the root of that formula. The repeated success of that game is evidence of the importance of playful learning in teaching our students seemingly complex concepts in an intuitive way.

GOOD DAY SUNSHINE: THE JOY OF ACADEMIC READING

If there is another concept as ubiquitous as the time value of money in accounting courses, it is the efficient market hypothesis (Fama 1970). If markets are efficient, then all information is already incorporated into prices, and so there is no way to 'beat' the market because there are no undervalued or overvalued securities available. This has important ramifications for accounting students because it undermines the work of the accountant. For example, if it is not possible to discover overpriced or underpriced stocks, what is the point of the financial statement analysis? Even worse, if all information is already incorporated into prices, what is the value of accounting numbers such as profit and loss? The good news for accountants though is, unlike their earlier counterparts, recent evidence suggests that markets are far from efficient (Shleifer 2000).

The logic behind the market efficiency hypothesis is that although an individual investor may make mistakes (e.g. being fooled by manipulated accounting numbers), these individual mistakes are corrected instantly at the market level, by more knowledgeable and skilled participants. Although market efficiency or its lack thereof is a crucial subject for accounting students, it is a too abstract concept for most of them.

To teach the concept of market efficiency (or its inefficiency!), I use an academic article which makes the notion very concrete. The paper (Hirshleifer and Shumway, 2013) examines the relationship between the amount of sunshine in the locations of stock exchanges across 26 countries and the exchanges' daily index returns for 16 years, and is published in a peer-reviewed top journal. It finds that sunshine is significantly correlated with stock returns. What this means is that prices get higher when the sun shines and lower when it doesn't. In an efficient market no such correlation can exist; even when some investors get overly excited by good weather, this should be corrected instantly by more sophisticated market participants in efficient markets.

After my students read the study's introduction, which is less than three pages long but summarises the study thoroughly, I ask them if this correlation could persist if markets were efficient. They instantly grasp the idea that in an efficient market this could have never taken place. And, in turn, they understand how market efficiency works: better informed participants correct the mistakes of less informed ones. Students learn this by having fun; lots of jokes go around after reading this article. I remember one student saying, 'if all investors behaved like this, the London Stock Exchange would have been in big time trouble', pointing to the lack of sunshine in London on a typical day. And most importantly, perhaps, such fun and opportunity to teach a difficult concept comes from a very unexpected place: an academic article. This, I think, is very good news for us, as educators. We can find informative fun everywhere; the key is to look, and to inform each other about what we have found.

THE BBC'S SARAH MONTAGUE AND JOHN HUMPHRYS AND ACCOUNTING: A PLAYFUL LEARNING OPPORTUNITY THROUGH VIDEO AND NEWSPAPER CLIPS

If there is any validity in the stereotypes of accountants, it is that accountants are numbers people; they believe in numbers and respect them and are a bit sceptical towards the qualitative side of things. This is also valid for accounting students. They have a hard time appreciating how any module which does not directly deal with numbers is related to accounting. I have discovered this during my conversations with my students in various contexts, such as personal tutoring and after-class hallway conversations and office hours. Particularly, accounting students have a hard time understanding how their qualitative modules such as sustainability have anything to do with accounting. This lack of understanding is not a trivial issue; although it is true that accounting is about numbers, many issues not directly linked to any calculations, including sustainability, have an impact on the numbers, and the profit or loss figure produced by the accounting system is the summary of the cumulative impact of all such issues. This lack of understanding suggests that accounting students are missing the big picture.

I teach accounting through a case study where we analyse a real company by examining its financial reports. Particularly, among other things, we examine the annual report of the company which includes sections about sustainability, such as the gender pay gap report. The examination of the gender pay gap report in our case study gives me the perfect opportunity to explain how these issues are related to the 'numbers' my students are so keen about! I first ask students, as accountants, why do we care about such reports? Not surprisingly, at this instance, none of the students comes up with answers linking the gender pay gap to accounting numbers. I then start the playful part to help students grasp the link.

Students first watch a short clip of Sarah Montague and John Humphrys co-hosting the BBC's *Today* programme on Radio 4. This clip helps students understand that these presenters are doing exactly the same job on the same show. Then they see a newspaper clipping, which reports that when it was revealed that John Humphrys was earning a salary as high as five times her own, Sarah Montague won a settlement from the BBC worth £400,000. We then watch a clip of the top ten salary earners at the BBC and their salaries, of which the top seven are all men.

Next we examine two sets of newspaper clippings. One highlights yet another female presenter winning a victory against the BBC due to the gender pay gap, and the other highlights the job cuts planned by the BBC amidst financial pressure, linking it partially to the existing and potential lawsuits or settlements due to the gender pay gap. The argument is that the high amount of settlement that the BBC pays/is expected to pay is creating financial difficulties for the corporation. This contemporary development enables students to capture how issues such as being fair to one's employees can have an effect on a corporation's financial status. When I ask them my initial question about the relevance of the gender pay gap report in our case study again, their answers can now link matters related to sustainability and social responsibility to the accounting numbers. This practice not only enables students to learn in a playful way, because it is based on a story, it also helps them to retain the knowledge longer in their memories (Bower and Clark 1969). I leave the class being grateful for BBC veterans Sarah Montague and John Humphrys; not only for their years of service to us as listeners, but also for their help to my students in grasping the bigger picture of accounting.

ASSESSMENTS CAN BE FUN TOO!

I began this chapter by talking about attendance, which is very important to accounting education, and am finishing it with a method to encourage attendance, namely continuous assessments. Continuous assessments are mainly 'pop quizzes' which could happen at any time. This unpredictability encourages students to attend the classes so as not to miss any marks from continuous assessments. At the beginning of the term, I give my students information about these assessments, mainly their weight on the final mark and their structure.

What is the fun part of these tests? What makes them fun is that each of these tests is linked to a polling game delivered through a student response system, Vevox. Right before each test I ask the class to answer ten multiple-choice questions on Vevox about the content of the lecture we have just finished, with students submitting their responses via their mobile phones. Vevox has a game-like feature instructors can use if they wish to. It shows participants the distribution of answers to each question so that they can change their minds. This feature is like the 'Ask the audience' option in the famous quiz show *Who Wants to be a Millionaire?* Students can revert to the answer given by the majority of the audience, but sometimes the audience is wrong. Therefore, a student may as well change his or her correct answer to go with the tide. I am hoping, in those instances, that the game teaches students to be confident in their abilities. We go over each question and discuss the results, as well as students' overall performance. Right after this game, students work on their continuous assessments and are typically asked questions very similar to those in the Vevox game, although not entirely the same. For example, the Vevox question could be about the impact on the inventory turnover ratio of a company of an acquisition that took place at the end of the fiscal year, whereas the quiz would ask for the impact if the acquisition took place at the beginning rather than at the end of the year.

Students enjoy this combination. Indeed, when asked about the best part of the module, several of them say that Vevox and the continuous assessments are the parts they most enjoy.

There is yet another fun aspect of the continuous assessments. To access the online quiz, students have to provide a password that I give them just before the quiz. Each quiz has a different password, and I try to make the passwords fun. For example, the password for the quiz taken on St Valentine's Day was 'Love'. Students react to these passwords by giggling when they appear on the screen; a good way to start taking a test! As for the academic reading part above, I hope that this part gives the audience the encouragement to look for fun; it can be found anywhere, even in assessments!

Before concluding, I would like to say a few words about the student response system as a mechanism to engage students. I use this tool in every single session, whether or not there is a quiz at the end. The anonymity embedded in such tools encourages even the quietest student to engage with it. Indeed, almost all my students engage with Vevox (the system lets the instructor know how many students submitted answers), it always brings some excitement to the class, and hence it is a very good method with which to review material; students see where they are in understanding the concepts of the session. One student summarised their experience with the following remark after the mid-term module feedback:

It's engaging and actually raises the mood and activity of the class.

CONCLUSION

Playful learning has one overarching aim: making the learning process fun. When we have fun whilst engaged in an activity, we want more of that activity. As an educator, I want my students to enjoy the learning experience, so much so that they would want to continue that fun when we are inevitably no longer in their lives, and as such, they become lifelong learners.

REFERENCES

Bougen, P. D. (1994). Joking apart: The serious side to the accountant stereotype. *Accounting, Organizations and Society, 19*(3), 319–335.

Bower, G. H. and Clark, M. C. (1969). Narrative stories as mediators for serial learning. *Psychonomic Science, 14*(4), 181–182.

Fama, E. F. (1970). Efficient capital markets: A review of theory and empirical work. *The Journal of Finance, 25*(2), 383–417.

Haywood, M. E., McMullen, D. A. and Wygal, D. E. (2004). Using games to enhance student understanding of professional and ethical responsibilities. *Issues in Accounting Education, 19*(1), 85–99.

Hirshleifer, D., and Shumway, T. (2003). Good day sunshine: Stock returns and the weather. *The Journal of Finance, 58*(3), 1009–1032.

Jensen, M. C. and Meckling, W. H. (1976). Theory of the firm: Managerial behavior, agency costs and ownership structure. *Journal of Financial Economics, 3*(4), 305–360.

Marriott, N. (2004). Using computerized business simulations and spreadsheet models in accounting education: a case study. *Accounting Education, 13*(sup1), 55–57.

Moncada, S. M. and Moncada, T. P. (2014). Gamification of learning in accounting education. *Journal of Higher Education Theory and Practice, 14*(3), 9.

Shleifer, A. (2000). *Inefficient markets: An introduction to behavioural finance.* Oxford: Oxford University Press.

Springer, C. W. and Faye Borthick, A. (2004). Business simulation to stage critical thinking in introductory accounting: Rationale, design, and implementation. *Issues in Accounting Education, 19*(3), 277–303.

Toffler, B. L. and Reingold, J. (2004). *Final accounting: Ambition, greed, and the fall of Arthur Andersen.* New York: Doubleday Business.

Tooze, A. (2018). *Crashed: How a decade of financial crises changed the world.* London: Penguin.

Wayman, T. (1993). *Did I miss anything?: Selected poems, 1973–1993.* Madeira Park, BC: Harbour Pub.

SHORT THOUGHT: PLAYFUL LEARNING IN ACCOUNTING EDUCATION

Ozlem Arikan

If there was one overarching message I tried to emphasise in this chapter, it would be that every aspect of teaching can be made playful, even the dreaded assessments and academic readings! One just needs to search for it. I learnt, and am still learning, how to search for fun from my wonderful colleagues, particularly those at Aston who take teaching most seriously. Although our aim is to make learning fun, a serious effort has to be put in for that to work, and as with every other effort to make the world a nicer place, it becomes easier when experiences are shared. Had I not learnt from other academics, whether my former professors who made teaching fun for me, or my peers who are at least as enthusiastic as I am when it comes to making education as interesting as possible, I would not have been able to write this chapter. Hence, I feel really excited about this book; I am finally able to pay back my fellow educators by sharing my own experiences with them.

Some of the activities I included in this chapter are given in an accounting context, such as the role-playing game to teach students the rationale behind discounted cash flow formulas, the news and video clips to discuss how sustainability is related to accounting numbers, and the academic article related to market efficiency. However, all these can also be applied to non-accounting contexts. A role-playing game can be used for any concept to encourage students to think critically. Empirical academic studies are drawn from the behaviour of people, so they are of great help in making abstract concepts concrete for students. Newspaper or video scripts can help tell a story which is known to improve sense-making and memory. Yet other activities such as using poetry to communicate the importance of attendance or merging classroom tests with the playful nature of student response systems are context free and can be applied to any subject.

The playful learning concepts I include in this chapter serve two aims. The first is to make some necessary evils such as assessments more bearable for students by bringing in some sense of humour and interaction. The second is to teach concepts which are difficult to learn with traditional methods because of their abstractness or because of the fact that the inherent rationale is not straightforward. This second point helps me underline the importance of innovative teaching practices; they are not only fun, they also improve the learning process by encouraging students to be critical thinkers, by allowing them to learn from their mistakes in a safe environment by ensuring their anonymity, and by simplifying the concepts for them.

18. 'Models' of ethical behaviour

Lauren Traczykowski

INTRODUCTION

Students often find theory application difficult, especially in written assessments and when the theory is new or in some way foreign to their way of thinking. One possible reason for this is that students have not unpacked the theory for themselves. It may also be that their language skills are not developed enough, they may not be confident in their ability to understand, or even that they have never been asked to do something like this before. It is our job, as educators, to 'focus on what the student does', to know what it means to 'understand' the theory and methods of application, and to consider and integrate the kind of activities which will enable the student to understand as well (Biggs, 2012).

Ethical decision making is a common activity in our day-to-day lives. Many people 'know' what is ethical and what isn't, but cannot break it down to the theoretical level and truly 'understand' why that is so. This breaking down of a decision to its component parts – theory, application, practice – is not something done day to day. Hence, when we ask students to do so we are not just asking them to learn a theory and apply it, we are also asking students to challenge their own understanding of what is ethical and question whether they are consistently applying that understanding. This is intellectually challenging and often emotionally charged and thereby contributes to the difficulties inherent in applying ethical theory to practice.

The kind of activities necessary to support students develop skills in unpacking and applying theory can be found in a playful learning approach. Critical thinking for learning and applying ethics requires that we 'treat knowledge as problematic', confront it within a context and approach it logically (Giroux, 1994). Playful learning provides a creative context which is self-formed instead of teacher-imposed (Giroux, 1994). In fact, playful learning offers the student choice: how to learn and how to convey knowledge in a way that suits them.

'"Models" of Ethical Behaviour' is a playful learning technique which uses art activities to encourage multisensory learning and ethical behaviour. Project creation and representation of an answer is not a new style of learning and teaching. What makes this different is the central role of ethics: using ethical theories to build ethical models in an ethical environment.

In what follows I offer a playful learning approach to teaching students to understand and apply normative ethical theory creatively and critically, and within a logical context that works for each of them individually. I begin with an analysis of the problems and hurdles associated with teaching theory application and engagement with critical analysis. I then offer the methodology and concept behind '"Models" of Ethical Behaviour'. From this, I can explain some direct benefits of using this technique, namely the provision of a multimedia, multisensory, inclusive learning environment. Observations and informal feedback from students and academics on how this method of learning is useful are included.

TEACHING ETHICAL THEORY AND CRITICAL ANALYSIS

Aristotle breaks knowledge into three groups: theoretical, productive and practical (Ostwald, 1999, pp. xiii–xvii). Those studying the 'theoretical nature' of something are interested in knowledge for its own sake – say, how a geologist is interested in rock formations or rock properties for the sake of knowing about rocks. The 'producers' are interested in what you can make with the rock, say, a hammer or spade. Whereas the 'practical' area of knowledge is what we can do with the spade once we have it, understanding and applying it to our lives. Ethics is a practical knowledge whose aim "is to act in a certain way" and hence to understand and apply it to our lives (Ostwald, 1999).

Immanuel Kant's ethics is an 'analytic' system or procedure by which he aims to find a singular 'principle of morality'. If everyone acts on these same principles, we "would generate a community of free and equal members, each of whom would in the process of realizing his own purposes also further the aims of his fellows" (Wick, 1994). So, whilst we might theorise and produce tools, it is ultimately what we do with ethics, how we understand and apply norms to our actions, that matters to ourselves and to society. Through practice, we learn ethical ways of being – what is 'good' (Ostwald, 1999).

Ethics is, therefore, more than simply instructions or rules, but rather action, a way of being and a mechanism for determining how to be the best versions of ourselves, morally speaking. According to Caza et al., "Ethical principles serve as fixed points. They indicate what is right and wrong, appropriate and inappropriate, by reference to universal standards" (2004). But ethics confuses us; ethics provides an opportunity for us to decide what we *should* do (Tong, 2002). Without the analysis component, or the practice of ethics, we are left with a product devoid of context and removed from – or, rather, unintegrated into – our lives.

Here is where critical analysis is necessary. Critical analysis is an advanced mechanism of problem-solving. It encourages the student to engage with learning how to learn, not simply learning a series of data or material. Instead students learn to 'think about thinking', challenge concepts, evaluate, etc.; application of that which is taught or read is crucial to an individual's ability to solve current and future problems (Snyder & Snyder, 2008). We want our students to move beyond regurgitation to utilisation of knowledge and hence an improved ability to problem-solve. Ethics must be practised, acted out, in order to fulfil its existence. We must do, not simply learn, ethics. Hence teaching ethics through critical analysis gives students the freedom, the space, to think about and discover the material (not simply memorise it) (Snyder & Snyder, 2008).

'Doing' ethics can be, and usually is, done discursively. Through oral debate and/or written critical analysis, we engage with theory by applying it to a scenario or situation. In this way we attempt to be 'good' for ourselves and society. Critical analysis should contain: (1) a problem, (2) a question posed regarding that problem, (3) student engagement with the problem and question within a given framework, and then (4) an opportunity to learn from that new thinking (Snyder & Snyder, 2008). That said, 'doing' critical analysis of ethics is also possible through play.

BUILDING 'MODELS' OF ETHICAL BEHAVIOUR

Play is linked to ethics, first, in that it tests the virtues of the player. A musician may practise 'fortitude': practising the instrument, improving upon his or her skill, avoiding ego, etc. (Huizinga, 2016, pp. 160–162). Second, we 'know' play to be play when it exists separate to a goal or necessary function of life. Instead, it is "a contest *for* something or a representation *of* something" (Huizinga, 2016, p. 13). Likewise, the art created from play takes on the ethical value of that thing. In 'playing' a participant creates a thing, separate to that which was imagined before or could be replicated in future. In this way it becomes a representation of something else.

Instead of practising ethics through verbal or written discussion, there is space to creatively engage with theory and apply critical analysis through playful learning. In this section I will explain the process of building '"Models" of Ethical Behaviour' to teach ethical decision making by leading the reader through the phases/steps of this kind of critical analysis training via a playful professional ethics activity.

1.   The problem: Students were asked to pick a scenario from a list of stand-ard professional scenarios as their 'problem' (Huizinga, 2016, p. 162). For example: (a) 'I was late to work'; (b) 'A gender pay gap exists in your organisation.'

2.   Question posed: (a) 'I was late to work, *should I tell my boss why?*'; (b) '*How should we address* the gender pay gap in our organisation?' These scenarios/questions were structured in such a way as to require an ethics-based response. By using the word 'should', students were led to consider the normative, instead of simply the practical, response.

3.   Student engagement within a given framework: this part of the critical analysis framework of student engagement required that students provide an answer to one of the everyday ethics questions posed via a piece of art.[1] Participants were asked to consider a normative ethical theory (utilitari-anism, deontology, virtue ethics or feminist ethics), after some traditional lecture-style instruction and pre-reading. This provided the tools with which students could 'think' about the answer.

     As is important in playful learning, learners should not be constrained to learn a specific outcome within a bounded set of rules or guidelines (Whitton & Moseley, 2019). Instead, the term 'art' was used so that stu-dents could pick their medium and with it their approach to the question. With this, I suggested that a song, a dance, a drawing, a sculpture, etc. were all acceptable 'arts' for submission. In my instruction, I only speci-fied that the piece/installation/activity made clear the question answered, the normative ethical theory used, and the answer being given. Hence, students could demonstrate understanding of the theory and how to apply it through their choice of medium.

A quick digression into the element of play used. The fundamental character-istics of play dictate that play is free (or rather, freedom, unconstrained by any boundaries the materials used might create), limited and is a representation of the real (Huizinga, 2016). In '"Models" of Ethical Behaviour', it can be argued that the 'play' involved in this activity only adheres to two of the three fundamental characteristics of play. Students have usually picked a sculp-ture or drawing as their 'piece of art'. (I have not yet had a student write or perform a song through which an answer was thought and developed.) It can be argued that 'plastic' arts or the visual arts of painting, sculpting, theatre, etc. are bound to matter and therefore do not constitute elements of play. A painting, for example, only exists as paints and canvas and requires a viewer. The 'plastic' arts can be said to be 'limitless' in that time does not constrain them and hence they are not truly playful. Play requires a time boundary such that the completion of play and return to reality can be marked, though not necessarily hard marks (Huizinga, 2016; Sicart, 2014). The 'plastic' arts, it is argued, are, however, consistent with the third characteristic of play in that they are a depiction or representation of real life and thus *not* real life; it is created/'done' for a non-functional purpose.

I would argue, though, that classroom play is constrained and in this way will never be free. If we are working within a given room, with other classes going on beside us, we must work within the boundaries of our room – in terms of substance, sound/noise, etc. Likewise, the 'limited' duration of the play is artificial in that we will not be able to 'play' until play is over – we will be forced to complete a task within a given portion of the lesson's activities.

I do not think that either of these constraints on classroom play hinder the playful nature of the activity used. These are better understood, I would argue, as fluid terms to guide our understanding of play. But with that, what is important in our use of play in classroom environments is that it removes students from the real. It provides an opportunity for students to tap into their own creativity and freely apply that to the task at hand. Indeed, I would agree with Sicart that "play is finding expression; it is letting us understand the world and, through that understanding, challenging the establishment, leading for knowledge, and creating new ties or breaking old ones" (2014, p. 18).

I return now to the playful framework involved in this kind of activity. Students were asked to play with materials, with art forms, with concepts, and show an answer. An example will help. Consider one of the above scenarios: 'You are late to work. Should you tell your manager the truthful reason why?' The expected response to this question, based on the lectures previously given, is 'yes, because Kant has a categorical imperative against lying'. However, that does not always sit well with students. Instead, they often prefer to use Utilitarianism, specifically Mill's Utilitarianism from which we can say that certain things bring about more happiness than others and, hence, if maximising happiness is the most ethical thing to do, as is the central claim of Utilitarianism, one must do those things that bring about the greatest happiness.

But this is actually advanced theory application and critical analysis if one is interpreting a scenario, applying a theory, and having to think of an answer completely on one's own.

4. Learning from new thinking. This brings us to the fourth component of critical analysis accounted for in this playful learning technique. Armed with a new theory and a scenario to which they can apply it, students had to think of an answer. There were no right or wrong answers, simply correct or incorrect understandings and application of theory. With this, students were free to make mistakes, ask questions which aided their

own particular understanding of the applied theory and adapt their art accordingly.

Once participants can visualise an answer, the description and written engagement with theory application becomes easier. Restating/explaining a theory that uses antiquated language is incredibly difficult. So, instead of struggling to simply restate theory, students have an opportunity to explain their own 'model' of the answer represented in their art.

Because workshop participants have built the 'model' themselves they are in a position to answer critical questions – how does the theory figure in to your artwork? Why should we view the answer in the way you have explained? Etc. (Snyder & Snyder, 2008). Again, though, they are not answering theory questions in the abstract. Students are answering questions about their interpretation and application of theory and hence responses are grounded in critical analysis. The student has done the hard work of understanding the theory in order to create the art itself.

Consider the advanced critical analysis involved in this activity. If a student has said that they are using 'Mill's Utilitarianism' but there isn't a hierarchy of preferences to make sense of maximum happiness, have they really used Mill's theory? Students are in a much better position to respond to such possible critiques and/or identified gaps in their understanding and hence to engage with critical analysis and self-correct when the corrections are part of their art. They can literally see the gaps in their own theory application.

Equally important, the learner has had the opportunity to engage with the question and answer creatively. By using '"Models" of Ethical Behaviour', a student is not searching for right or wrong answers, they are encouraged to think for themselves and adapt their own learning as necessary: reading more, asking for clarification, reviewing notes, etc. The art provides a 'correct' answer if it is consistent with the theory being applied, no matter how whimsical or far-fetched the art presented (or answer) is.

Further, Gomes argues that the "act of jointly attending to works of art can play a role in one's coming to understand and share another's ethical framework" (2013). By seeing the piece together we can come to understand the ethical person who created the piece. Equally, the viewer of the art need not be 'engaged' with the ethical concept being portrayed. One can assess and understand the validity of the theories being applied without agreeing with the norm (Gomes, 2013).[2] This is important as the creation of art gives students the freedom to express an understanding of an ethical norm without having to convince the teacher and/or worry about being 'right' in their response. Likewise, students can work with controversial responses for the purpose of seeing what/if works ethically in a given scenario. This art gives students a freedom only possible in the world of play.

Before submission, students were asked to 'write up' a description of their piece (i.e. using a museum label or abstract) and include how it answers the question posed. Whilst students were asked for a 'description', this was based on the critical analysis done to create the art originally. The evaluation of the problem, the structure of the answer, and the reasoning behind the student's answer to 'Should I tell my boss the truth?' was already playfully built into the activity so that it was not an added stress for the student (Learn Higher, 2020). Students were only asked to verbally describe what they have already constructed in their minds and art. This gives learners the space to answer and identify gaps or flaws in the piece and self-correct (Snyder & Snyder, 2008).

In Higher Education, it is much easier to be judged (by peers and lecturers) for poor art skills than to be judged for not understanding a concept. Anecdotally, students find it much easier to correct mistakes, hear criticism and understand flaws in their representation of the answer than of their answer itself. It is fun; it isn't 'real'. Any 'mistakes' will be missing or incorrect in the art piece and thus can be adapted as necessary. Alternatively, correcting a verbal or written response requires a keen understanding of the words being used, not just the concepts being explained.

Hence, as teacher I can comment on how I think the student wants me to understand the art. If that is consistent with their intended answer and with the correct application of the theory, then the answer will be clear. If not, the student has an opportunity to adapt the model based on questions I ask so as to complete the response in the way s/he intended. Regardless, the student need only adapt their art if it is inconsistent with that which s/he is trying to explain. This is a confidence-building aspect of playful learning, and particularly using art to understand ethics. Individual creativity to create art, even the 'plastic arts', offers freedom.

BENEFITS OF 'MODELS' OF ETHICAL BEHAVIOUR

There are several pedagogical benefits to using playful learning technique such as '"Models" of Ethical Behaviour', namely, that it is multimedia, multisensory and inclusive.

Multimedia

By putting words and pictures together, people learn better, and by extension they are better able to apply this learning to new situations (Mayer, 2019). So, if I want to explain an ethics thought experiment like, say, the Trolley Problem, I should provide a verbal or written description and a picture or cartoon. With multiple media, students can process the information through two cognitive pathways (verbal and visual).

For the purpose of this chapter, though, I am interested in how the student is supported in their own development, not how the teacher teaches/provides the material. By using '"Models" of Ethical Behaviour', teachers are in a position to guide "the cognitive processing of the material" that students are doing on their own (Mayer, 2019). Students will benefit from the use of multimedia tools in their own guided study, as it increases the amount of information with which they are able to make connections. Then educators should provide those tools for their independent engagement with and application of ethical theory.[3]

Indeed, multimedia instruction, where students choose their media, provides an opportunity to learn what they want/need to learn. Students can then adapt their materials and media to account for any gaps in their own understanding of the topic or theory. Learner-managed learning in this way will enhance memorisation (Mayer, 2019). I am not concerned with cognitive overload in my activity because most students come to this module with no background in ethics; reducing working memory load and hence the dual pathway of knowledge integration can be effective (Kalyuga, 2020). Altogether, engaging with multiple media, in a structured environment, improves students' retention and application of information.

Multisensory

At its core, multisensory teaching accounts for the use of multiple and layered human senses – touch, taste, sight, hearing. It is one way of providing students with a learning experience which makes learning 'richer and more motivating' (Teaching and Learning Programme, 2008). Multisensory learning, within the context of this project/object, "invokes a variety of senses and encourages a form of interactive or experiential learning" which contributes to experiential learning highlighted in the Kolb cycle (Chatterjee et al., 2015).

As an active learning technique, object-based, multisensory learning is aligned to discovery learning and constructivism. It provides learners with the opportunity to see and do the learning which, again, contributes to the ways and repetitions of information being fed into the brain (Chatterjee et al., 2015). Further, if each of us is able to learn through different media (and we are not visual vs. kinaesthetic vs. verbal learners), providing all mechanisms of learning gives students a chance to absorb the information in the way that makes sense to them at the time and/or absorb the information without having to think about learning it in a 'preferred' way (Dodgson, 2018). In this ethical art project, students are quite literally constructing their own understanding of concepts.

Most importantly, we know that individuals do not learn by specific 'learning styles'. However, we do know that using two or more senses for learning reinforces memory and allows for creative learning which provides students with creative and relaxed spaces. This, in turn, encourages broader thinking and critical analysis (Ratty, 2018).

Inclusivity

Moreover, '"Models" of Ethical Behaviour' as an example of a playful, multi-sensory learning activity, is inclusive. Students with dyslexia or other learning challenges have an opportunity to engage with the concepts being taught in ways that helps them make sense of the information. This (type of) activity also ensures that those with certain disabilities will not be excluded from learning. The use of multiple senses means that some aspect of the activity will be accessible and there is an opportunity to develop *all* senses (Teaching and Learning Programme, 2008).

Additionally, I have found that student confidence in writing increases as a result of this activity. Self-evaluation of understanding is happening constantly as students 'practise' their understanding of key ethical concepts. With this, when students approach a write-up phase, they are not facing a blank page. They know and understand where and why they began their art project in the way that they did, what criticisms or questions they had to address in developing the piece of art, how they went about adapting the work, and what this means for the final analysis and answer. Just as mind maps help to focus, structure and apply different concepts to a problem, a playful 'model', free from the constraints of certain pedagogical tools, will enhance a student's ability to make sense of the material and effectively answer a question posed (Monash University, 2020). Writing is easier when the structure is already represented for you, by you.

CONCLUSION

In sum, '"Models" of Ethical Behaviour' encourages inclusive, multisensory learning. Critical analysis and ethical theory application are easily surmountable hurdles when students are given the freedom to engage with the material playfully. Within the classroom and beyond, this approach can build student confidence in their own understanding of ethical theories and application. This in turn means that ethical decision making becomes relevant and practical in real-world scenarios.

NOTES

1. For reasons of space, I have not considered aesthetics in this analysis. Likewise, I have not evaluated the possible link between making these projects to *learn* ethics and ethics as beautiful in itself (the art project's end as an ethical ideal).
2. Please note that whilst I mention aesthetic/ethical concepts, this is not intended to be, nor is it remotely, aesthetic analysis of 'models' of ethical behaviour. That would require an additional, separate study.
3. Future possible research would consider the most effective medium for making the most of cognitive processing in ethical decision making.

BIBLIOGRAPHY

Biggs, J., 2012. What the Student Does: Teaching for Enhanced Learning. *Higher Education Research & Development*, 31(1), pp. 39–55.

Caza, A., Barker, B. & Cameron, K., 2004. Ethics and Ethos: The Buffering and Amplifying Effects of Ethical Behavior and Virtuousness. *Journal of Business Ethics*, 52, pp. 169–178.

Chatterjee, H., Hannan, L. & Thomson, L., 2015. An Introduction to Object-based Learning and Multisensory Engagement. In H. Chatterjee & L. Hannan, eds, *Engaging the Senses: Object-based Learning in Higher Education*. Abingdon: Routledge.

Dodgson, L., 2018. The Idea That We Each Have a 'Learning Style' is Bogus – Here's Why. *Business Insider*, April.

Frasca, G., 2003. Simulation versus Narrative. In M. Wolf and B. Perron, eds, *The Video Game Theory Reader*. Abingdon: Routledge, pp. 221–235.

Giroux, H., 1994. Toward a Pedagogy of Critical Thinking. In K. Walters, ed., *Re-Thinking Reason: New Perspectives in Critical Thinking*. Albany: State University of New York Press.

Gomes, A., 2013. Iris Murdoch on Art, Ethics, and Attention. *British Journal of Aesthetics*, 53(3), pp. 321–337.

Hines, C., 2018. Unintended Lessons: What Typically Developing Students Learn from the Inclusion and Exclusion of Students Who Receive Special Education Services. *Analytic Teaching and Philosophical Praxis*, 39(1).

Huizinga, J., 2016. *Homo Ludens: A Study of the Play-Element in Culture*. Kettering, OH: Angelico Press.

Kalyuga, S., 2020. Expertise Reversal Effect and its Instructional Implications. *Impact: Journal of the Chartered College of Teaching*, January.

Learn Higher, 2020. *What's the Difference Between Description and Critical Analysis*. [Online] Available at: http://www.learnhigher.ac.uk/learning-at-university/critical -thinking-and-reflection/whats-the-difference-between-description-and-critical -analysis/ (accessed 12 August 2020).

Mayer, R., 2019. How Multimedia Can Improve Learning and Instruction. *Impact: Journal of the Chartered College of Teaching*, January.

Monash University, 2020. *Brainstorming: Mind Mapping*. S.l.: Monash University.

Ostwald, M., 1999. Translator's Introduction. In *Nicomachean Ethics*. New Jersey: Prentice Hall.

Ratty, M., 2018. Multisensory Classroom as a Pedagogic Innovation. *Education and New Developments*.

Sicart, M., 2014. *Play Matters*. Cambridge, MA: The MIT Press.

Snyder, L. & Snyder, M., 2008. Teaching Critical Thinking and Problem Solving Skills. *The Delta Pi Epsilon Journal*, 50(2), pp. 90–99.

Teaching and Learning Programme, 2008. *Effective Teaching and Learning*. Learning Wales.

Tong, R., 2002. Teaching Bioethics in the New Millennium: Holding Theories Accountable to Actual Practices and Real People. *Journal of Medicine and Philosophy*, 27(4), pp. 417–432.

Whitton, N. & Moseley, A., 2019. Play and Learning in Adulthood. In N. Whitton & A. Moseley, eds, *Playful Learning Events and Activities to Engage Adults*. New York: Routledge, pp. 11–24.

Wick, W., 1994. Introduction. In *Immanuel Kant: Ethical Philosophy*, 2nd edn. Indianapolis: Hackett Publishing Company, Inc.

19. 'Quality lecturing is like a walk in the park': making learning more tactile and fun through location-based strategies

Kris Lines

INTRODUCTION

A lot of what we do as lecturers is within either a physical, or virtual, class-room. Our world is the pages of a textbook, a video clip or the visuals we conjure from our speech. Yet, even the very best descriptions are just that, descriptions. Our experiences are necessarily mediated through and constrained to a one-dimensional lens. This chapter will explore how learning can be made more tactile, experiential and visceral, particularly by incorporating considerations of 'location' into and out of the classroom.

The first part of the chapter discusses the creation of a self-guided walking map, from its initial design and underpinning pedagogies, to its practical application in the classroom as a formative extra-curricular activity for students on the core 'Law of Torts' module. The second part of the chapter then discusses my best practice recommendations for anyone wishing to incorporate adventures outside of the formal learning spaces. For ease of reading, I have grouped these reflections into four themes: the medium of the map (whether it is published physically, or virtually); when it should be followed (e.g. synchronously or asynchronously); whether any route is fixed or variable; and finally whether there are special legal considerations.

CREATING A MAP: GENERAL PRINCIPLES

Many years ago, my status as a stranger on campus was starkly exposed when I had to attend a training event, off site. At the time, I was working at another university based on three semi-interlinked campuses. Although, I had been at the Law School for a while, I lived quite a distance away in another part of the country and commuted in. My knowledge of the local area was therefore somewhat limited. I knew most of the campus, the major arterial roads and the train station, but put me 500m outside of this zone and I would have no idea where I was! Needless to say, getting to this training location without a sat nav proved a bit of a challenge.

What was interesting was when I recounted this experience to some of my students after a lecture, many felt the same. Many of us were not locals, and our sense of belonging was missing. While the campus (and its people) were super-friendly, the campus's self-contained nature made it very tempting to view it more like a temporary island than an integral part of the community or neighbourhood.

When I later moved to work at a different university, the first thing that I wanted to do was find some way of encouraging students to explore their surroundings and develop this affinity with where they were studying. I also wanted a way of bringing my subject (the Law of Torts) to life. The break-through came when I realised that one of the major landmark cases in the liability for economic loss, still in use today, occurred at a factory that had been situated one mile down the road from the Law School. The more I researched the local area, the more cases I found. This led to the creation of a series of five self-guided maps. Between them, they detailed 50 legal cases across a range of subjects and locations, from civic centres to neighbourhood disputes, falls while out shopping to road traffic accidents, even defamation from the evening newspaper. Each route went off in a different direction from campus before looping back to the reception area. The routes were about 7km long and focused on approximately 15 points of interest (eight to ten legal cases, and the remainder points of local, cultural or historical interest). Between them, the routes also covered all of the local railway and coach stations, as well as the major shopping areas in the city.

Importantly, while aspects of the routes and the cases located on them were discussed in class, the routes themselves were purely extra-curricular and led to no additional credit if a student completed them. This decision was the product of a number of debates – perhaps, chiefly, if it is not compulsory, whether the students will actually use them.

Ultimately though, it was felt that as the maps were designed as an induction tool and a chance for students to explore the area around them at their own pace and without supervision, making them available, but not mandatory, accomplished that aim. I have however come across a range of courses where engagement with local geography has been assessed summatively. Where this assessment has occurred, typically, the activity itself is just a tool, and it is the product of the walk (whether this is photographs, a reflection or research) that determines any mark. There is however no right or wrong approach. The remainder of this chapter will therefore explore how the use of walking routes could be integrated into classes, and any advantages or disadvantages to how this can be accomplished.

CREATING A MAP: TECHNICAL DETAILS

Unfortunately, even now, there do not seem to be many practical academic resources on how to create self-guided maps. Instead, the best resources that I found on map design came from outside of academia. One such example, from the tourism, travel and leisure sector, 'Designing Urban Walks', is included in the references at the end of this chapter (Reponnen, 2015). The article is an excellent walk-through (pun intended!) on how to create the graphics of the map itself; it also includes sample detail for some of the stops along the route. Although the article was written from the perspective of an American designer embarking on the design of a new tour guide app for New York, many of the conclusions are equally valid when the map is employed in a learning and teaching setting.

For those interested in the more abstract and visual aspects of creating a map, I would also recommend exploring the cartographic material contained in role-playing games (RPGs). While this material is often based on a fantasy-historical rather than modern setting, it can sometimes provide a useful 'bird's-eye view' of what should be contained on a map, with all of the embellishments, flourishes, legends and iconography that accompanies such an approach.

In contrast to the more practical design-based resources, there are lots of (mainly sociological) articles on learning spaces and distributed learning. Although these tend to focus on the design and management of physical teaching spaces, rather than the wider environment beyond the classroom, they can be useful for justifying how playful learning can be located in the gaps between formal timetabled sessions.

From a pedagogical perspective, I would also recommend some of the work on either 'legal geography' or 'urban history' to draw out some of the more hidden themes inherent in the environment, such as power or privilege. For example, in cities, particularly London, while land such as Canary Wharf may appear on the face of it to be public, in reality these areas are privately owned public space (POPS) with restrictions enforced by private security companies. This may have little practical effect for day-to-day activities, and many people will not notice any differences; however, it is worth noting that private landowners do have powers over prohibiting commercial filming and demonstrations, as well as restricting access for rough sleepers.

What map you ultimately create will depend on three key decisions (explored in the rest of this chapter):

1. The medium of the map (e.g. whether it is published physically, or virtually).
2. When any route should be followed by participants (e.g. synchronously or asynchronously).
3. Whether any route is fixed or variable.

> **Teaching Tip:** It is important to be clear from the start what the objectives and purpose of the map will be. How does it align with the learning objectives for the module/course? Will the activity be assessed formatively, summatively or is it simply an extra-curricular activity?

THE MEDIUM OF THE MAP

Lange and Smith argue in chapter 6 of the edited collection *Learning Space Design in Higher Education* (Scott-Webber et al., 2014) that space can be conceptualised into three areas: physical (geographic), virtual (online), or conceptual (state of mind). This is also an important choice to make for anybody wishing to use a map with their students.

A conceptual map is by the far the easiest mapping option to publish, since it may simply utilise excerpts from open-access public maps (in the case of a larger area), or a street name (in the case of a more discrete zone). For example, students might be told to explore from point A to point B along a street. In doing so, they might be encouraged to use critical thinking and reflection, to identify the invisible barriers, structures or challenging ethical concepts along this route. This type of conceptual tour demands a higher degree of engagement and maturity from students and may therefore be more appropriate for pairs or groups.

If, by contrast, the activity was intended as a tour, or orientation, a physical paper map is by the far the easiest mapping option. Depending on the degree of professionalism required, the route could be hand-drawn or word-processed; and either photocopied or uploaded on a learning management system/website for users to download and print. Although this will add more expense to the project, the use of either a graphics tablet (such as the 'Wacom Bamboo' range), or a precision stylus (such as the 'Apple Pencil'), will allow you to create more detailed routes, or create hand-drawn tracings. Both tools are relatively easy to use, and are compatible with most leading graphics packages. They will however add an extra degree of complexity and cost to the project.

Providing a virtual version of the map will significantly increase the time and cost of production; however, it will allow it to be used effectively on mobile devices, or with real-time locations. At its simplest, a virtual map can be overlaid onto a pre-existing map template such as Google Maps, OpenStreetMap (https://www.openstreetmap.org) or Mappa Mercia (http://www.mappa-mercia.org/fullscreen-maps/mapnik/). By creating and adding a new 'layer' onto the software, it is possible to make annotations onto an existing map, before sharing this with other users. This approach has a number of advantages, not least that the detailed map has already been built. Ironically, this is also its chief disadvantage, as it may be difficult to customise or alter an off-the-shelf map, particularly if you wanted to simplify the data displayed. A good example of this was the Open Law Map (https://openlawmap.co.uk). The map was designed as a user-generated map, accompanied by short blog entries and photographs. It later inspired the London Law Map (london-lawmap.blogspot.com).

If a virtual map could be created and overlaid on to an existing map, for example via a downloadable app, this would give universities the opportunity to widen the scope of the project to other subjects within their portfolio. It also would reduce the reliance on external hosting by a third-party server. As discussed earlier, the inclusion of key cultural, local or historical sites would be common to whichever route was used, regardless of the subject being studied. However, mixing a new layer per subject could allow the substitution of subject-specific landmarks or case studies. For example, an accounting department could bookmark the location of a Greggs store to introduce the differential tax treatment of eating a hot vs. a cold sausage roll; or a local supermarket could be identified as a place to debate whether Jaffa cakes are cakes or biscuits. Similarly, marketing departments could use brands such as the Body Shop or Nike to illustrate ethical concepts; there also seems to be no shortage of examples of recent corporate insolvency and governance debates around brands such as Debenhams or Sports Direct.

In these latter examples, it is less likely that the local branch in question was responsible for the decision making leading to the issue; however, if this is made clear in any description, the value of the map becomes a starting point for discussion rather than a definitive historical record.

Teaching Tip: Many Town and City Councils have tourist information centres that have already compiled maps or visitor information notices. These may be helpful for identifying other generic locations, such as parking, public toilets or transportation hubs.

TREASURE HUNTS, AR!

Whether you intend the maps to be used by the students during a specific week/time (synchronously), or at their own leisure through the course (asynchronously), will determine how interactive the maps are.

The advantage of a self-guided map is that all of the necessary information is contained in one resource, and there are no pressures to complete it within a particular timescale, or possibly at all. The map therefore has to be an exciting enough prospect that students see the value in using it. Good examples of this type of resource can be found as induction or outreach activities. However, caution should be used that the routes are checked periodically, and that roads and footpaths are still open to the public, or that shops have not moved elsewhere, or out.

A good example of how this trail might work in practice was described by Jeremy Donald in 'Blood on the Stacks' (Donald, 2008). In particular, Jeremy discusses how American students completing self-guided treasure hunt-based orientation tours had higher satisfaction ratings and demonstrated better knowledge than a more traditional control group.

Where the map is intended to be interactive, this may be less of an issue because the timescale is more condensed, but it might also be more of an issue, particularly if it relies on the use of supplementary signage or posters. For example, one way of testing competency and engagement might be to provide students with only a partial route, forcing them to receive instructions for the next phase as they progress along it. This could be achieved through notices with text instructions, scannable QR codes or via marshals at checkpoints. If these resources are particularly vulnerable to vandalism or loss it may be worth exploring whether they could be protected in display cabinets (although this will obviously be easier where the trail is located on campus).

I had also intended to discuss the use of augmented reality (AR) within this section. As technology has developed and smartphones have become more powerful, it is becoming increasingly possible to superimpose digital content in real time over what the camera sees. For example, if you point at a specific object, this might trigger additional media or descriptions. In this way, route maps and educational experiences can be overlaid as a virtual experience without affecting the physical world. Perhaps the most common examples of this can be found in Snapchat filters, and Pokémon GO.

At the time of writing, the two most popular, user-friendly AR creator apps (HP Reveal and Aurasma) have been withdrawn. While there is a new company that has just been launched, this seems to still be in Beta-testing; however, by the time of publication, this may be stable enough to support educational experiences. Alternatively, it is possible for experienced web designers to create their own AR apps utilising either Google Lens or the Apple ARKit/RealityKit; however, these are specialist programmes and, as such, beyond the scope of many academics without institutional IT support.

Teaching Tip: When creating any route (whether interactive or self-guided), it is worth making sure that there are very clear landmarks at regular intervals along the way. Students may drift off track or miss scheduled checkpoints, therefore the inclusion of a distinctive landmark may allow them to reorient themselves easily.

FIXED OR VARIABLE ROUTES?

It is possible to identify at least three schools of thought involving the integration of walking and learning. For some people, like Aristotle, walking could be combined with teaching, and students engaged in conversation and thinking as they travelled from place to place.

Conventional route maps are fixed and shepherd the user through certain designated checkpoints. While the route is predictable, the excitement and the learning occurs in bite-sized chunks at each stop. This has certain advantages for classroom activities as each route can be allocated an appropriate completion time and an anticipated total distance. It is also possible to identify any potential hazards or accessibility issues in advance of participation.

Alternatively, for others, like Debord or Rousseau, the action of walking necessarily involves an examination of the world around you, all of the time. Debord calls this the act of *dérive* ('drift'):

> Participants put aside their usual reasons for moving and acting, including those tied to work and leisure, and immersed themselves within urban currents, attracted or repulsed by existing terrains. But, referring to the etymology of dérive, the LI also highlighted its other associations, among them the active sense of diverting water along with the inflection from the English word 'drive'. The group further proffered: 'to undo what is riveted' (LI 1996a [1956]: 60). Through gaining awareness of the powerful forces that channel and condition urban space and life, the dérive offered means of *undoing* them. It was a detouring, a process of appropriating, diverting and rerouting. (Pinder, 2019)

Routes are typically not fixed, nor indeed easy to schedule since the experience may be different for everyone. While this approach might initially seem too abstract and philosophical for the typical undergraduate in a business school, it does however share some similarities with conventional scavenger hunts. In a scavenger hunt, students do not have a fixed route, but their learning might consist of a 'photo-safari' or the documentation of experiences or objects they discovered during their journey. This approach is very strongly student-driven and will involve the sharing of (often very different) experiences. A good recent example of this can be seen in Nigel Hudson's 'PropertyMon Go!: Gotta Catch 'em all' (2017), where students were tasked with photographing aspects of buildings and structures that might identify issues such as easements or mortgages.

Teaching Tip: Consider the extent to which students should develop an emotional connection to their locations. The more personal, and individual, the experience, the more intense this may be. Conversely, if the learning outcome is based on creating a more general familiarity with the neighbour-hood, this may not be achieved if a student focuses more in-depth at a particular location, instead of venturing more widely; or if they mechanically follow a set route.

SOME IMPORTANT LEGAL BITS

Finally, in any discussion of organised (or semi-structured) walking activities, it is important to reinforce a number of key safety principles. Risk assessments should be carried out for the environment in which the walk will take place, although if the route is self-paced and extra-curricular, responsibility could be passed to the students. While university students will all be adults, it is however still important to remind them of the importance of walking in pairs or groups rather than individually, and to cross roads, where possible, at designated crossing points.

If the task or route involves taking photographs, it also will be important to reinforce the need to be cautious about their use. Stopping to take a photograph will advertise the presence of the device to thieves, particularly if students are distracted or focused on where they are moving to next. It is also worth highlighting that although it is legal in England to take photographs of public places, some governmental, civic or sensitive buildings may trigger additional concerns from authorities, particularly over anti-terror sensitivities. This will be particularly important in relation to court buildings, since it is a criminal offence to take photographs of a courtroom, and this will also include its immediate vicinity and the access route on the pavement outside.

Useful guidance, policy and resources on walking safely within the built environment can also be found at https://livingstreets.org.uk/

CONCLUSION

The use of walking as an integral element of education has been with us since ancient Greece. Now, as we transition to a post-COVID-19 world, we are all being encouraged to spend more time walking – whether this is for health reasons, as a break from constant screen time, or as a more environmentally conscious method of commuting. This chapter would argue that learning and teaching should also be included in that list of reasons.

Walking activities might be structured, scheduled or merely self-paced, but what is important is that they allow students the chance to engage with and fully experience their surroundings. In some locations, these routes might be supplemented by specific and meaningful landmarks or commemorative plaques; however, this is not essential, and engaging activities can still be accomplished along much shorter, discrete routes if the purpose of the walk aligns to a more reflective and individual task. The key challenge for academics is working out exactly what they want to achieve from these activities, and designing the routes accordingly to support these outcomes.

BIBLIOGRAPHY

Braverman, Irus, Blomley, Nicholas, Delaney, David and Kedar, Alexandre (Sandy) (2013). 'The Expanding Spaces of Law: A Timely Legal Geography'. *Buffalo Legal Studies Research Paper Series* (032).
Donald, Jeremy (2008). 'The "Blood on the Stacks" ARG: Immersive Marketing Meets Library New Student Orientation', in Amy Harris and Scott Rice (eds), *Gaming in Academic Libraries: Collections, Marketing, and Information Literacy*. Chicago, IL: Association of College and Research Libraries.
Hudson, Nigel (2017). 'PropertyMon Go!: Gotta Catch 'em all'. Nottingham Law School – Centre for Legal Education Conference.
Pinder, David (2019). 'Transforming Cities: On the Passage of Situationist dérive', *A Journal of the Performing Arts* 23(7), 18–28.
Reponnen, Anton (2015). 'Designing Urban Walks: A Story Behind Design Process of a Walking Tour App'. Available at: https://medium.com/@repponen/designing -urban-walks-9b521d51dcae (last accessed 14 September 2020).
Scott-Webber, Lennie, Branch, John, Bartholomew, Paul and Nygaard, Claus (eds) (2014). *Learning Space Design in Higher Education*. London: Libri Publishing.
Walker, Rob (2019). 'The Art of Noticing: Five Ways to Experience a City Differently', *The Guardian*, 9 May.

SHORT THOUGHT: PLAYFUL LEARNING SHOULD NOT JUST BE RESTRICTED TO THE STUDENTS!

Kris Lines

Lockdown and the transition to online teaching has forced all of us to re-evaluate our teaching, and the material that we use. While there is nothing particularly novel, nor technically demanding, about editing traditional lectures into bite-sized chunks to be interspersed by a variety of short, interactive clips, what can be more challenging is the search for appropriate academic content to supplement these. It was during one such search that I rediscovered the 'brickfilm' phenomenon.

Essentially, a 'brickfilm' is a stop-motion animation made entirely out of LEGO bricks. These films are painstakingly animated via thousands of photographs, as the mini-figures are moved one millimetre at a time to simulate movement. The photographs are subsequently downloaded to a computer and stitched together with an audio track to recreate iconic movie scenes, or funny dance videos.

I've always been a fan of both LEGO and the cinema, and I was struck by the realisation that this medium could illustrate clips for my Medical Law and Ethics classes that would traditionally be too gory or specialised to find as an academic video. I could also customise these short films to suit my own context and the time I needed to fill.

Interestingly, exploring how to create these clips has enhanced my 'normal' lecture recordings as it has forced me to re-evaluate the lighting used, the angle of the camera shots, the type of microphone and (lack of) pop filter, and the storyboarding of my content.

While I feel reasonably confident that some students will appreciate the inclusion of an animated short film, I do worry that the use of LEGO will be a distraction from the more serious ethical questions illustrated in the clips. It also raises an interesting question as to whether the use of this medium creates a cognitive dissonance with the medical topic, or whether it increases engagement by making the subject easier to understand. Only time will tell.

In September 2020, newspapers reported that LEGO's global sales rose 7% year on year in the first six months of 2020 (a trend attributed primarily to lockdown) (Butler and Jolly, 2020). I wonder just how much of that is due to academics teaching themselves stop-motion animation ...?

Reference

Butler, Sarah and Jolly, Jasper (2020). 'Lego-playing Kidults Help Build UK Toy Sales During Covid Lockdown', *The Guardian*, 2 September.

20. Jeux sans frontières? A critical angle on the use of games/simulations and 'play' in higher education

David Yates and Ivo De Loo

1. INTRODUCTION

Gamification involves the application of game-based principles or rewards to otherwise non-gamified aspects of life (Nicholson, 2015). This can include, inter alia: offering incentives, points scoring mechanisms, achievements and awards (Robson, Plangger, Kietzmann, McCarthy & Pitt, 2015). Gamification is deployed in education as a pedagogical technique, which while carrying other benefits, can make learning more appealing and interesting to the student (Moncada & Moncada, 2014). In this chapter, we engage with theoretical stances on play and games, discussing the field of business simulations/serious games and critically assessing their impact on the gamification of education. More specifically, we consider the potential wider (and possibly detrimental) effects of the growth in the gamification of business education within higher education (HE) institutions. We present several conceivable consequences of the deployment of games and simulations in HE, and effects of gamification on everyday life that may arise as a result.

In section two we introduce a theoretical stance on play and the playful subject, drawing primarily on Huizinga's (1936, 1955) conception of 'play', its components, and the role that it occupies as part of everyday life. We supplement Huizinga's thoughts with that of other scholars who focus on the concept of play and subjectivity. In section three we discuss playful learning in business simulations and games more explicitly, referring to the philosophical approaches outlined in section two. In section four, we focus on the ethical dimensions of gamification and game-/simulation-based learning. The conclusion to this chapter is contained in section five. There, we mainly consider the wider implications of gamification in education. We also outline some potential further lines of enquiry on this subject from a research perspective. Finally, we advise caution when deploying games and simulations to student cohorts for a number of reasons, including wider considerations associated with the gamification of 'real life', namely the effects of the educational experiences that students encounter, and carry with them for the rest of their lives.

2.   THE IMPORTANCE OF PLAY

2.1   Play and the Playful Subject

Huizinga (1955) purports that man (sic) is a playful character who needs to play in confined spaces and at specific times in order to be able to handle and effectively engage in the seriousness of everyday or 'real' life. When individuals agree to engage in play in specific ways, they create what Huizinga calls the "magic circle" (p. 10). In these circles, cultural themes and ways of living tend to be dramatised and evaluated. Instances of play impact and (re)shape culture through the experiences of the players engaged therein. Episodes of play also have their own organisational forces, as Huizinga (1936, p. 176) argues:

> a large part of social life is carried on in the form of play, that is to say, within an artificial mental sphere governed by rules of its own and temporarily encompassing all conduct in a voluntarily accepted system of action. A conventional proceeding takes the place of the direct pursuit of utility or pleasure.

Within this statement, Huizinga brings in a number of key elements of play. Huizinga outlines five of these, which will inform our theorisation as we move forward through this chapter.

1.   An individual's motivation to engage in play is assumed to be voluntary and purely based on the fun or excitement that play generates. Therefore play is seen to offer freedom, practically from the sense that it offers an escape from 'real' life, but also that a player engages of their own free choice. In this sense, play is also freedom in itself.
2.   Play is not part of the 'real' life experience but is (quite literally) 'extra-ordinary'.
3.   Play is distinct from 'ordinary life', and takes place in a particular space and time.
4.   Play creates order, in that there are rules that govern play.
5.   Play is not connected to material interest or profit, nor can profit be gained from engaging in it.

Players are given the opportunity to step back from 'real' life in play, and because of play's place within culture, they can consequently reconsider their ways of living. In line with this view, Marcuse (1964) suggests that notions of play are essential to bring about societal change, which otherwise

might could excessively technology-, production- and output-oriented otherwise. This carries implications for business-themed games and simulations,
which remove the individual from the 'real' of 'real' life but present 'play'
through the simulation of business activity, constituting a (technological)
representation of that which is considered part of 'real' life, i.e. the context of
a business-orientated organisation.

Both rituals and games are seen by Huizinga (1955) as examples of play.
In order for play to progress, it is important that its players adhere to certain
predefined rules that govern the 'magic circle'. When these rules are broken,
play (temporarily) stalls and one returns to 'real' life, possibly to restore the
conditions of the episode of play in question. Deliberately stalling an episode
of play is called 'foul play' and may result in one or more players being penal-
ised or expelled. It may also be, however, that play is cut short when rules
have been broken (extensively).[1] In that case, the particular play has not come
to its natural end, and there may be spillovers to everyday life as a result.[2] The
assistance of an arbitrator may have to be called upon, to determine whether
play can continue or not.

Huizinga asserts that if an episode of play is participated in seriously and
willingly, it may appeal to, and effectively control, one's competitive impulses
and prevent mayhem and distress in 'real' life. When competitive impulses
start to dominate and (largely) determine one's behaviour in 'real' life,
however (as may happen in the case of 'foul' play), a play is no longer a 'true'
play and individuals and/or a community may enter a state of what Huizinga
calls 'puerilism'. The term is attributed to mental illness, and refers to childish
behaviour in an adult.

Puerility manifests itself when the boundary between play and 'real' life
breaks down, so that the two flow into each other and their meaning becomes
conflated or flipped. Huizinga sees puerilism as a widespread and potentially
detrimental phenomenon in society, which can lead to war[3] and the collapse
of human values and interaction, because the moral responsibility people have
towards one another (Levinas, 1991, 2006) is diluted, as one continuously
believes themselves to be in competition with others. Morality consequently
is framed as if it were an element of play, while it should in fact be treated
seriously, and with a degree of separation. Societies that are affected by
puerilism attribute too much seriousness to episodes of play (for example,
football-related violence), and can show signs of treating serious elements of
'real' life as games (for example: driving too fast, hazing practices or even the
early management of the recent COVID-19 pandemic).

2.2.   Work Hard, Play Hard? – Business and Play

Linking play to the realm of business, and in particular business education, some linguistic/terminological crossovers can be observed. For example, 'competition' resides as a concept in both fields, and the notion of competing to be a (market) 'leader' shows a borrowing of linguistic terms from competitive games. Notions of 'position' in markets share the use of the term with runners in a race, or players on a baseball field. Equally, the similarities with militaristic terms and language can be asserted (e.g. captain, 'midfield battle', 'commanding a defence', etc.).

Considering playful learning, Huizinga's take on play raises some questions as to how these two practices reconcile/combine. Business is considered as a 'real-life' phenomenon, dictated by, and supportive of, the economic system within which it operates. Individuals make decisions, within markets, utilising forms of capital and ownership to generate wealth. When considering capitalist societies, this notion forms the heart of the rules that govern society. Laws, social rules, norms and practices fit within the support of this ideology, protecting the wealth of individuals and organisations, and also (supposedly) regulating the over-accumulation of such wealth (e.g. through taxation and legislation).

How can play, as defined by Huizinga (1936, 1955) fit within this serious, ideologically driven method for life? When considering business-themed games and simulations, the inseparability of play and non-play (i.e. real life) is made explicit. The combination of these two phenomena therefore makes for a complex and conflicted situation for the subject who is 'caught up in the game' of business life (and potentially, in a business educational setting). The voluntary entry into play on the part of the subject is therefore not an option. They are a player by default, regardless of whether they desire to be one. In addition, can the escape into play ever be realised when play itself is so realistic to the subject, and carries with it consequences for everyday life, personal prospects, relationships and perceived success? The following sections of this chapter seek to explore these themes and provide a discussion of the role of play within UKHE and wider business education.

3.   RISK FREE SANDBOXES?

One of the most popular and regularly cited claims regarding games and simulations is that they offer an environment where the user can make mistakes freely, with little or no (negative) consequences (cf. Anderson & Lawton, 2009). However, this notion resides far too close to the surface-level thinking concerning the interaction between an individual and a particular game. Although it is ostensibly correct that mistakes often bear little apparent consequences in, for instance, a business simulation/game, the user of the software still derives meaning from the actions they take, and has responsibility in taking those actions, be they only virtual.

Engagement with simulations or games in business education may often be linked to a student's assessment, even if the claim is made that the relative success or failure of the student or their team does not (immediately) affect their assessment. We postulate that the user engages with the game/simulation while playing it and will cognitively revisit this experience when preparing an assessment. The notion that these two elements can be distinctly separated would also belittle the case for lasting impact (e.g. claims of enhancing employability) of such a learning innovation, if the student simply forgot the experience and instead reverted to a transactional analysis following their engagement with the game/simulation.

Therefore, the actions undertaken by a student in the context of a business game (in an educational setting) take place in an environment realised by assessment, obligations to peers (team-mates/fellow group members playing the game) and the experience of the environment created by the game. What is lacking compared to everyday life is the responsibility to subjects within the game: fictional employees, suppliers, customers. The face of the Other becomes encrusted (see Levinas, 1969, 1991) by the process of simulation, and representation inherent to a game/simulation. These representations can be complemented by the augmentations of human video and voice acting. This issue has the potential to be further exacerbated by referring to games as 'simulations' (presumably of 'everyday life') and 'serious games'. What comes from this is the question of whether playful learning (through simulation and games) can ever truly be 'playful' when education is such a serious affair within the ideological framework of Western society.

4.   FURTHER CONCERNS REGARDING GAMES AND SIMULATIONS IN BUSINESS EDUCATION

4.1   Identity Implications

While at play, an individual will often (temporarily) assume another identity, in the form of a specific 'character', for example: a CEO, concerned parent, animal, investor or broker. Related specifically to 'serious games'/'simulations' commonly deployed in the field of business-related studies, this character often will be a company manager or director, carrying with them the responsibilities associated with their position, provided that the team polices this throughout the duration of the simulation/game.[4]

Not only is the player characterised when in 'play', but also the associated subjectivity that they experience is also different on a deeper level. The inability to feel consequences of actions as deeply as in real life, with interactions with other living beings and objects taking a virtual form, allows a notion of invincibility to be felt by the subject at play. Even when losing the game, the player can continue, either beginning the game again, 'virtually' rewinding time to the start, or continuing as if there are little consequences to their past failings. This absurd notion of being,[5] which can lead to excessive risk-taking, is realised through play, rather than outside of it, but can spill over into everyday life nevertheless.

Marriott (2004), drawing on Kolb (1984), reflects on "concrete experiences" derived from games and gaming in education, emphasising not only their value, but also the wider-reaching effects of the often deeply emotive and realistic experiences of the game/simulation for the individual subject. Playful learning through simulations forces an identity onto the subject that they may or may not relate to, resulting in learning effects that they may respond to in varied and multiple ways. This sharply contrasts with Huizinga's view that play is entered into on a voluntary basis. What comes from this is not 'true' play, compliant with Huizinga's five dimensions mentioned in section two, but instead a set of compulsory subject positions that the individual is forced into for the duration of play. A parallel in popular culture: in the television show *Quantum Leap*, the main protagonist of the story (Dr Sam Beckett) is thrust into different identities, and different realities, against his will. He is faced with the completion of different tasks, before he can move on, with the aim of finally making it home at some point, as he 'leaps' through time and space. When Sam believes he has made it home, he discovers this 'home' to be markedly different from the one he left before, and so too himself.

The analogy with gamification in education is that modules based around games are often compulsory. If we are to believe Huizinga's point regarding games residing outside of everyday life, and recognise the profound effect that games can have on people's mindsets, then students are effectively thrust into the role of Sam in *Quantum Leap*, becoming finance directors, CEOs and other characters within virtual organisations that they have little connection to. The tasks that they must complete involve running the virtual business round by round, but also the spillovers into the real environment outside of the game in the form of assignments, meetings, presentations, reflections, etc., that they must complete to move on through their degree – which could be viewed as another arguably over-gamified aspect of ordinary life.[6]

4.2 The Panopticon of Reporting and Accounting

When engaging with business simulations, a commonly utilised information source will be of the annual report document produced each 'turn' within the simulation. This is often the only link between players and their virtual organisation within non-serious games/business simulations. This level of interaction limits perception to the symbolic representation of events provided by the scope of the report produced by the game/simulation. Reporting such as this can only provide a symbolic representation of business activity, and if relied upon too much can be confused with reflections of 'real life' (Roberts, 2009, 2018).

The potential to reinforce the 'managing by the numbers' approach seen in accounting and wider everyday life (Ezzamel, Hoskin & Macve, 1990; Hopwood, 1994; Johnson & Kaplan, 1987) exists within the use of educational games/simulations. The approach implies that accounting and finance information is seen as adequate, reliable and (largely) a complete representation of business life, even though it is, in fact, riddled with assumptions. It should be acknowledged that accounting is inherently subjective and loose – irrespective of what may be claimed. For example, accounting is based on assumptions of the future of which it is uncertain whether they will materialise (e.g. about future returns, depreciation and demand). It has an inherent problem in capturing activities that have financial implications and/or in quantifying what those implications are (Lowe & Puxty, 1989). Still, it is generally believed and assumed that accounting is neutral and manages to apprehend business life 'as it is', which is clearly not the case, and most certainly not in the context of a game. Managing by the numbers neglects more qualitative aspects of doing business, management and other business-related activities (e.g. visiting a shop floor and experiencing such activity 'first-hand'). Marriott (2004) touches on this point, citing the development of 'algorithmic thinking' as a potential consequence of engaging with such business simulations/games. The misrecognition of human activity contained within the practice of business (or in this case, 'simulated human activity'), provided by reporting, offers up a potential pitfall in learning, should this not be taught with a critical eye in mind. The illusion of transparency through reporting (Roberts, 2009) has the potential to be perpetuated. Even as more sophisticated simulations offer manuals or other guides to wider factors affecting the way the simulation works, the absence of human emotion and action, etc., remains within this simulated experience. Should the designers of such simulations even attempt to reflect the wider business environment, when in truth they can only provide an account or experience of the algorithms contained within them?

4.3   Moral Neutralisation – All's Fair in Love and Games?

Moral neutralisation refers to how humans morally justify and excuse themselves when undertaking what may be considered unethical action. For instance, slaughtering animals for consumption could be justified for human survival, economic reasons, maintenance of tradition or religious beliefs, etc.

All of these reasons can be deployed within the process of moral neutralisation, trumping the ethical responsibility due to the animal (Levinas, 1991).

Relating this to the business context (although economic reasoning through 'managing by the numbers' has already been suggested), let us take a common business decision: whether or not to fire an employee. To many, this would conjure up emotions associated with removing the livelihood of someone known on a personal level, perhaps a colleague of a number of years. This action plunges their family into financial peril. Children and partners suffer. The door to abuse is opened. The wider-reaching ethical implications of the action to fire someone are apparent in everyday life, provided that empathy or some form of compassion endures.

However, within the game, the apparent simulation of 'real life', moral justification is not required. The individual being fired no longer needs to be reduced to bare life, and simply exits the game. No doxa of moral neutralisation such as 'we don't owe them a living' or 'they should have done their job better' is required to justify firing the virtual employee. Such action can be undertaken at speed, with little reflection, save the utilitarian view of the lost labour provided (e.g. fewer units produced in the simulation this turn). Decisions and wider ethical consequences are significantly detached from a form of realisation outside that of the player through their virtual organisation. Part of this is due to the rules that dictate the play within the 'magic circle' of the game allowing for this behaviour (Huizinga, 1955). Within the magic circle, this does not represent any sort of problem, due to the rules that govern this form of play. There are no virtual families at home deprived of welfare, no social issues as a consequence of firing a virtual worker. However, when we make claims that games promote skills that can be applied in real life, then a consideration of wider ethics stares back at us from the abyss.

If the skills learned within the realm of play are transferred to the outside world, then presumably habits practised within the game environment (such as that described above) can be too. Should this be taken to extreme, then life itself may become (or may already be) a game. Therefore, the role of education in the wider world should be an issue of constant debate and critical thought. If business education is simply to feed business with a supply of relatively skilled labour, schooled in economic logics and the ideology of capitalism (as is encouraged in some business schools), then business education faces being relegated to a purpose of state ideological administration, and a factor in the maintenance of the status quo. This is hardly the innovative, forward thinking sector as often repeated within learning and teaching rhetoric.

5.   CONCLUSION

In this chapter we have engaged with a philosophical stance on the phenomenon of play. We relate this stance to that of the gamification of business education through simulations and serious games.

Business-themed simulations can complement existing degrees and curricula, offering diversity in terms of module execution, assessment and appealing to more diverse learning groups. Games and simulations also offer diversity in terms of how business education is delivered, potentially reaching wider audiences, and therefore contribution to promoting inclusivity in education, overcoming barriers that otherwise would deter some potential learners.

The prospect of escape from otherwise ordinary aspects of life can entice the player to engage more freely than say with an activity that does not possess some playful elements. The allure of promoting student engagement carries a certain allure to teachers in an increasingly marketised, transactional, 'customer-service provider' HE environment, where student engagement is an issue (Miller, Rycek & Fritson, 2011; Soilemetzidis, Bennett, Buckley, Hillman & Stoakes, 2014).

Despite these benefits, there are potential negative connotations of utilising simulations and games that require consideration, and that should not be dismissed easily. Over-simulation and over-deployment of such simulations can result in a detachment from the educational experience as part of university life. The novelty of simulation-based modules quickly wears off, particularly if the same simulation software is used across different modules.

The potential spillovers of realistic simulation into the world outside of play also warrant concern for the reflective academic in deploying simulation- and game-based learning. What is permitted within the magic circle of play may not be socially acceptable, legal, moral or ethical when the subject returns to 'ordinary life', following the conclusion of play. We believe that the potential for puerilism in this regard is increased with the strong 'real-world' connotations of the playful learning in question, i.e. achievement in the eyes of onlookers through quantification of module performance. This examination of play could render spillovers more likely to occur and therefore again blur the boundary between play and ordinary life.

As academics, we have a duty of care towards students, and also a moral duty to the wider society and societal well-being. Education as a public good (although increasingly exclusive fee levels and large class sizes for HE push it towards the private category) functions not only as a support for private enterprise but for wider society. As such, this wider role in society informs our conclusions on the use of play and playful learning when it comes to the deployment of business game/simulations in HE. We argue that the potential negative connotations associated with utilising play as a learning medium are too easily 'swept under the rug', in favour of recognising supposed positive cases for deploying such methods. Also, the drive towards innovation in higher education, and the need for educators to appear innovative to the onlooker, creates a motivation to utilise play as an element of individual academic identity, in a narcissistic form (see Lacan, 1977; Roberts, 2001); with 'innovation' becoming an object of desire, games and simulations represent a tangible, particularised method of showing engagement with this theme. The academic can portray themselves as a pioneer, innovative and creative by engaging with games and simulations, and therefore this self-interest is an issue to be considered, particularly in highly individualised (see Roberts, 1991, 1996) staff performance appraisal systems.

In deploying games and simulations to student cohorts in HE we therefore recommend caution, and call for more holistic thinking when it comes to curriculum design, especially in technical business subjects such as accounting for example. We also call for an end to management by student satisfaction, and the potentially dysfunctional use of play (and the prioritisation of student fun/ enjoyment) it can encourage when faced with the alternatives of traditional, arguably more philosophically informed, scholarship and curriculum design. Moments of withdrawal from this seeking of satisfaction or enjoyment are necessary in order to promote reflection, revitalisation (Žižek, 2020) and higher-level learning, and to allow also for the detachment of play from the 'real world' allowing for it to serve the function that Huizinga (1955) emphasises: a release from other aspects of everyday life. Education must challenge students, allow them to consider uncomfortable topics, and encourage thought and reflection for not only the subject matter but also the values they hold and carry with them through the rest of their lives. For if everything was fun, if everything was playful, and if everything was tailored to provide 'satisfaction', then would anything be worth pursuing?

NOTES

1. For example, the 2002 'Battle of Bramall Lane' football match remains the only English professional football match to be abandoned due to lack of players. Sheffield United were eventually reduced to six players, after three players were sent off for infringements, and two left the field through injury with no remaining substitutions available.
2. For example, the public vilification of a footballer for injuring another player, whether deliberate or not, can be seen as a case in point (e.g. Long, 2016).
3. "Aren't the Arabs terrified? Aren't the Iraqis terrified? Don't Arab and Iraqi women weep when their children die? ... What fools we are to live in a generation for which war is a computer game for our children, and just an interesting little Channel Four news item." Tony Benn sought it necessary to refer to games and

puerilism during his commons speech against foreign military intervention in 1998 by expressing these views.

4. Too often, we have personally witnessed groups of students begin with rigid roles and responsibilities and quickly descend into authoritarian operation of their virtual organisations, or, worse still, anarchy, when engaging in business simulation exercises.

5. An alternative view could compare this repeated 'starting, failing, starting again' pattern discussed by Camus (1955). Such an educational process (if allowed to occur) could fit well with a more general view of the absurdity of 'everyday life', considering the careers frequently pursued by business graduates.

6. For example: complete this module (particular 'level' of a game), achieve a high score (mark), receive symbolic recognition of achievement(s) (degree certificate, classification, designatory letters), etc.

REFERENCES

Anderson, P. H., & Lawton, L. (2009). Business simulations and cognitive learning: Developments, desires, and future directions. *Simulation & Gaming, 40*(2), 193–216.

Camus, A. (1955). *The Myth of Sisyphus and Other Essays*. London: Hamish Hamilton Limited.

Ezzamel, M., Hoskin, K., & Macve, R. (1990). Managing it all by numbers: A review of Johnson & Kaplan's 'Relevance Lost'. *Accounting and Business Research, 20*(78), 153–166. doi:10.1080/00014788.1990.9728873

Hopwood, A. (1994). Accounting and the Pursuit of Efficiency. In D. MeKevitt & A. Lawton (eds), *Public Sector Management: Theory, Critique and Practice* (pp. 145–159). London: Sage.

Huizinga, J. (1936). *In the Shadow of Tomorrow*. New York: W. W. Norton & Company.

Huizinga, J. (1955). *Homo Ludens: A Study of the Play Element in Culture*. Boston, MA: Beacon Press.

Johnson, H. T., & Kaplan, R. (1987). *Relevance Lost*. Boston, MA: Harvard Business School Press.

Kolb, D. (1984). *Experiential Learning*. Englewood Cliffs, NJ: Prentice Hall.

Lacan, J. (1977). *Ecrits* (Trans. A. Sheridan). London: Tavistock.

Levinas, E. (1969). *Totality and Infinity* (Trans. A. Lingis). Pittsburgh, PA: Duquesne University Press.

Levinas, E. (1991). *Otherwise Than Being or Beyond Essence* (Trans. A. Lingis). Dordrecht: Kluwer Academic Publishers.

Levinas, E. (2006). *Humanism of the Other* (Trans. N. Poller). Chicago: University of Illinois Press.

Long, S. (2016). 'Ryan Shawcross: Aaton Ramsey tackle affected my public persona – but no-one should feel sorry for me'. *Evening Standard.* Retrieved from https://www.standard.co.uk/sport/football/ryan-shawcross-aaron-ramsey-tackle-affected-my-public-persona-but-noone-should-feel-sorry-for-me-a3209661.html

Lowe, T., & Puxty, T. (1989). The Problems of a Paradigm: A Critique of the Prevailing Orthodoxy in Management Control. In W. F. Chua, T. Lowe & T. Puxty (eds), *Critical Perspectives in Management Control* (pp. 9–26). Basingstoke: Macmillan.

Marcuse, H. (1964). *One-Dimensional Man: Studies in the Ideology of Advanced Industrial Society*. Boston, MA: Beacon Press.

Marriott, N. (2004). Using computerized business simulations and spreadsheet models in accounting education: A case study. *Accounting Education, 13*(sup1), 55–70.

Miller, R. L., Rycek, R. F., & Fritson, K. (2011). The effects of high impact learning experiences on student engagement. *Procedia-Social and Behavioral Sciences, 15,* 53–59.

Moncada, S. M., & Moncada, T. P. (2014). Gamification of learning in accounting education. *Journal of Higher Education Theory and Practice, 14*(3), 9.

Nicholson, S. (2015). A recipe for meaningful gamification. In T. Reiners & L. Wood (eds), *Gamification in Education and Business* (pp. 1–20). Springer International Publishing.

Roberts, J. (1991). The possibilities of accountability. *Accounting, Organizations and Society, 16*(4), 355–368.

Roberts, J. (1996). From Discipline to Dialogue: Individualizing and Socializing forms of Accountability. In R. Munro & J. Mouritsen (eds), *Accountability: Power, Ethos and the Technologies of Managing.* London: Thompson.

Roberts, J. (2001). Corporate governance and the ethics of Narcissus. *Business Ethics Quarterly, 11*(1), 109–127.

Roberts, J. (2009). No one is perfect; the limits of transparency and an ethic for 'intelligent' accountability. *Accounting, Organizations and Society, 34,* 957–970.

Roberts, J. (2018). Managing only with transparency: The strategic functions of ignorance. *Critical Perspectives on Accounting, 55,* 53–60.

Robson, K., Plangger, K., Kietzmann, J. H., McCarthy, I., & Pitt, L. (2015). Is it all a game? Understanding the principles of gamification. *Business Horizons, 58*(4), 411–420.

Soilemetzidis, I., Bennett, P., Buckley, A., Hillman, N., & Stoakes, G. (2014). The HEPI-HEA Student Academic Experience Survey 2014. Higher Education Academy.

Žižek, S. (2020). *Pandemic! COVID-19 Shakes the World.* New York: OR Books.

Index

Printed and bound by CPI Group (UK) Ltd, Croydon, CR0 4YY

16/04/2025

14658486-0001